Thunderstruck Fiddle

*The Remarkable True Story
of Charles Morris Cobb and His Hill Farm
Community in 1850s Vermont*

By Leslie Askwith

From the journals of Charles Morris Cobb
of Woodstock, Vermont

Illustrations by Calum McGhee

Front cover design by Asha Hossain Design LLC

Interior design by William Hoard, BookCreate.com

Printed by Blurb Books

Cover photograph of Charles Morris Cobb,
courtesy of Woodstock History Center

2017

PREFACE

My interest in genealogy began when my mother gave me a small box of black leather-bound diaries, the common ones kept by so many people in the nineteenth century. They'd been saved by an ancestor named Emma Graves. Her thirty-six years "passed pleasantly although there were always some clouds to obscure the fairest sky."

I knew there was more to Emma than doing the wash, feeling the pain of an occasional toothache and noticing the weather. What were her worries, hopes, feelings? What did she do every day? How, exactly, did she do the wash? I visited nineteenth century historic villages, lived as she did without electricity or indoor plumbing and listened to the silence outside the rural schools where she'd been a young schoolmarm, trying to understand more about her life. I still couldn't grasp what she was like as a unique individual.

Her gravestone was near Mary Cobb's, her sister, my great-great-grandmother. When I added that last name to my Graves family investigations, I made an astounding discovery.

In the basement of the Woodstock (Vermont) Historical Society, Jennifer Donaldson, librarian at the time, produced a treasure trove of Cobb memorabilia – old hand-written memoranda, later records of expenses and income, other Cobb diaries and a thick sheath of papers. This was the transcript of a journal kept over thirteen years by Charles Morris Cobb, a teen-age hill-farm boy and musician in the 1850s, my second cousin, fourth removed. Unlike Emma Graves, whose brief memos told only the most basic facts of the day, Charles felt so compelled to record every detail of his life that he considered it useless labor to play a game of cards unless he kept a record of the proceedings. He described himself. "In my old coat over t'other, hair a foot long, face and hands unwashed six weeks and tanned like thunder, I do look bad enough to scare crows." That was the kind of detail I wanted. He described everything he did and much of what his neighbors did, and how he felt about it day after day for thirteen years.

  The Vermont Historical Society in Barre has the original journals, small pages hand-sewn into booklets. Every square inch of each page is filled with tiny writing. Fortunately for me and other researchers, Michael McKernan transcribed these journals in 1988 as part of a Cate Fellowship research grant from the Vermont Historical Society. His work is a marvel of painstaking diligence, and I wondered as I studied them, how his eyes survived the effort. Paul Carnahan, librarian at the Leahy Library, gave me a copy of the CD containing the transcription. Without that CD, this book would have been almost impossible to write. From the CDs, I realized Charles wrote 497,241 words describing his life from about 1839 when he was four years old until 1862 when he was twenty-six. [Original journals are collection number MSA 480.]

  The library also owns Charles' Universal Musician or his "big book of music," as Charles called it, begun when he was thirteen years old and continued until his death. In Middlebury College Library's (Vermont) special collections, Rebekah Irwin and Joseph Watson showed me writings from the collection of musical folklorist Helen Hartness Flanders who said the large book had been saved from a burn barrel in the 1930s. What did she find? "A great spread of what was currently sung a hundred years ago," every inch of six hundred pages set with "closely penned stanzas and music-notation ... words and airs, fiddle tunes, and calls for dances."

Countless exploratory drives on the roads winding through the hills north of Woodstock eventually led me to where Charles lived during his journal-writing years. He called it Rum Street. It's now known as Vondell Road. Nothing remains of his community other than a few stone foundations and seven cellar holes. Most of these are little more than depressions in the ground obscured by brush, leaves, and the stones of collapsed walls. The road is a mile as the crow flies from my grandfather's farm and the hills I roamed one hundred years later.

The author with her Cobb family grandfather, Rupert Lewis, in Woodstock, Vermont.

This book is memoir, biography, and narrative non-fiction, a combination of my own and Charles' words. With a few minor exceptions, the events in the story happened. It is Charles' truth of his own life, how he saw his world. It contains teen-age judgments, personal biases, opinions, and sometimes gossip. He tried hard to limit himself to the truth but admitted he couldn't "help soaring above it in some cases."

Charles wrote about more than two hundred people who lived in Woodstock in the middle 1800s. Not everyone he mentioned is included in this book although everyone mentioned is real and their actual names have been used with rare exceptions where I thought Charles' opinions may have strayed too much into the realm of hurtful gossip.

I tracked down Charles' great-granddaughter, her son and others of the family. They helped me with information about his later life – photos and old diaries and papers, some of which have been donated to the Woodstock History Center.

Charles' life was most extraordinary because he left

such a remarkable record, a sensitive and insightful first-hand view of the lives of one community of poor hill farmers in 1850s Vermont.

Charles was thirteen when he wrote, "July 1, 1849. It is the actual starting point. I shall commence with this motto. 'Take care of the present, and the past will take care of itself.' We will have a Memorandum and a History of the great Author's life, instead of a few good-for nothing scraps. Friend read on. Perhaps you'll find a long story, for it will be a history of the World. I know this will end in a lot of time wasted, paper cut up and writing which I am eternally scared to death for fear someone will lay their paws on, and read. But HOPE is one of the largest bumps I have got on my skull. Now go ahead, you will see that although we begin poor, foolish and ridiculous, that at least we shall improve. We have said a QUEER beginning always ends well and so of course a good ending must always begin queer."

I feel sure he would think this is a good ending.

About the Author

Leslie Askwith and Charles Cobb are both descendants of Benney and Azubah Cobb who settled in Vermont in the late 1700s, salt-of-the earth people who farmed the land in the hills surrounding the village of Woodstock. When Leslie came upon the Cobb journals, she loved the fact that his writing was about common folks and that his stories weren't bound by tradition or correctness, only the truth of what he thought and saw.

Leslie, like Charles, has always felt compelled to write, working for and writing for northern Michigan newspapers and magazines and producing booklets and a newspaper of her own that supported small farms and local food. She's won awards for her writing about the Great Lakes, nature, small farming, local food and the stories of ordinary people.

Leslie spent most of her childhood summers on her grandparents' farm in Woodstock, Vermont, roaming the hills only a mile from where Charles Cobb lived a century earlier. She now lives in Sault Ste. Marie in Michigan's Upper Peninsula where she raises chickens and gardens cooperatively. She lived off-the-grid through three winters and learned to appreciate the difficulty of house-keeping with water hauled from a lake and working by the dim light of a kerosene lamp. She also learned something of the value of Charles Cobb's way of life.

Acknowledgments

I thank my family and friends for offering help and standing by me during this long process, particularly my husband Richard Askwith and my children Grace Watson and Will Eger. I am also grateful to librarians and historians in Vermont, especially those at the Woodstock History Center, for their whole-hearted assistance. Without them, books such as this would be impossible. Many people read, edited and commented on this manuscript, and I thank every one of them for their frank observations and insights. And I thank Charles Cobb's descendants, particularly John Beauvais for his generosity, cooperation, and enthusiasm.

Dedication

This book is dedicated to my grandparents, Rupert Milo Lewis and Ruth Blakely Lewis, whose Woodstock farm gave me roots in Vermont.

Table of Contents

Part 1

1	Nothing But the Truth	2
2	A Small Boy on the Flat	6
3	The Move to Rum Street	10
4	Christian to the Very Uttermost	14
5	Waxing Into a Great Gawkey	16
6	Addison Holmes as Company	22
7	The Ways of the Mammoth Man	24
8	The Woodstock-Shadigee Touch-Hole Old-Iron Company	27
9	Making the Cider Run	30
10	Wasting Wisdom	34
11	Mice Were Thicker than Pudding	39
12	The Essential Skill of Swapping	44
13	Itinerant Medicine Peddler	48
14	Political Disquietude	50
15	Fiddling and My Great Book Of Music	55

Part 2

16	Hill Farmers	62
17	The Abode of Satan's Poverty-Strickens	64
18	The Farm Years	67
	Sugaring	67
	Grafting	73
	Fixing Fence	75
	Fixing The Road	78
	Hoeing	80
	Watching Bees	82
	Haying	84
	Herdsgrass, Oats And Beans	88

	Elisha Raymond's Mill	91
	Work and Play	93
19	Norman Cobb Leaves Woodstock	94
20	Fiddle Mania	100
21	Mother's Sickness	104
22	Hopeless	107

Part 3

23	A Celebrated Musician	114
24	Fiddling And Dancing Down Tew Hell	117
25	Tremendous Bad Times	120
26	Leaving Woodstock	129
27	Studies with Pushee	135
28	Father's Miserable State of Affairs	138
29	The Rise and Fall of Spiritualizm on Rum Street	141
30	From the Women's Perspective, Hell Right Here on Airth	150
31	Gold	157
32	Fishing for Horned Pouts	161
33	The Old House	163
34	Coming Down Low in Every Way	167
35	"Adversity Is the First Path to Truth"	169

Part 4

36	Joining the Band	174
37	Astonishing the Band	179
38	Not a Great Greeny	182
39	Playing with the Greatest Bugle Player in the World	186
40	Broken Up and Scattered	189
41	Tempests of Sweet and Magnificent Sounds	192

- xi -

42 Raking Down the Crowd	195
43 Teaching the Tweed River Brass Band	198
44 The Life of a Musician	202
45 Finding a Wife	206
Epilogue	210
Characters	218
Chapter Notes	236

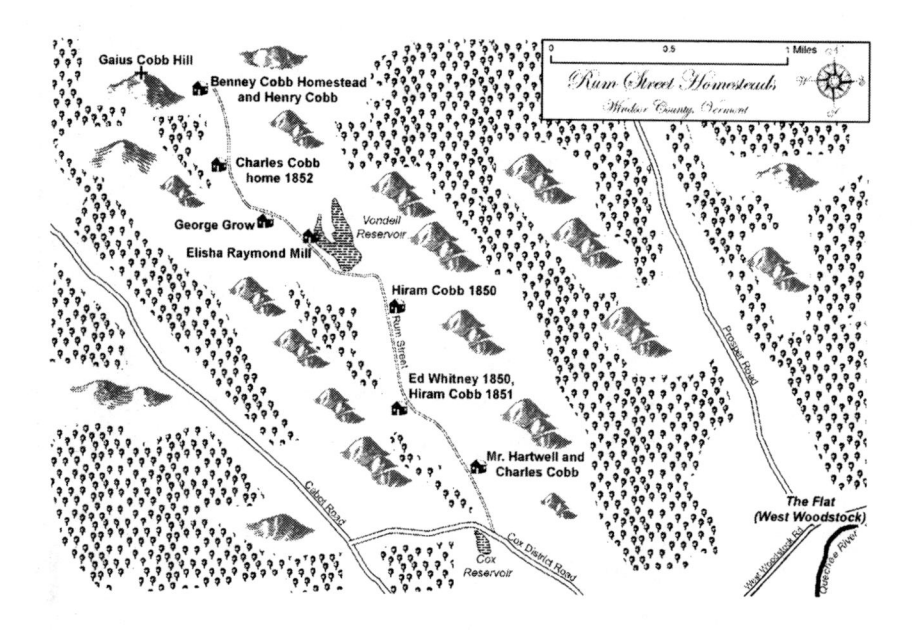

Map of Rum Street and surrounding area created by Will Eger using ESRI ArcGIS. The map was created using the U.S. censuses of 1840, 1850 and 1860; an 1832 map drawn by the Woodstock Institute; a map hand-drawn by Charles in about 1850; a survey map of Windsor County drawn in 1856 by Hosea Doton; the F.W. Beers map of 1869; Google Earth; a Woodstock Aqueduct map drawn in 1953 during planning for the Vondell Reservoir and by finding evidence of old buildings on foot.

Facing page: Photo courtesy of Woodstock History Center, Vermont

PART ONE

Chapter 1

Nothing But the Truth

Our house was poor. In winter my ink froze and had to be thawed on the stove. When it rained, water dripped from the ceiling and made a puddle within two feet of my writing stand.

I, Charles Morris Cobb, was born on December 20, 1835, and raised in the prosperous community of Woodstock, Vermont. But it wasn't on the village Green that I lived, where women knew to use napkins and men voted for temperance, but in the hills that circled the town. We grubbed our livings from the worn out land and carried what little we produced to the Green. Our lives were humble and our houses shabby.

I began keeping a journal when we moved up into the hills

onto a road I called Rum Street, for purposes of characterizing the neighborhood in two words. I was 6 years old. I often wrote in my bedroom so nobody could see my words. Also, Mother was a great talker which distracted me so, that I couldn't make my words hang together. I couldn't think what I was writing about any more than a toad under a harrow. If Father and Mother had gone to bed and no longer needed it, I lit our oil lamp. The house was silent then, but for the soft thumps of moths flitting against the hot glass chimney, the scratch of my pen and the crackle of fire in my fireplace.

Our house was poor. In winter my ink froze and had to be thawed on the stove. When it rained, water dripped from the

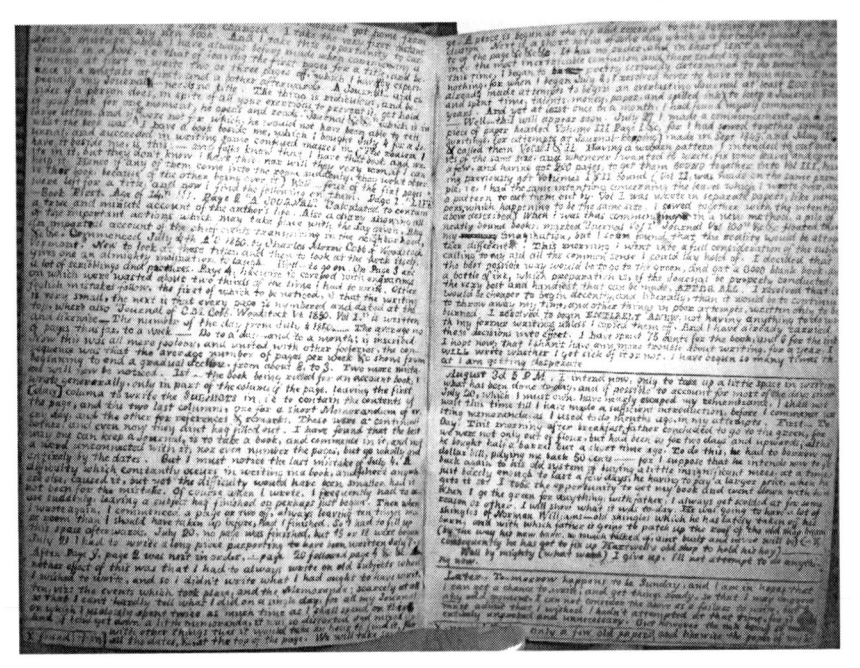

These pages are from Charles' original writings which he called his memoranda. Loose papers such as this accumulated in his trunk in a disorganized fashion that discouraged him until he came up with the system of small books. Then, he copied his memorandum onto pages cut to the same size, correcting mistakes and exaggerations along the way and including only "all that was necessary." Thus were created his journals, the small hand sewn booklets he described once as "small newspapers" now stored at the Vermont Historical Society Leahy Library in Barre and transcribed by Michael McKernan in 1988. Many of these original memoranda are stored at the Woodstock History Center, which is the source of this photo.

ceiling and made a puddle within two feet of my writing stand.

At first I wrote with a quill pen that left blotches on the page. I wrote on whatever paper I could scrounge up — the backs of old letters, empty corners of earlier writings, or single sheets bought at the Green where we bought nearly everything we couldn't make ourselves. My colt skin trunk was filled with so many of these writings that they were in an abominable confusion. Father made the trunk from the hide of a colt that belonged to our neighbor, Geo Grow. Its unexpected death had about ruined Geo. He'd claimed the colt as worth $60 on the Grand List in an effort to swell his wealth so the mother of his intended wouldn't be adverse to their marriage. She opposed the union and told Uncle Hiram's wife, Sarah Cobb, that giving her daughter a good spanking should end it. Soon the entire neighborhood heard of it since Sarah repeated everything she heard whether it was the truth or not.

I'd tried various ways of organizing my pages into a journal and failed upwards of a hundred times. Then one night in March of 1849, when I was 13 years old, I'd well nigh run squizzle of paper when Father surprised me with five sheets and a gold Knickerbocker pen. He'd paid $2 for the pen, a sum we could ill afford. With my new writing materials, I was inspired to begin a new system of organization. I made a pattern five by three-and-a-half inches and cut my pages all the same size. When I had enough, I sewed them together into small books. At first my pages and bindings were dirty, so I began washing my hands, something I'd rarely done before.

I vowed to follow three strict rules. I would not divide syllables at the ends of lines. I would average at least a page a day, even if I had to use brown paper and my blood for ink. I would tell no lies.

I copied my earlier writings into these books in order to correct places where I'd stretched the truth. Doing so tested my self-confidence so much that I wished for a box of pain killer to be close at hand. I felt I couldn't write a word that had anything but the stamp of foolishness on it. Still I wondered if my journals would reveal my wit and wisdom, qualities so far undetected by others, or should I consign them to the fire as Palmer Kingsley had done with his poetry?

Kingsley had taken a notion he could write poetry and

when he tried it he became fully convinced that such was the case. He continued to write now and then for six months perhaps, never looking at a piece after it was finished. At the end of that period he was astounded that his verses had changed much for the worse. "They were enough to make a dog vomit," he told Hiram. That night he committed them all to the flames. I wondered if my "Vermont Collections" might come to a similar end.

For a time I was inspired by the elegant writing of "Gowdie or The King's Pot." The story used such stylish sentences as "The calm and tempestuous breezes rippled the glassy sky, as they swept across the bosom of the plain and bent the umbrageous rocks, that reared their smiling heads upon the summits of each meandering hill-side." I hoped to write similar sentences myself someday but found that such poetic license interfered with the truth.

I had wanted my writing to be a little romantic so I'm sorry to say that I began to put in a little fiction for fact. But when I wrote or said a thing, I desired to be believed. When I read my journals 20 years hence, I wanted to know full well that what I was reading was strictly true. Seeing that such was the case, I thought it best not to stretch little stories that were of no consequence. I meant to tell the truth but I soon learned how difficult it was to understand what the truth was, much less write it.

For example I didn't know how to describe the neighbors without dwelling on their bad qualities and habits. I didn't wish to run down the whole neighborhood and all of its inhabitants, but it seemed necessary if I were to tell the truth. So I vowed to make every character appear as favorable as I could.

I wanted to write. I felt I MUST write. When Father proposed that he get me some meeting clothes and I go to meeting, I said that I must write on Sundays. I got so that I considered it useless labor to play a game of cards unless I kept a record of the proceedings. If I had no paper or no ink I kept entirely out of sight of my writing materials so as not to become discouraged.

I wrote for 13 years before abandoning my keeping of a journal for more pressing needs.

The stories I'm about to tell come from those journals. They are the truth, the whole truth and nothing but the truth as close as I can come, given the difficulty of understanding what the truth is.

Chapter 2

A Small Boy on the Flat

*The Flat, now known as West Woodstock, in the 19th Century.
Photo courtesy of Woodstock History Center, Vermont*

My first house, where I was born and lived as a child, was on the Flat, a part of Woodstock named as it was because it was built on a wide plain alongside the Quechee River. Common working people lived there in a community of dozen or 15 wood-shingled and clapboarded houses clustered along the Stage Road. In the early 1840s the Flat had a blacksmith shop, candy store, school, and two political readings rooms during elections — one for the Whigs and another for the Democrats.

The Stage Road was 18 feet wide and connected Rutland and Sherburne to the west with the Woodstock Green, so named because of its central park surrounded by shops and fine homes. That was downtown Woodstock, where people went to conduct business. From the Green the road continued east on to White River Junction and eventually, 142 miles further on to the southeast, it reached Boston.

I lived there until I was 6, playing with the other small boys, often in the road. We watched out for slow country oxcarts and wagons as well as the stage that clattered through twice a day. Our mothers warned us to be particularly careful of the stage because its driver, John Bravard, was sometimes drunk. In winter people switched from wheels to runners. The packed snow made travel fast and quiet and it was the best time of year to go places. Folks socialized until early morning, gliding home by the light of the moon and stars, covered with buffalo robes which we referred to as buffaloes.

Most of the men on the Flat worked at Reuben Daniel's machine shop turning out machines and other articles used in the woolen business. The shop smelled of oil and clanged with the turning of belts and pulleys, powered by the flow of water over the dam across a side-channel of the Quechee River. Across the road Elisha Buck kept a boarding house for unmarried hands. Aaron Whitney, the foreman at the machine shop, tried to keep the hands in order by requiring them to practice temperance and to vote Whig.

When the large boys practiced marches during their juvenile trainings, we small boys followed. We wore uniforms of shirts trimmed off with red and paper hats.

THUNDERSTRUCK FIDDLE

Farmers, including my grandfather, raised merino sheep in the hills that rose north of the Flat and sold the wool to mills nearby.

When we lived on the Flat, Father shoemaked in a small shop attached to the house, which was the second house north of Mill Road. I was one of a mob of small boys, thin, with dirty pantaloons and untidy hair. We played run-round, dug ditches and built tiny towers for our pet spiders, picked spruce gum in trees up on the hills and boiled eggs in a small hollow near a large tree in Mrs. Holmes' pasture.

When the large boys practiced marches during their juvenile trainings, we small boys followed. We wore uniforms of shirts trimmed off with red and paper hats. Walter Scales accompanied us on the big drum that belonged to my Uncle Henry. Walter's father was a drunkard whose fears of poverty were as common and schemes for success as fruitless as most of the other men on the Flat, so, like most of us, Walter had learned, at a young age, of the importance of earning money. He charged 10 cents for his services on the drum. I was the company's lieutenant so it was my job to collect one-cent pieces from the other small boys.

The threat of the poorhouse hung over many of the folks on the Flat all the years I was growing up. When one of the large boy's folks was sent there it seemed like even more of a possibility for my folks. For example, when Jim Peterson's father ran away, Jim and his mother and sisters had to move in with Bill Cleveland's folks. Mr. Cleveland was a drunkard and temperance was running high so the owners and hands of the machine shop helped them some, gave him work, and kept him sober. He died about 1847 because of rum or the want of it, or effect of it, or consumption or something else of the sort, leaving nobody to support Jim's family. Jim was put out to work and everyone else was sent to the poorhouse, much against their will. Jim had always been accused of all the mischief done on the Flat, whether guilty or not, which he sometimes was, so I considered the poorhouse to be the salvation of the lot.

Among my own folks, Father's youngest brother, Hosea, failed first, by buying Reuben Daniels' silkworm business for $300. Hosea's plans and schemes changed every day. He said "I'll grow mulberry trees in the hot house. Charles and Almira can pick the leaves. It's the ideal job for children. The silk factory in Woodstock will buy the silk." Almira was Hosea's young sister, my aunt, but close enough to my age to feel more like a cousin.

Reuben Daniels was well known as a speculator in improved methods of farming and a man with an eye for profit. He once bought some land from Laura Dunham and immediately cleared the timber, getting enough gain on it to almost pay for the land. Laura felt cheated and was mad. I thought it showed a mean disposition to spoil land to make a little money.

So when Hosea suggested buying the silkworm business, Mother said "If Daniels is selling, it's because he can't make a profit."

Hosea bought the silk business anyway and it soon failed.

Father was next. He thought he would do devilish large things in the beekeeping business. "Your grandfather told me to invest in merino sheep," said Father, "but the wool market is failing. The price has dropped to less then half what it was–to 25 cents a pound. We can't compete."

Father studied Mr. John Weeks' Manual of Beekeeping and became convinced that the Vermont Beehive was "the first improvement by which honey could be gotten without destroying the bees." It was the future of beekeeping in Vermont. He borrowed against his house to set himself up in hives, bees and southern honey to feed them. He intended to take his northern honey to Boston, $200 worth each time. I remember seeing Father hitch our good-for-nothing Arabian horse to the wagon filled with boxes of honey and pull out onto the Stage Road. The horse's hooves raised small puffs of dust as he drove down the road on the 140-mile trip. Father's wagon joined the stream of farm goods headed towards Boston, maneuvering along increasingly congested roads, circling slow herds of pigs, avoiding teamsters driving wagons loaded high with cargo, and being passed by fast-moving chaises and people on horseback.

But the project didn't prove as lucrative as the brochures had promised. Father started with 40 swarms of bees worth $200 that first winter, but it was a long one, and in the spring all the bees he had left were in one honey box. He built a Concord wagon to pay off part of his debt to Weeks and sold his house to pay the rest.

Chapter 3

The Move to Rum Street

*Three sheep, Tom, Dick and Harry, raised their heads briefly,
and a turkey eyed me menacingly.*

That spring I was 6 years old when we loaded our belongings into Father's wagon and headed up into the steep hills north of the Flat. We were to live with Grandfather, Uncle Henry, and Aunt Laura. It was a distance of only three miles but it felt like a vast distance from the world I'd known so far and so isolated that few people even knew of the road's existence.

As our wagon rolled away from the Flat we left the smooth dirt road and turned onto another that was bumpy and eroded from spring runoff. The brook that ran alongside the road flowed fast and high, swelled by spring freshets and I heard a certain strange noise which was said to be caused by a new sort of downeast bird called a snipe.

Father clucked and slapped the reins dispiritedly,

encouraging our horse as the hills grew steeper. Father pointed out the tall butternut trees that gave the best nuts. Apple orchards were frothy pink, signaling a good crop, and green pastures unrolled like carpeting, dotted with gangly sheep shorn of their wool. We passed a few old houses, most of them faded from lack of whitewash with cloth where panes of glass should be. Just past a mill, we turned up a hill so steep the horse strained to keep going, so Mother and I got out and walked. Near the top we turned into the dooryard of Grandfather's house. Henry and Laura came out and welcomed us warmly.

We'd reached the end of Rum Street where Cobbs had been living since my great-grandfather Benney joined the exodus up-country to the new state of Vermont in the second half of the 18th century. He'd been lured by advertisements inviting settlers to develop the wilderness and stories sent back to Middleborough, Massachusetts, from neighbors who'd settled in Woodstock. More than 50 families left Middleborough to settle in Woodstock towards the last of the 18th century, sending word back about the Green and the Flat with its saw mill and grist mill, clothing and fulling mills, and by about 1793, a public schoolhouse 50 feet long with two chimneys and separate entrances for boys and girls.

Along with the Cobbs, the Churchills, Powers, Woods, Bennetts, Raymonds, Darlings, Sampsons and Thomases moved north, buying land and building houses near their old neighbors. They cut trees and sent the logs to the mill on the Quechee River to be planed into boards, burned the rest and sold the ashes to Captain Williams' perlash works. They pulled stumps and wrestled stones onto walls along the edges of their property. They planted buckwheat and rye and created pastures for merino sheep that produced thick wool for the mills on the Flat and a profitable crop of spring lambs. They also cleared the forests of the wolves, coyote, bear, and cougar that threatened their flocks.

Great-grandfather Benney Cobb arrived in 1790 with his three youngest children, Gaius, Elias, and Isaac, about the time Vermont achieved statehood. He settled on 75 acres in rather a back place and on very high ground, overlooking everything. North and west were three high hills which kept the wind off grand. His wife, Azubah, followed later. An older son, Binney Cobb, came later with his wife, also named Azubah, and settled over the hill in the community called English Mills.

At that time downtown Woodstock, called simply the Green, was the new frontier to southern New England with a courthouse, tavern, dwelling houses, run-down grist and sawmill and a 30 by 40-foot barn that housed a church. By 1791, mail arrived once a week. That year 180 letters were received and 120 were mailed out. The population totaled 1,597, but most of them, like my great-grandfather, had settled in the hills surrounding the town.

By 1798 Great-grandfather had a 544-square-foot house and 500-square-foot barn worth $488 in the eyes of the assessors. He paid $1.39 in taxes. By the time old Benney Cobb died in 1817, his estate had increased in value to $1,297.89.

His son, Gaius S. Cobb, my grandfather, remained in the family homestead until his death. He raised seven children to adulthood with his wife Betsey Palmer, who was from Calais, Vermont where she belonged to a branch of Zion, a congregation of "upwards of 40 members, almost half of whom were under the age of 21 years." This I learned from letters she saved that were passed on to me 46 years later. Needless to say I enjoyed reading them immensely since letters were so few.

I learned that Grandfather may have won her from a suitor by the name of L.W. Kingsley who wrote, on January 18, 1804, "I hope you will pardon my boldness in writing to you. I am sensible that many will think it very indecent for us to have a correspondence with one another by writing, but I think we may if we have the glory of God uppermost in our minds. Zion shall prosper: therefor let us try by the grace of God to put on the whole armor of God that we may be able to stand an evil day. But I do not feel so much engaged as I have done sometimes but I find no discouragement in the way, but of the way briars and thorns stand thick, which the lord has placed there to keep us in the way."

A "brother," Oliver Holmes wrote "Stand fast in the faith, where with Christ has made you free and be not entangled again with the yoake of bondage, keep the work under your feet, take up your cause, live with self denial, live watchful and prayerful, live near the bleeding side of our savior. Be earnest in the throne of grace by prayer."

Great-grandfather's household must have been a place

where new religious thought flourished. Grandmother brought her Zionist views and Grandfather and his brothers argued about how to interpret the Bible. They weren't involved in any organized religion in Woodstock, such as Congregationalism, until the Christian Church arose at the beginning of the 19th century. The Christian Church believed everyone should decide for themselves what the Bible said and not be bound by the dictates of a minister. This suited them very well.

Grandfather sold wool from his merino sheep at a good profit, bought up neighboring farms so as to have additional grazing areas, and reaped the financial benefits of a market that had jumped to 57 cents per pound of wool in 1835. By 1845 he owned four farms.

It was into this family that my father, Gaius Palmer Cobb, was born in 1807, the eldest of a family of brothers and sisters who arrived regularly for the next 18 years. Seven survived to adulthood. Grandfather and Grandmother added to their household by taking in neighborhood boys who needed homes. According to Hiram's tell, the lot used to have good times.

Mother and Father were distantly related, both descended from Henry Cobb, who'd come to the new world from England in 1631. Mother's grandfather, one of the settlers from Middleborough, arrived in Woodstock in 1777 and built a log cabin near the Pogue Hole, a pond with a reputation for mystery. It was perfectly round and high on the slopes of Mount Tom. Some said it was bottomless, maybe the crater of an extinct volcano. We young people had a tradition of gathering there on May Day where we picked checkerberry leaves and ate poison low hemlock berries while repeating stories of deaths that had occurred there — how Samson was shot dead by a hunter — how Elisha Cox dropped dead from apoplexy, all alone in his field.

Grandfather was a solidly respectable man and a founding member of the Congregational Church. His wife, I was told, kept a tidy house and had a reputation for being smart and sensible.

Father met Mother, Lucia Cobb, when they were in their 20s. They married and moved from the hills where their parents and grandparents had farmed, into the Flat, where he built a house. That's where I was born on December 20, 1835.

Chapter 4

Christian to the Very Uttermost

"You're a hard worker but a poor manager," Grandfather said to Father when we arrived at the farm with our wagonload of possessions.

"Winter was long, hard on the bees," said Father. "'Twas bad luck."

"Good farming takes bad years into consideration—doesn't depend on luck," Grandfather replied.

His farm had a good house, barn, corncrib, shop, carriage house, and sheds. Grandfather was a big man, larger than any of his sons, six feet tall and 200 pounds, shrewd and frank about his opinions. He lived on the farm with my Uncle Henry who'd been given control over Grandfather's affairs by the court at the request of Father and my uncles. When Grandfather remarried after the death of Grandmother, they suspected his new wife of conducting his affairs to her own benefit.

I learned from Henry more than I ever did at school where I always hated to go. He had me work for him in haying and planting and I did so like a good fellow as he used to tell me stories and converse with me, a thing which Father would never do, except to chide or provoke by his cunningness.

Henry was willing to do a person a great many kindnesses without any recompense but he kept precise records of debts and credits. "Do unto others as you would that they should do unto you," he said. "But go ahead of them by saving all you can get."

I felt well provided for during the time we stayed with them. If something was amiss, my Aunt Laura set it firmly back in place. She was prudent, gentle, and kind, and she and Henry lived in harmony. She helped him farm in the summer, sometimes wearing breeches—the first woman in the neighborhood to do so—

when she picked potatoes and raked hay. She didn't leave the farm for months together.

She was a Christian to the very uttermost. "But," she said sternly, "I abhor bigotry, superstition, hypocrisy and persecution and will have none of it in this home," unlike some Orthodox Christian neighbors who thought observing the Sabbath and avoiding cards, dancing, and fiddling all that was necessary to be a true Christian.

Henry and Laura's only child died as an infant. I don't think she ever recovered. She read the *Christian Messenger*, passing copies around the neighborhood until they were returned limp and smudged. I liked to read them so I could better argue opposing philosophical viewpoints with Henry, who was fond of my investigations.

She took some queer spiritual turns during her lifetime. When I lived with her, she followed the alarming teachings of a Vermont farmer and evangelist named William Miller who claimed the world would end between March 21, 1843 and March 21, 1844, but certainly no later than October 21, 1844. He was specific as to the dates. She wasn't alone in believing him. Many people called themselves Millerites. They thought that only those who were saved by God would survive the final day. Since Henry was an outspoken infidel and Father and I hardly ever went to meeting, she prayed for all of us. I'm ashamed to say we laughed at her.

Father and I were at home making beeswax in the kitchen one afternoon in April of 1843. The sky darkened and the wind came up. Hailstones fell, thundering on the roof so hard, that it seemed the house would be crushed. Branches of trees whipped about and bits of bark and debris whirled in the air. The sound was deafening. We all rushed to the window except for

We all rushed to the window except for Laura, who offered up loud prayers, and Sarah Cobb, who wept into her hands

THUNDERSTRUCK FIDDLE

Laura, who offered up loud prayers, and Sarah Cobb, who wept into her hands.

When the storm ceased, the sun came out, glinting on the layer of ice pellets covering the ground. We all, with the exception of Laura, went back to our business as usual. She continued to believe Miller's predictions even after the final day came and went, praying for us even as Miller moved the predicted final day forward. That day passed uneventfully as well and Millerism faded from everyone's minds.

Chapter 5

Waxing into a Great Gawkey

Solomon wasn't a very grand scholar. He leaned with his elbows on his book and his chin on his hands and looked 'round the schoolhouse day after day.

By 1850, at the age of 14, I'd waxed into a great gawkey and found myself in the curious position of being one of the large boys. There was only one boy larger than myself, but there were several girls. If everyone didn't know I was a green one they must have been devoid of observation. I didn't know enough to warrant the silver key and $20 watch that Father had given me and I carried to school, or the wearing of my best clothes, which I did because I had no others.

I went to the Flat school

that year and sot between Solomon Wyman and Walter Scales in our three-seat benches. We were rarely spoken to for any other misbehavior than laughing. I can remember what painful times we had to "hold in" for half days together and how, four or five times each winter, unable to contain ourselves, we would get overhauled and scolded severely. Little did we study.

Solomon wasn't a very grand scholar. He leaned with his elbows on his book and his chin on his hands and looked 'round the schoolhouse day after day. He didn't advance much in four or five years. If anybody undertook to explain any new principle to him, they'd find they'd got their match. Once the master got rather vexed in explaining division of fractions. Said he, "I've told you this five or six times over, and now you don't know any more about it than Balaam's ass."

Solomon's name was wrong. He wasn't like the wise King Solomon. He always studied the same thing, going so far, then dropping it. He studied geography, then took up grammar, and stopped arithmetic halfway through. Yet viewed in every other light than that of a scholar, he was a smart enough boy and a good fellow. He could always find something in his books or do something that would make anybody laugh.

Once we'd got a map of the United States and were making shocking work of pronouncing the names of the Indian tribes such as Assinboines, Omahas, Osages, Clalams. Sol chanced to look in my eye and we got to laughing so hard we had a painful time to hold in. The master was very merciful, otherwise he would have whipped us all. As it was, he had a hard one trying to tell what we were laughing at.

We also played pranks like marking out words in my Webster's spelling book with a lead pencil that created phrases like, "our friends send forth an agreeable smell" and "the beams of a wood-house are upheld by God." Knowing the master wouldn't like it, we put the entire book in the wood stove.

During oral reading, Walter Scales studied his book to calculate exactly which paragraph was to come to him but once in a while he had to read one he had not prepared for. Then it came bad indeed. He made such disastrous blunders in pronunciation that to hear him was one of the greatest amusements of the school. He pretended not to be half so much aware of it as he was.

One time I was forced to stand up with him and read my

part from his book because earlier he'd loaned the master use of my book, for the master brought none of his own. It was hard to conceal my amusement at such a slight distance and besides I didn't like the smell of his breath very well. Walter wasn't a very darn'd brilliant speller either.

We had an exercise which I liked very much. All stood up. One was required to give the name of a town in Vermont and the next and so on. And when one could not give another, he was directed to be seated. Now, as I had always delighted in drawing maps, I could with all imaginable ease repeat the name of every town in Vermont in order, beginning at the southeast corner, and I could point out their exact situation. As no other scholar could name 30 particular towns out of the 239, and but few, 10 of them, I had a great advantage which did not fail to show itself, tho' I sot down instantly when I discovered no one standing but myself.

In 1852, the master, whose last name was Cobb — he was somewhat related to me — was relieved of his duties after he whipped a small boy, Stephen Taylor, who lived at Nathan T. Churchill's house. The master whipped him for quarreling outdoors with another of the small boys. That pretext alone was silly and insignificant and no reason for punishing him so but if I had been in the master's place I never would have borne the insulting looks and actions that Taylor had been guilty of all term. And, since the master and I were both named Cobb, I favored his side.

"He's a damned fool," said Solomon as we walked up the road to my house where I'd invited him to spend the evening. "Everyone says so."

"Taylor is a quarrelsome cuss," I said. "The schoolmaster should have whipped him sooner."

"Nathan Churchill says he's going to sue him and completely raise the Devil with him," said Solomon.

"I guess some folks are bitter against the schoolmaster," I said.

"He struck him 25 times," said Solomon.

"You've always hated the master," I said. "The master said that he counted the blows and there wasn't 25. I think that's true, tho' everybody says he LIED."

"Taylor's confined to his bed and almost in danger of his

life!" said Solomon.

"I saw him out in the road with my own eyes, in perfect health," said I.

"Folks say Taylor was a hero to stand up to it."

"My idea of heroes is devilishly different," I said. "Taylor didn't cry or show any compunction at all. He stayed at school till night and even read his composition after the whipping."

"How do you know?" asked Solomon

"I came to school late, after you'd gone home."

"Daniels and Whitney posted a paper at the schoolhouse and machine shop. It says the master's conduct was highly improper and immoral," said Solomon.

"Mr. Daniels is mad at Cobb because he fears he'll lose his note for $15. Daniels took his horse, which I shall not praise any, up to Cobb just at dark so Cobb couldn't see its faults. It was all a cheat to begin with. Daniels made Cobb give him his horse plus a note for $15. Now if Cobb loses his job, he won't be able to pay the $15, so Daniels tried to attach the horse and a sleigh and harness on top of it. But Cobb had already sold them all, so Daniels lost out on a swap he cheated on to begin with."

"How do you know about all that?" asked Solomon.

"Everyone knows it," I said.

"Everyone makes a story bigger than it really is," Solomon said.

"That's true about the whipping too," I said.

I knew Solomon was right but was still mad at Daniels for taking advantage of other people every chance he got.

Solomon turned to go home. I wished he had. Somehow no one but me could argue about anything without getting mad. But I tried to please him just as I would try to please anyone, and I was willing to have him come home with me for the sake of its being over with. Besides, Mother had swept the old kitchen as I'd asked her to, for it looked altogether too bad and Father had gotten pork sausages and opened a box of honey so that we might make a decent show of something to eat. We had no potatoes, since ours had frozen in the cellar.

After eating, I built a fire upstairs in the shop so we could play billiards on the workbench with buttons and bullets. I set up twelve buttons in a row and rolled bullets at them — took aim and won every game. Then we tried to slide down hill in

Norman's old sleigh bottom, but found it rather hard work so went up to Geo Grow's house to swap my cracked fife for an old jackknife worth 12 cents.

I was glad when Solomon went home.

The Cox District School which I attended when I was 16, was smaller than the Flat school — only 12 pupils! It was a mighty inferior affair. N. Carlos Thompson was the schoolmaster. He was only two years older than I was and I scrupled to call him a simpleton were it not for the melancholy fact that he knew a little more than I did. The previous fall Thompson had gone to Taftsville to school, which was about as grand as the Flat school and qualified him to teach our school, it being an intellectual mud hole.

A boy once told the schoolmaster (who boarded at his father's house) that the minister prayed for his school last Sunday! "How so?" said the master. "Why," replied the boy, "He prayed for the colleges and inferior institutions of learning," and if our school wasn't a most inferior institution of learning, there never was one.

I wanted to learn algebra and had got a *Davies' Algebra* second hand from Mrs. Eliphalet Dunham for 50 cents which I still owed her. Father had told me not to get it. But Thompson had studied that text and could ask me questions. The first day I showed him two sums that I couldn't do and he pronounced them undoable. But I went to work and at 11 am had 'em both on my slate, proved.

I began going to school later in the day, and then only to retain my position at the head of the competitive spelling exercises. I didn't care a cuss about the spelling, yet I wouldn't be beat by Benoni Shaw, my most formidable opponent. The competition was only among the two of us and Sarah Jane Cox, but Thompson wouldn't allow us to quit when we realized nobody else was benefitting. He said it interested us in our lessons and made us study. Oh God! It didn't make anybody study and made me neglect my algebra for I thought of nothing but winning. Finally Sarah started a revolution by refusing to stand when she corrected a word and we all followed suit and that was the end of the spelling contests.

I quit school during the winter term anyway, to take fiddle lessons — although if truth be told I quit because I wasn't learning much and was expected to read aloud in class. I managed to read a piece, *Battle of Ivry*, to the school, and did it with much agony and confusion but without shedding any tears and didn't intend to repeat the performance.

I wanted to go to a larger school where the teachers were better qualified. Mr. Daniels sent John Daniels to Kimball Union Academy in Meriden, New Hampshire. But John trained like Satan and was scolded at a great deal and was sent home two months before the term was out. It was to be expected. He'd been turned out of the Flat school too. He'd edified us boys with a peculiar kind of small song and picture book and also showed us his large dirk knife. Once he knocked my nose and it was bent to the left ever after even though I tried to fix it by always wiping with my right hand.

My friend, Mary Gibson, was sent to the private Thetford Academy. "You can't have companions in your room during study hours, play cards or smoke and you have to go to meeting on Sundays," she'd told us when she was sent back home to Woodstock for disobeying the rules.

A man named Decatur Randall — we called him Kate — offered me a chance to go to the bigger public school in Woodstock. He rode up to our house on horseback with an umbrella and a greyhound one afternoon to swap an old sleigh for part of an old harness of Father's and the remains of Uncle Norman's old pleasure wagon. He asked me to fiddle some. The first tune I played very flatly and indifferently and he began to flatter me very foolishly which I refused to acknowledge as there was no need of it. He wanted I should come to the Green and do chores for my board and go to the Green school. Father said I wasn't fit for the place for I couldn't milk nor get up early, but I could have done both were it necessary. I couldn't do better than to go but Father wanted to keep me at home because I wouldn't get any wages at Randall's. Thus ended any hope of a decent education.

Chapter 6

Addison Holmes as Company

Even though Addison Holmes and I, at 14, were large boys, Ad still played with the small boys down on the Flat. One morning during sugar season he came up to keep me company. Having arrived he thought we had better go to play at once and concluded that playing war would be good business. The first thing was to whittle sticks for soldiers. When he had finished two he threw down his knife and said "You make 'em. I want to see your daddy shoemake."

But I persuaded him to continue with the game and after I made about 60, we set them up behind shingle forts on the banking. Said he "you set them up and I'll throw at 'em." Another trouble with the fun was that we had to find stones. In a short time I had a large pile while he threw his as fast as he got them. Then he was in favor of having only one pile and I, sensible enough to please, shared mine. When we had killed all the sticks once, Ad was too lazy to set them up again, and so we quit the play.

Then he proposed playing in the dirt on the bank and, unfortunately, I opposed it a very little, at which he was decidedly indignant and said he was going home. But he was easily dissuaded from this and we went down into Mr. Hartwell's barn. Ad got over into the haymow and I said that we had better go up to our barn if he wanted to lay down in the hay, for Mr. Hartwell might scold. "Let Hartwell go to grass. I won't hurt his old hay none," said Addison. He ought to have added "I don't care how much he scolds at you, it won't hurt me any."

Eventually he came down and pulled out a piece of newspaper that was rolled up to light a lamp with. "Go up to the house and light my cigar!" he said. But I couldn't keep it lighted till I got back, so he gave up the idea.

He didn't stay satisfied long, so next he said we should go up to the house and look at fiddles. He took the best one, not needing any assistance in that, and began to saw on it. Getting sick of this, he stuck it into my face and desired me to play him "Old Dan Tucker".

This examination over, he said we should go up to the great rock in the hog yard, and build forts thereon. So of course we went. Two mighty forts were commenced. But mine entirely eclipsed his in a short time and he became sick of the business and having knocked his over went to snowballing mine. Soon this species of sport was condemned as totally insufficient and Ad wished he was at home.

Instead, we went down to eat dinner. There he wanted to see my picture books but I told him I hadn't any at which he was surprised and grieved. Not long after dinner he said that he was darned hungry and must go home but some butternuts answered. After this, as I had to gather Mother's sap tree, bring in wood and water, and do numerous other little chores, he went up to see Father shoemake. At three o'clock I told him I had to go up to the sugar place and asked him to go with me and then stay all night. That, he instantly declined and went home.

He went off with the old clarinet Father had loaned him but soon returned it. Probably Mrs. Holmes, who suspected any music as being the work of the Devil, didn't like our tucking him off with it. Or maybe she recognized that it sounded much like a last year tur-key because of the poor ivory reed he'd whittled out and put on. Such was Mr. Holmes as a visitor.

"Go up to the house and light my cigar!" he said.
But I couldn't keep it lighted till I got back, so he gave up the idea.

THUNDERSTRUCK FIDDLE

Chapter 7

The Ways of the Mammoth Man

Mrs. Holmes' voice was heard on high so all the village knew that I was there plaguing her, hindering the saintly Byron, and forcing the industrious Addison away from his work. I wished myself a mile off.

When I was a small boy, the other small boys and I were kicked out of the large boys' lyceum so we formed our own. Our lyceum's aim was to write stories that ridiculed people we were mad at, often because they'd scolded us. These stories unfolded as we took turns writing parts. We named ourselves the Slab City Lyceum or the Mammoth Lyceum depending on the subject.

Our Mammoth Lyceum ridiculed Father. We called him Mammoth Man, as in "the ways of the Mammoth Man are inscrutable," because he, for example, worked till nine at night on yet another trunk, me holding the oil lamp, when I saw no need for any trunk at all, and everything necessary in the house was left undone. Mother was out of wood again and I'd chopped up the last piece at the door, the one Father had been intending to make a sled tongue with. Naturally, this madded the Mammoth Man mightily so he sot down, "awaiting orders." Father was always abominably behind in his work.

Our Mammoth Lyceum pieces were cussedly ridiculous, but our Slab City Lyceum pieces were more laughable. We modeled our stories after the cartoon-style book, *Jeremiah Saddlebags' Journey to The Gold Diggins*. Often we invented parts of the Bible that might have been left out and featured Bezer Thomas, a very strict orthodox who lived near us on Rum Street. He'd earned his place in our stories by scolding us boys for playing in his fine mowing when it was just ready to be cut.

Addison and I wrote one Bezer story at Ad's house on the Flat. I suggested, "View 1. God takes Bezer's rib to make Eve when a dog suddenly springs forward and snatches it away from him."

"That's not right," said Addison. "The Bible doesn't say that. That's sacrilege."

I said, "Probably Moses left it out for want of room when he wrote the Pentateuch. We're making the Bible laughable."

"It's a sin to laugh at the Bible," he said.

"All right, don't laugh then," said I. "Think of it this way. If two persons talk about the same thing, their stories never agree. They're telling the truth in different ways. This is just another way to tell the story of Adam and Eve."

"It sounds like a lie. The Bible is the truth," said Addison.

"Well, it's not really a lie, it's more of a story. The kind Sarah Cobb tells where almost everything is made up. Everybody knows it. She might have been a good novel writer had she been educated. As 'tis, she tells novels and calls 'em facts."

Addison's brother, Byron, had been eating candy in the next room and listening in. "Go and do your work deacon," he yelled at Addison. Addison had a three hour wood chopping stint which he'd been neglecting for three days.

"Hold your tongue and do your own work," said Addison. "I have company."

I was sorely tempted to go off, but sot him to work and helped him. He soon had another quarrel with Byron who was sawing close by. "I've done my stint and that's enough for one day," said Addison and went off into the house crying.

Quite a scene occurred. Addison bawled. Byron scolded and laid down his saw and went into the house saying that he wouldn't work if Addison didn't. Mrs. Holmes scolded so loud her voice was heard on high, so all the village knew that I was there plaguing her, hindering the saintly Byron and forcing the industrious Addison away from his work. I wished myself a mile off. Mrs. Holmes was a good woman, but too pious and she had given her sons the sort of religious education that made them quarrelsome and superstitious, also lacking in common sense.

When everything settled down, Addison and I went up to the graveyard to continue our Slab City Lyceum piece. The graveyard stood northeast of the machine shop at the edge of a 40 or 50-foot high caving bank that slanted clear down to the river road. More people were buried there than any other ground in town. Unfortunately it belonged to a devout orthodox and Sabbath school teacher who kept his sheep and cattle in it, so the town suffered the destruction of about 10 gravestones every year.

We settled down next to a gravestone marked 1718 although the town wasn't settled till much later.

I said. "View 2. God grabs the dog by the tail."

"And the dog gets away minus his tail," said Addison. "God made Eve with the tail and glued her together with mutton tallow."

"View 3. Now, it's present times," I said. "Adam is looking for his rib. Bezer is locked into his room in the attic, dressing for church. He has on his best coat and waistcoat. His boots and stockings lie in a heap near him and in his hands he holds his pantaloons and views, with dreadful astonishment, a super immense hole in the seat of 'em. Fortunately, Bezer has a most worthy and excellent helpmate named Mrs. Thomas."

"You mean my aunt? That Mrs. Thomas?" said Addison.

"Well, not her exactly, but someone like her."

"Oh."

"View 4. Mrs. Thomas stirs cream in a large sap tub which she holds in her lap, with one leg across t'other in front of the fireplace. On her right are some large chunks of butter in a jar."

"And a dog holds one hind leg elevated above the butter," said Addison.

"View 5. Bezer shows Mrs. Thomas his pants and in comes Miss Carroll and sits down to sew 'em up," I said, flustered at the thought of the amiable young seamstress on the Green named Harriet B. Carroll.

"View of Bezer Thomas" continued through several hilarious episodes involving Bezer tricking Miss Carroll into sharing his quarters. Addison was shocked. "I hope no one gets hold of this."

Neighbors burst in, tables tip over, Bezer jumps out the window to escape and falls into the pork barrel and finally escapes to the woods in his shirt flaps. Mrs. Thomas and all the other old women gabbling in Bezer's room agree it was the work of his satanic majesty.

It was a smart collection of foolery.

CHAPTER 8

THE WOODSTOCK-SHADIGEE TOUCH-HOLE OLD-IRON COMPANY

We boys celebrated July 4th in grand style. In 1848 when I was 11, we met on the mill logs at the Flat to collect enough money to buy gunpowder so as to celebrate the holiday appropriately. I called our company the "Woodstock-Shadigee Touch-hole Old-Iron Company." Shadigee was a section of the next town of Bridgewater that was like Tophet — all rocks and woods and badly out of creation.

We went up the hill to John D. Perkin's house with money enough to buy about six pounds of gunpowder. Mr. Perkins and Alonzo Gibbs were jawing at each other, both of them remarkable mad. We waited a long while to get our powder. I told Father later that they jawed like the Devil, which he interpreted to mean they swore. Swearing was a serious offense and Father was thick skulled to have misunderstood me. Anyway, he rebuked Gibbs, who denied it of course.

We stayed up until 10 o'clock, cleaning and fixing our guns and cannons, which were rather small. We'd slept only two hours when we were awakened by the sound of blasting. We jumped out of bed, got our coal stove and iron and went out to find that someone had fired Solomon's cannon twice. So we limbered up and went up the road in the rain, firing at every house. We soon raised all the rest—Geo Grow, Lute Raymond, Ed Woodward and others. I didn't load my gun very heavy at first, but afterwards I put in more powder and it made a good deal of noise. Geo Grow had only a quarter of a pound. He put it in freely. His gun made considerable of a crack, kicked like Satan, and got sprung severely. But Lute had an old King's Arm. He put in powder by the double handful and made more noise than all the rest. Ed Woodward had Ches Raymond's old Springfield which had to be touch-holed off.

We fixed in Lish's shed till three o'clock in the morning, when it stopped raining a little. Then we went down along on a run firing at every house, fired several times forward of the schoolhouse at the Flat, then went up onto Charles Thomas' hill where the shop hands were firing the old anvil, and fired till four-thirty. Lute's gun actually made as much noise as their cannon. At Nathan Churchill's, I loaded Geo Grow's gun. I put in a heavy charge but he kept yelling "more, more," and I poured it in till he said, "There's too much in." And then I slyly put in a little more, put in a tow wad, and rammed it like the Devil. He was foolish enough to hold the breech to his guts and it fairly kicked him out of the road.

We finished at nine o'clock, left our battery, and went to breakfast. It was a curious time for breakfast for it seemed as though it was at least four o'clock in the afternoon. We took a nap between two mill logs and, after sleeping two hours, got up and took a boat ride with some of the boys from the Flat. We put the boat ashore and then, according to agreement, some of us jumped back into the boat and left the rest on dry land. They jumped into the water up to their necks, caught hold of

*He was foolish enough to hold the breech to his guts
and it fairly kicked him out of the road.*

the paddles, and were spattered and dowsed all over. Then they threw sticks at us, but we'd taken in a cargo of stones, rowed just within throwing distance, and gave it to them. This attack not satisfying us, we made a sortie, landed, and drove the others entirely away.

After this land and sea fight, we swabbed out our cannons and stationed ourselves about halfway up the hill and began firing. We had more than 40 people firing there before we finished. I went home that afternoon rather crooked and occupied both sides of the road. Father and Mother had company and I played the fiddle for them, but Father said I made it squeak so and played so loud and harsh that I spoiled it all. I wondered what had got into the fiddle to prevent its making any noise so I rosined the bow again and bore on with all my might. I was so deafened by the explosions that my fiddling sounded very faint.

That night I went to bed early and I had a continual ringing in my ears for six months afterward. For the next three days I couldn't hear hardly anything. If someone wished to be understood they had to holler three times at least.

Chapter 9

Making the Cider Run

I passed beneath a giant wooden eagle glaring out over the entrance, warning me not to treat the Cadets of Temperance frivolously.

Temperance ran high when I was growing up. The Sons of Temperance, as part of their mission to convert everyone, formed a Cadets of Temperance and I was invited to join when I was nine. It was an honor, but considering that plenty of the boys from the Flat were there, it was less one than I'd supposed. Their meetings were in the Sons of Temperance Hall in Stevens Tavern at the Eagle Hotel on the Green. To get there, we passed beneath a giant wooden eagle glaring out over the entrance, warning us not to treat the Cadets frivolously.

I was uncomfortable even going to the Green where the big folk lived — doctors, lawyers and merchants. We came down from the ramshackle neighborhood of Rum Street to the Flat where houses were only slightly better — wood and plain and somewhat poor — to the Green with its intimidating streets of stately brick and white painted houses fronted by pillars, shutters, wide porches, and fenced dooryards. Sometimes I'd walk through the park or green, shaded by a high canopy of trees, for which the village was named, past the imposing courthouse and into the shops where I felt the shabbiness of my clothing. The overcoat Father wore to the Green was so devilish ragged that he didn't wear it into a house or store—he left it in the sleigh.

Cadets meetings were instructive and secretive. I went through a formal rite of initiation, in which I pledged not to tell any of the secrets of the group and was given a secret password. At meetings we debated important issues like did farmers or mechanics benefit society more? Farmers won. Had the Indians suffered more than the Blacks from the Whites? The majority decided not. I thought that decision was against truth or common sense. Every officer voted in the affirmative. I thought every fool voted in the negative.

I stopped going to meetings after about a year because I didn't tolerate fools and was disgusted about Walter Scales breaking the pledge of secrecy a thousand times. The Cadets discharged him with honor but I thought he ought to have been kicked out and fined a dollar. I'd also lost the election for secretary and importantly, had trouble paying the dues.

Once I was no longer a member I decided it could be no treachery to write the proceedings of the meetings in my journal, or anything and everything else that I could seize hold of, but if it was treachery, I was soon guilty of it.

I didn't like drunkenness long before I joined the Cadets. I remembered how in 1840 when I was 4, the machine shop hands gladly showed their support for the Whig candidate for president, William Harrison, Old Tip, by setting up a great hard cider tub outside of the machine shop. Harrison appealed to voters with a campaign symbol of a barrel of hard cider and log cabin. They got so very badly done to before heading off to the Old Tip July 4th celebration in Windsor that they drove under the covered bridge at the Green without taking down the flag and broke it off in the twinkling of a bedpost. The wagon came home a very complete smash with all hands drunk. I was highly impressed by the scandal.

I named our road "Rum Street" for good reason. One night around 1845 when I was 9, I was playing the fiddle at Hiram's house. He and Jim Willis had a rum jug on the table and got pretty high. They danced and jumped 'round, hopped up and down and cut capers and acted like fools. If I stopped playing they stopped dancing. I might have kept them exercising till noon the next day provided the rum held out. I didn't get off 'til one o'clock in the morning.

My uncles, Henry and Hiram, were both troubled for

breath. Henry said he had asthma and when he worked in his herdsgrass, the blow poisoned him. I could hear him sneeze for three miles off. Hiram had it badly–called it the phthisic and drank rum to help control it. He got jugs of it at the Green — once even on a Sunday — and got rather blue-y on it. I feared it was a poor way to cure the phthisic but it was darned hard not to be able to draw a breath. Even when he was drunk he could walk and work well enough but his actions were — well — drunk.

    The first time I got drunk was on the smell from a bottle of rum Hiram had in his overcoat pocket when he and I went to the circus in Cornish. It operated so powerfully on me that I must have passed for drunk all that day. I kept on my legs with much difficulty. I didn't get entirely over it for three days.

    Our neighbor, Ed Whitney, had sober spells and drunk spells. When he got below the surface of the rum he was at the bottom for three days, and more than 20 times said that the next fit would be his last. When he was drunk, he thrashed his wife most abominably. He had the worst tug just after his wife went away, so joined the Sons of Temperance, expecting, I suppose, that his wife would come back, but she didn't. He wasn't at all dangerous when sober and kept his room very slick.

    Whitney bought the next house above ours and arrived with his father, Old Dolph, in a great wagon drawn by two abominable looking horses even though it was a Sunday. They always had a bottle on the wagon. Ed was what we used to call a "smart chap." He didn't do a great deal of work. Old Dolph did it for him. His name was not Dolphus or Adolphus, but Rodolphus. I saw in the town auditor's report, where the two towns of Woodstock and Hartland had been contending together to see which should have the honor of his birth, but as a little drawback, the one that got it had also got to support him partly.

    We'd made cider every fall since before I knew anything. The neighbors took turns grinding apples at Lucius Raymond's mill on Rum Street. Our cellars almost always had barrels of cider in them unless it was all drunk up. We gave it out freely when people came by.

    Oramel Churchill visited often to get his boots mended. His boots needed mending more than any other person in Woodstock. He arrived a little tight, helped himself to cider and went away with nary a stitch put into his boots. He was the most entire and professional drunkard that I ever clapped eyes on.

His visits though, kept us abreast of the local news. It was from him that we learned that the public at the Flat had been threatening to tear down a woman's house because she entertained so many gentlemen lodgers! I'll admit Oramel's stories verged on gossip more than news sometimes.

Mr. Hartwell, whose house we lived in for a long time, said Oramel stopped by only for the cider but I don't think that was true. He helped Father chop wood, pick apples, make hay, and thresh beans, oats, and herdsgrass. In exchange, Father mended Oramel's boots, sleighs, harness and anything else that needed repair. They'd been swapping labor, cider, and various items for years but when I tried to balance Father's accounts, I couldn't ever find a single item charged against his friend. Father was quite wroth when I alluded to it.

Vermont's liquor laws changed almost every year between 1844 and 1853. A new restriction would be passed and when people figured how to get around it, another took its place. All the poor miserable devils voted against liquor laws and the middle classes and all the great men, such as Jacob Collamer, Norman Williams, Julius Converse, voted for them. I persuaded Father to vote for the restrictions, even though it was hard on him and my uncles.

As the liquor laws became stricter, the Sons of Temperance started watching Oramel. They wanted to know where he was getting intoxicated. It wasn't only at our house.

At first, when it was legal to sell cider but not for drinking, Father gave Oramel gallons of cider for his sister to make vinegar of. The Mt. Tom Sons of Temperance considered the matter and sent my uncle, Chas Raymond, up to warn Father.

"The next time you sell to Oramel, contrary to law, it'll cost you $20. The prosecutor is making no exceptions," he said. "He fined Dr. Gibbs of Stockbridge $17.55 for selling a woman half a pint of alcohol even though it was mixed with camphor!"

So Father started selling Oramel cider by the barrel because, by law, a man could sell it in quantities of five gallons or more. Oramel got hot again. The Sons sent Chas up again to warn Father. I told Chas that "Oramel was drunk when he arrived and our cider was hardly a fart in a whirlwind to the whole."

After that, Oramel escaped detection by crossing through the nine acre lot behind our house with his jug hidden in a bag of beans. Finally Father drew off the cider in the cellar — there wasn't but a little left — and put it into the vinegar. Even after that, the next Saturday Oramel came for some "shoemaking" but somehow made the cider run. Father learned he'd gotten the hang of getting the cider out of barrels that Father had left in Hiram's cellar. When Father found two barrels of whole cider and a barrel and a half of water cider missing, he locked the remaining barrel in the wagon house.

And that was the end of the cider. But through all of it Father and Oramel continued as friends, whether cider was part of the relationship or not. Probably Oramel got his cider somehow even with all the laws. I don't think he could have gotten along without it.

Chapter 10

Wasting Wisdom

"I never thought Daniel Webster's mind would be produced from cabbages, but it must be so," said Solomon. "But that still doesn't account for the soul."

Solomon Wyman and I wasted a good deal of wisdom talking on large subjects such as religion, politics and domestic topics. He flattered himself that he was superior to me but I put it down to his ability to speak a piece without visitings of conscience whereas my conscience troubled me a great deal, particularly when it came to the truth.

Solomon's mother was a strong Congregationalist and very pious. Old Square Damon, her father, lived with them. He prayed night and morning and asked a blessing before every meal. Solomon's father, Ashley Wyman, had a good farm worth about $3,500, a good deal more than any of the farms on Rum Street. Ours was worth about $1,000. Unlike Father, Ashley Wyman raised stuff to sell every year. He was a church member too but not half so absurdly superstitious and strict as were many others.

Sometimes I thought that Solomon was indeed my superior although most of the time I couldn't convince myself of it fully. He was mighty difficult to explain a thing to. One Sunday he, Jo Pratt, and I snuck into the corn house, me with Mother's Bible so I could read aloud some verses of interest I'd found in Deuteronomy. They described the consequences of lying with another man's betrothed and the punishment that would fall upon the wife who falsely claimed to be a virgin on her wedding day. Solomon didn't relish it and told me so.

"What about the soul?" said Solomon one rather cold and windy Sunday as we climbed the hill, headed up towards Henry's house. "It's certain that men have souls. How do you account for its existence?"

He'd taken a notion that he wanted to go fishing and come up Rum Street to see if I'd go along. I'd already tried to get out of helping Father, who'd suddenly decided that drawing manure that very day was essential. I reminded him that Sunday was a day of rest and amusement. So Sol's arrival suited me well. We dug some worms and rigged ourselves so that we could fish in the brook that flowed down along Rum Street to Mr. Leach's on the Cox District Road.

"Men must have souls to make it reasonable to suppose that we live after death. The soul isn't matter in any way and must somehow be created when a man is born," I said.

"Yes," said Sol.

"The intellect a man or even a dog has when he is born, is nothing but matter— the brain," I said. "A full grown man knows more than an infant, so the extra intellect must be made from what he eats, smells, and breathes."

"And intellect is different than the soul," said Sol. "Animals have minds and intellect but do not have souls."

"The soul may be similar to a particle of life," I said. "That particle of life is the same, whether animal or vegetable. Vegetable life produces animal life as everyone that eats knows, and when animal life decays, 'twill produce vegetable life. Since no particle of matter can be destroyed or lost, it assumes another form. Maybe the soul is the same."

"I never thought Daniel Webster's mind would be produced from cabbages, but it must be so," said Solomon. "But that still doesn't account for the soul."

"The soul, like life, has no form, weight, or location. It is nowhere but it must be somewhere," I said. "It cannot be proved."

"Then its existence must be taken on faith," said Sol.

"Then folks have the right to believe what they have a mind to about it—the Bible, Koran, book of Mormon, Swedenborg and the spirits, or Thomas Paine," I said.

Solomon, being a believer in the Bible's word, wasn't happy with my conclusion but couldn't reason farther, backward or forward.

I'd caught one trout and was greatly encouraged. We took a rest and I picked some spruce gum which I pressed onto one of my teeth to make an impression of the hole I knew was there. It was larger than I'd supposed.

"It's the same with the earth," continued Solomon suddenly. He'd been quiet for some time. "The Bible says God gathered dirt together in a heap in one place and made dry land and it's supposed that the two great oceans went one east and t'other west to the very extremes of created space."

"The Bible is nonsensical in places. Everyone knows the earth is round," I said.

"The Bible's words can be turned into anything as new things are brought to light," said Solomon. "Everyone knows that."

"Then that must mean that man is ignorant to believe just exactly what the Bible says," I said.

"It's folly to doubt the Bible!" said Solomon.

"It's folly to take arguments from that which I do not believe," I said.

"That is Atheism!" At that, Solomon stalked off. We were at an impasse. I thought he should have been flummoxed by my powers of reasoning but he based so much of his belief on faith, that he was never discouraged by lack of scientific evidence.

The unpromising end of our fracas and lack of fishing success forced the truth upon me. Fishing was small business. I should have been helping Father or writing in my journal or practicing the fiddle, so I quit. Solomon had caught four trout and I, only one. I had never caught but three trouts before in my life and I was convinced that there was something about fishing that I was not aware of.

As I returned home through the woods, I noticed a tree with H.P. 1842 carved into the trunk. I took out my jackknife and added "Died 1851" and finished the name, Hosea Palmer. Hosea had made his bed in Hell uncalled for by hanging himself in his barn. He was a good enough man although a miserable cuss when he drank rum. I reflected on the thought that I'd never kill myself and added my name and birth date to the tree.

Was Hosea in heaven or hell? Did Hell even exist? Some, like Mother's sister, Polly Woodruff, said, "Only an insane fool would doubt that there was a Hell."

Sometimes during a February cold snap I told myself I wouldn't be homesick in Hell, but it was only a figure of speech. The word "Hell" that we used so freely to mean the worst of anything, wasn't a real place for me although it was for many.

Mother and Father and my uncles and aunts, talked often of the Bible, God, Hell, and keeping the Sabbath. So I studied the Bible and everything else I could in order to win these arguments.

I found the *Classical Dictionary* at Henry's house. The Cobbs had lived in that house for three generations and it was where I found most of my literature–*Treasure Island, Ivanhoe, Sardanapalus* by Lord George Byron, William Cowper's *Task*. Henry and I often read for a while after dinner, before beginning the afternoon's work.

In the *Classical Dictionary* I read about Babylon, Nineveh, Palmyra, Persepolis, Jerusalem, Thebes, Memphis etc.

I learned that we knew of things that took place 12,000 years ago, and that 8,000 years ago the world was almost as civilized as it is now. The Bible said the world was created only 6,000 years ago and that in 2,048 B.C., all the inhabitants but Noah and his family had been destroyed. They would have had to increase most awfully fast to have founded empires 160 or 200 years afterwards.

Lord George Byron's *Vision of Judgement*, was the best thing I ever saw of the kind. It brought up Bible ideas so that it appeared most infinitely ridiculous every line or two. It was the most laughable thing I ever read and not with a fool's reason either.

Granny Morey was one of many who opposed my views. Among her contrary and firmly held beliefs was that the "airth" was a flat strip of land floating at the center of the universe. She said she was too far advanced in knowledge to harbor such nonsense as that the world turned around.

"The truth's writ in the Bible by Moses who was expired by God,' she said.

Another was Mr. Grow, who often loaned us Sabbath School books in the vain hope of saving our souls and encouraging us to observe the Sabbath. He didn't think we observed the day very well.

Our practice of religion, if it could be called that, was most in keeping with the Christian Church's that expected such discussion so that we could decide what to believe. Many of us Cobbs belonged to the first Christian Church congregation in English Mills in the early 1800s. Grandfather's brother, Elias Cobb who lived on Rum Street, was an elder in the early English Mills congregation.

The new church departed ways with the traditional churches by believing that everyone should interpret the Bible for themselves. It was started by others who believed as we did–Abner Jones of Bridgewater and Elias Smith, who'd lived in Woodstock's South Village.

The Christian Church didn't have pastors, because it believed that no person, only the Bible, was our authority. Leaders called themselves elders. The first Christian Church pastor in our town to take the title "Reverend" was Moses Kidder. He performed our funerals, marriages, and baptisms but didn't tell us what to believe.

The Christian church permitted instrumental music in meetings including the violin which at the time was widely thought to be worldly and profane, even outside the church. It allowed the ordination of women and opposed slavery.

Elias Cobb's congregation at English Mills was the first in Vermont to last more than a few years. In 1808 they held a baptism for nine people in the brook that ran behind Brother McKenzie's door yard down in north Woodstock. It was attended by 500 or 600 people according to Elias Smith's newspaper, *The Herald of Gospel Liberty*, "notwithstanding the appointment was at five o'clock in the morning. The people were so numerous and so unexpected, that many of the brethren could not come near enough to hear the candidates tell what the Lord had done for them." Five of the people baptized that day were Congregationalists and nobody cared if they went back to their own church after the baptism. Such was their strength of commitment to individual freedom.

CHAPTER 11

MICE WERE THICKER THAN PUDDING

Mother got sick one morning in September of 1852. I found her with no fire in the room nor signs of breakfast so I got Mrs. Hoisington to come down. Since there wasn't any firewood at the door and nothing to cook, I went up to the orchard and got some sweet apples to bake and picked up burnables here and there as much as I could. Henry and Laura came down at night. Laura thought Mother was sick from eating too many black cherries but I feared typhus fever would be the result.

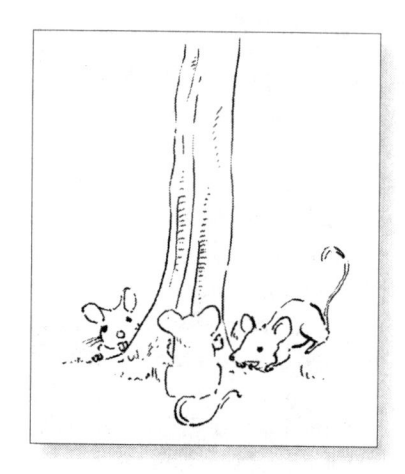

Nearly all the predators were removed from our land. As a result, mice were thicker than pudding in 1851, and I sought to kill all that crossed me.

Laura had recently been dangerously sick with typhoid fever as a result of having the mumps. Dr. Tom Powers visited her every day. Eliza Briggs stayed with her for five days, then her sister, Lucia Jaquith, came from Barnard. They all seemed to blame Henry and said if she died, Henry would be just as guilty of her murder as though he had cut her throat! An alarming and astonishing statement based, I suppose, on him having the mumps first and Laura catching them from him.

When Mother got sick, Father went down to get Dr. Perkins to prescribe for her, but not to come up. "Give her gin and a tea of thoroughwort, camomile and yarrow," he said. I got the camomile at Henry's and found a great plenty of thoroughwort in Grow's hay, the principle part of his hay being swamp grass, rushes and thistles. Father got the yarrow from somewhere.

It didn't do any good and so Father got Dr. Powers to come up. He gave her a puke and said to make a tea of mountain ash bark and a broth of red or gray squirrel. He also played my fiddle and pronounced it inferior to his.

I'd planted some mountain ash trees I'd gotten up on Fletcher's hill during a hunting trip with Geo Grow. When Laura Churchill from the Flat heard we were going, she sent word to get "one or two mountain ash trees for her." I suppose she thought they were quite plenty. I made her loan me *Don Quixote de la Mancha* to pay for them. I planted the rest but our cows had trimmed them up so the previous spring that I didn't want to cut off any more limbs. Fortunately, Hiram had a dozen-year-old mountain ash tree so I took two limbs from that.

The broth was more trouble. I hadn't seen two of any kind of squirrels all that year. Father washed out the gun and got four or five charges of ammunition from Henry for five cents. But lo and behold — the gun wouldn't go off. I wormed the powder out, found it all mud, wormed out the charge because it wouldn't come primed and so on, until it finally fired off. Father took it when he went to milking. He hunted around Henry's fence where I thought I might have seen a red squirrel, but he didn't make his appearance and after considerable more searching, returned home with nothing.

Emeline Cobb, Uncle Norman's wife, helped do our washing the next day, and Mrs. Hoisington spent the afternoon reading aloud to Mother from the *Spiritual Telegraph*. She didn't dare to read it at Old Grow's where she lived, they thinking communication with spirits of the dead, which was what it was about, to be the work of the Devil. More about that later.

Father said that Mother's being sick a week cost $6 — $2 for the doctor's bill, $2 for Mrs. Hoisington (including board), and $2 for Father's time. He asked Mother how she was going to pay for it.

I thought I might dry apples enough to balance the doctor's bill at least. The apples that year were small and I got along with the paring discouragingly slow. Then I couldn't find the darning needle to string with and the foolishness of having lost it struck me so forcibly that it spoilt my appetite for labor. Eventually I pared 12 strings which filled the rack and put up some back of the stove pipe. In the end we took 52 strings of apples down to the Green weighing 22 pounds 7 ounces, with 23 more strings on the rack. We got one dollar.

The reason Father didn't get any squirrels for Mother's broth was because Geo Grow had shot them all on our side of the mountain. Geo was three years older than I and confoundedly lazy. He hadn't any energy of mind or to work unless he was obliged to. Even though he was an inferior cuss, when I had nothing to do I liked to be with him.

One Sunday, Geo wanted to go a-hunting on Fletcher hill — that time I got the mountain ash trees — for he'd heard squirrels were plenty there and he had a little powder for his gun. So we set off to do some "mighty hunting before the Lord" but couldn't get our guns off. Mine wouldn't snap a cap while Grow's gun would sometimes crack a cap but wouldn't go off. Finally he made a fire with some paper by cracking a cap in powder. He took his gun barrel off from the stock and heated it till it went off. So much for hunting on Sunday.

Geo Grow bragged a good deal about his gun being better

than mine. I admitted it to be the best in all considerations but four—mine had the best stock, lock, ramrod, and barrel. He also thought he was the best shooter among us. But on one occasion at least, I must have taken the best aim or something, for I caused five deaths in seven shots, while he killed three in six, so was palpably beaten.

Father and Henry called our shooting "extremely poor business." They agreed with Zadock Thompson, who, when he was a boy, had lived just over the hills in Bridgewater. He described shooting as "barbarous" in his book, *History of Vermont, Natural, Civil and Statistical*, published in 1842. Not only had we "ruthlessly warred on all the tribes of animated nature," but we did not "protect the birds which prey on the insects most destructive to harvests."

Geo Grow, and sometimes I, shot at crows and hawks because we didn't want them to carry off our chickens or eat our corn, although Geo's hunting was more for sport. But Father and Henry, as well as Thompson, knew that crows were also eating the grubs that were ruining our corn. Hawks may have taken a chicken, but they also ate mice. In Thompson's view, we were killing God's creatures and destroying nature's balance

Hunting had become nearly hopeless. I called it "gudgeon hunting." Large creatures had been eliminated long ago. In 1851 Lute and John Raymond went off to the mountains in Plymouth to hunt bears. Five had been killed there in 1850, but they didn't see any. Chas Raymond traveled to New York State to hunt deer.

I grew weary of the sight of a gun. I found more sport in going a-hunting alone and without any gun. Meanwhile Geo Grow shot at chipmunks, skunks, woodchucks, coons at night, and birds — owls, pigeon hawks, hen hawks, snow birds, partridge. When nothing better presented itself, he shot at sap tubs and apples and had the presumption to shoot Morey's dog.

Nearly all the predators were removed from our land. As a result, mice were thicker than pudding in 1851 and I sought to kill all that crossed me. They were completely overrunning us. Old Moses, our tomcat who'd got home one day with one eye put out, scared them some. Mr. Hartwell put gate-spring covers on his little trees to keep them off. They got nearly the whole of Father's herdsgrass. Henry said the seed was worth $3.50 a bushel, had he been able to get any. Mice overran our bushels of Meacham, round Pink Eye, and Long John potatoes, and they carried off our shucked corn. They managed to gnaw around and kill three or four of Father's very best Northern Spy apple trees. They stole buckwheat from Old Grow and Chas Raymond and stored it in Father's beehouse. I feared they'd eat all my papers.

Not only were we destroying the balance of nature by killing predators, but our soil was eroding, carried down our steep hillsides by spring freshets. In the spring of 1850 a great freshet caused a landslide. It rained as if the windows of heaven were wide open. The creeks were so full that the bridge near our house went off, raising the Devil with everything.

Our land was so steep in places, we used sidehill plows and at least once our wagons nearly tipped over. Father and Hiram were drawing home two loads of excellent hay when Hiram's load went on one wheel for three feet. Father hallowed to him — once he'd gotten his own load balanced — and it was almost a complete miracle that both didn't tip over.

We were hill farmers. "Hill farming" implied hardship, difficulty and deprivation for good reason. Our hillside land was worn out after 55 years of farming. Trees were cut, stones removed and fields plowed, causing soil and its nutrients to wash down to our creek and out to the Quechee River.

Father saw what was happening. I thought it was just shiftlessness but it may have been his conscience that prevented him from skinning the good timber off the Pierce Place before he sold it. He had to cut trees on his remaining land because we depended on them to live. He chopped down hemlock for stakes, eve spouts, and water troughs, then used the bark for its tannin to tan hides. In 1852, Father hollowed out a hemlock log 20 feet long for a trough to put in the barnyard. By its rings, it counted more than 300 years. We cut slippery elm for plank and wheel hubs and used the bark to make straw beehives and to string corn fields to discourage crows from uprooting corn sprouts. We used birch for planks, butternut for fence posts and barn sills and spruce for sleepers and shingles. All of us burned vast quantities of wood for heat, cooking, and maple sugaring. One year Hiram burned enough popple to take 569 bushels of charcoal down to the blacksmith on the Flat, the Frenchman Veyette.

In 1853, Father wanted to know how many trees we had left so I went up onto the hill with paper and pencil and counted them. On Father's 20 acres he had 149 maples, 86 beeches, 11 basswoods, 12 ashes, 35 butternuts, 95 hemlocks, 4 mountain ashes or remans, 12 birches, 2 spruce, 3 dogwoods, 4 elms, 125 apple trees, and 1 black cherry tree, for a grand total of 539.

Even as we struggled to farm up on Rum Street, the environmental conservation movement was beginning. Essays, books, articles, paintings, and talks at local clubs popularized scenery, birds, and nature. Within a few years the United States Department of Interior was established. In 1854, Henry David Thoreau declared that "in wildness is the preservation of the world" and wrote *Walden*.

The Vermont Department of Fish and Wildlife was established two years after Marsh published *Man and Nature* in 1864. He could have been describing our farm when he wrote, "Steep hill-sides and rocky ledges ... [are] well suited to the permanent growth of wood, but when in the rage for improvement they are improvidently stripped of this protection, the action of sun and wind and rain soon deprives them of their thin coating of vegetable mould, and this, when exhausted, cannot be restored by ordinary husbandry."

Chapter 12

The Essential Skill of Swapping

I never saw so much horse jockeying before the day Ed Whitney moved onto our road. Everybody that passed by stopped to swap horses and instead of talking and examining two days and then fearing to swap, they were ready and willing to swap at first sight and always thought they made $20. The way the miserable old horses flew about was a caution to conscience.

Whitney began with a gun worth $1.50 and ended with a horse, watch and cash worth $75.

One swap beat all the rest. Whitney began with a gun worth $1.50 and ended with a horse, watch and cash worth $75. It happened this way. First he swapped with Geo Grow, who loved to swap but wasn't good at it, by giving him the gun and receiving, in exchange, a gun worth $3, cloth worth $1.12 and $1.50 cash. Whitney swapped that gun and $5 worth of boards for a horse. He then swapped again and gave $5 to boot. The same again and $4 more to boot. Then he swapped with Orlando Richmond and acquired a horse valued at $30, a watch worth $25, and $20 cash.

Father and Hiram benefitted in the end. Whitney sold his horse to Hiram for an old white horse I valued at $5 and Father's note for $10 to boot, and Hiram's promise to chop eight cords of wood. Father and Hiram sold the horse for $25 cash, so they got a good trade.

Whitney's watch continued swelling in value, from $30 less than nothing to $23 when he swapped it with Alden Thomas for a $12 watch plus $11 to boot. Then it declined precipitously when Alden swapped it for a pistol and sold the pistol to Chas Raymond for $2.

That's the truth, every word of it — or so I was told. We repeated stories of such swaps again and again, making legends of some men like Ed Whitney and fools of others like Geo Grow

THUNDERSTRUCK FIDDLE

and Alden Thomas. I admit some of the stories may have been exaggerated in the re-telling.

I liked to swap with Geo Grow because he liked to do it so well and I stood no chance of being cheated. I thought Geo did credit to his bringing up because he didn't know enough to be tight. His father, Old Grow, was so almighty tight he never would pass on the skill of it, even to his son.

When Geo needed a horse to take his intended, Amanda Hathaway, out riding, he offered his gun — he called it worth $5 — to Hiram in exchange for a log chain and 50 cents in horse hire. He let Father have the log chain for a knife worth 62.5 cents and a shave worth 50 cents. He then let Henry have the shave for an old fife worth 62.5 cents. In the end Geo owned $1.25 worth of knife and fife and took his intended for a ride, for his $5 gun.

On October 7, 1849, when I was 13 years old, Father had a notion of making an inventory of his worth. I was ready to help him by mighty and started by listing the value of our possessions. Father's livestock consisted of a horse, a dun cow, a black cow that was a little sick, 2 calves, 17 roosters and 5 hens, and a pig weighing about 35 pounds.

I calculated our five and a half tons of hay from the upper mowing to be worth $42 minus costs — the time Father and I spent on the cutting, wages for hired workers, dinners provided by Mother and the oxens' work. I listed 37 items — furniture, pots and kettles, barrels and tubs, fiddles, bushels of corn, swarms of bees, a wagon house, wagon, sleigh and so on, plus thousands of things worth ninepence apiece. I tried to list their value but Father was mad before I'd asked a dozen simple questions so I gave up.

Even though I assigned a dollar value to all our possessions, nobody on Rum Street had much cash so it was more likely that our stove was worth a bushel of beans than $3.50.

I figured the red fiddle to be worth $6, but Father swapped it along with a 50-cent bow and our poorest fiddle box — which had cost him more than a week's labor to make — to Alvin Miles for a silver chain and neat little cylinder escapement watch, four holes jeweled.

When I tried to figure the watch's worth, everyone had a different thought. Miles said the chain alone was worth $2.50.

George Scales said the chain cost Miles only 50 cents and the watch, $12.50, and that Jerome Cox had paid Russell and Clarke $15 in wood for one exactly like it, only a little bigger. According to Henry's scales, the watch weighed in at $1.85 in silver. Then Russell and Clark's on the Green said the chain wasn't silver but that the watch was a good one.

When it came time to calculate Father's debts and credits, I found his financial records — kept in his daily memorandum — were almost no account at all. They were so brief and lacking in detail, that nobody, not even himself, could understand if they were credits or debits.

For example, he wrote, "Oct. 20 Sunday. Jarvis Richardson had 5 3/4 bushels of fall apples .70. Oramel Churchill 5 bush. .63."

"Oct. 26 Sat. Rainy. ... mended 4 shoes for S.P. McClay .30."

"Nov. 20 Wed. N.M. Cobb had the oxen & cart 1/2 a day .40. 1 hemlock log .60 One Elm .34."

I asked Father whether these amounts had been paid and found his memory to be remarkably untrustworthy. Father gave away a great many things that he would never collect.

I never knew a debt to be as obscure as the one between Father and Hiram. It started when they traded farms, leaving Father owing Hiram $80. That was in 1847. Over the next two years Hiram dressed off Father's hog, hewed timber for his shop, drew a load of wood, ground out a load of apples and received from Father flour, money, shoemaking, and other odd credits to some amount every day. In 1849, Hiram needed money to pay a debt, so Father mortgaged his own land, the piece we called the Pierce Place and gave Hiram $90 in cash. In 1850, Hiram gave Father oxen worth $75 and a note for $19.98. I thought that settled the debt.

Then in 1851, Hiram found himself owing money once again and feared that his possessions would be attached. So, even though the earlier loan was settled, Father took a suit out against Hiram for the old $90 debt. Hiram's things were sold at auction. Father bought them for $83.75 but left them in Hiram's possession. I wondered who really owned Hiram's things. I guessed Hiram did.

In the end, I concluded various people owed Father $27

and he owed $105 to merchants on the Green and others. I figured if we were to run away, our affairs would sell at auction for $700, debts paid. Father also owned 100 acres of land that was worth $1,500 or $1,700 or $2,000 or $1,200. I never could tell.

CHAPTER 13

ITINERANT MEDICINE PEDDLER

He was up on the hill watching Father milk. That was a worry! The peddler would have plenty of time to convince Father of anything.

A medicine peddler stopped by Grow's house when I was there one afternoon. He peddled medicine for W.W. Warner of Mt. Holly, over near Rutland, Vermont. He told me I was badly out of health — terrible bilious. The peddler was about six feet, four inches and weighed, say 250. He looked like he'd been blowed up somehow.

Grow's folks and Old Morey bought some of his medicine but I didn't buy anything, distrusting peddlers since the time I might have been cheated by one. I'd bought a *Smiley's Atlas* for 17 cents that he said should have cost 75 cents. Later I learned that it was an old one, published in 1839! Still I thought maybe I'd come out 17 cents ahead.

I'd learned to watch peddlers carefully. They were skilled at trading since they did it every day and I didn't trust Father's abilities in that department. So I was on guard the next time Mother told me a peddler had come by and had gone up on the hill to watch Father milk. That was a worry! The peddler would have plenty of time to convince Father of anything. So when they returned and the peddler began taking wares out of his wagon, I kept careful track of how much they agreed each item was worth. Father chose a glass honey dish with cover for 50 cents that soon got smashed, three tin pans for 60 cents, six tumblers, six sauce dishes, a tin pail with cover and a small tin pail, that we later learned leaked, and something else — oh yes, a dipper. I bought a shaving dish for 12 ½ cents although, God knew, I had no need of it yet.

The peddler took a box of honey for $1.42 and Father threw in an additional 2 ounces. I thought it worth $1.44, not including the extra ounces. He took four quarts of herdsgrass seed, calling it worth 42 cents. I thought it should have been 44 cents. The peddler stayed the night, Father asking 25 cents for his keeping, entire! He ate that much worth of honey!

I hadn't kept my figures as carefully as I'd hoped and when I did them over again, I thought Father owed either $2.59 or $2.80 and on the peddler's side, $2.55. It was all a muddle.

When Father handed over the last cent the peddler said, "No matter about the odd cent," just as he'd got it between his fingers. I was incensed. When he tried to swap knives with me, I knew he'd cheat, so I wouldn't.

That night the peddler looked my thunderstruck fiddle over carefully and admired it. I fiddled to him, and he recited a splendid epitaph ... "Beneath this sod John Esty lies; His Mouth and his grave, they were both of a size; Oh Reader! Quickly travel on; For should he gape Oh God! You're gone!"

Such was the visit from the peddler.

Chapter 14

Political Disquietude

*"The Whigs are going to win. It says so in The Standard!" said Solomon.
His claims were too much to bear.*

The first presidential election I remember was the one of 1844. I was 8. I became deeply involved, inflamed by the horrifying possibility of my candidate's loss. When the results arrived in Woodstock, I was elated while nearly everyone around me expressed shock and amazement. It felt like a personal victory. For I was a Democrat in a town of Whigs.

Elections in Vermont gave me plenty of chances to be in the minority, which is the side I preferred. I was a Democrat, not so much because of what the party stood for, but because Father was a Democrat and even more, because I always stood up for things despised. If everyone had been a Democrat, I would have been a Whig.

Father subscribed to the staunchly Democratic newspaper in Woodstock, the *Spirit of the Age*. He was among the initial subscribers in 1840 and maintained his subscription until his death in 1895. He was so loyal — except for the short time he neglected to pay his bill — that in his obituary, the newspaper called Father their "venerable democratic friend." By then, he was the last of the original subscribers. He nearly lost his subscription in 1851. In early March of that year, the newspaper sent a lawyer, Mr. S. R. Streeter, out from Barnard to collect the $6.75 Father owed. Fooled by the Flat road, which was dry, Mr. Streeter tried to make it summer on Rum Street by riding all the way up on wheels. But Rum Street, being up in the hills, was all snow and ice and he had a hard time getting through. Father gave him $4 for his trouble — all he had. I'd been in hopes that he'd gotten rid of that bill long ago since we were so poor.

Nearly everyone on the Flat and Rum Street, including all my friends, supported the Whigs. I was furious when, in the election of 1844, when Whig candidate, Henry Clay, opposed the Democratic candidate, James K. Polk, Solomon shouted out, "Polk's a coward!" Polk had refused to participate in a duel, even when insulted, a stance I considered highly honorable.

I responded with, "And Clay's a drunkard," repeating what newspapers claimed when they wanted to criticize him.

"The Whigs are going to win. It says so in *The Standard!*" said Solomon.

Aaron Whitney intervened, saying arguments such as ours were hurting the reputation of the Flat and the machine shop. He was foreman of the shop, and if you worked there you were expected to vote Whig. He made sure of it. Some years later, when Republicans replaced Whigs in the election of 1856, he told the men to vote Republican. He even made Alden Thomas stay home to vote although Alden had promised to go for his betrothed, Abby Hitchcock, in Lowell, Massachusetts, on that day. He'd gotten a house in readiness for her. I'd written Alden's love letters to Abby and so knew all about it.

Solomon Wyman's claims were too much to bear. Was *The Standard* right? I hurried to Father's shop and sweated again over my elaborate political maps, detailed lists of candidates and state by state predictions. Father had showed me how to add and subtract so I could keep track of the delegates from each state. I wouldn't have asked for any more interesting romance than a book containing all the election returns that had taken place in the United States since 1835. I shouldn't have wanted it to contain anything but names and figures, so intrigued was I by elections.

I loved politics, the competition, the fight for delegates, the passion over who was right, me or my friends — all of it. I didn't care much about the candidates' platforms. I thought them much the same on both sides. But if my candidate won, it was a personal victory.

When I was off alone, I imagined political campaigns. When I had settled one issue and one side had beat the other, I went on to the next year and brought the parties up again in different positions and the other side would generally beat. I didn't make up sets of principles for each party and change 'em at each campaign because principles could be got along without. The names alone were sufficient. In truth, I thought a Whig and Democrat could get together and not be able to agree as to what separated them.

My primary criteria for support was that they be in the minority. I would have made a poor judge, for if I heard a lawyer make a very eloquent plea, I would be against him. Then should the other side answer with most convincing and overwhelming proof, I would oppose him with my whole heart.

I read stories in the *Spirit of the Age* — stories like "Doom of the Tory's Guard" — working myself into a passion of righteous indignation over the powerful Tories, led by the cruel Teunis Van Loan who lorded it over the weak colonists, especially the handsome Reginald Mervale. The colonists happened to be Whigs during Revolutionary War times, but that didn't matter. They were the underdog.

I examined my numbers again. James Polk WAS losing ground! It was true! That night I trembled too bad to write a word and lay awake until morning. On the day the election results were expected, I ran down to the Green to wait for news. Polk won. Glory to God! Solomon paid me two cents.

Eight years later, in the election of 1852, Solomon again supported the Whig candidate. So did another friend, Austin English. Mother and I visited the Englishes that year. Father scolded about the visit because we hadn't finished haying, husking the corn, digging potatoes, picking apples, getting in wood or fixing the house for the winter. Nevertheless, I fixed up the horse, harness, and wagon to go. Betwixt us and our gear, I thought we should astonish the Englishes. I felt ashamed remembering Mrs. English's visit to us some time earlier. Mother didn't have any flour to make dinner with so instead she made johnnycake, a poor substitute, and served it with honey. I think it made Mrs. English about sick.

Austin's father was a successful rake maker in English Mills. He sold several hundred hay rakes each year and their home looked very different than ours. They had a shed full of dry wood and no jawing about it. While Mother went indoors to visit with Mrs. English, Austin and I went out to the workshop to see who could hold the most rake teeth in one hand.

"Pierce don't know nothing," Austin said. "He fainted away in Mexico and shit his breeches."

"If Franklin Pierce isn't elected, it'll be because the Free Soilers prevented it, damn 'em," I said. The Free Soilers had split off from the Democrats.

"Maintain your rank, vulgarity despise. To swear is neither brave, polite nor wise," said Austin.

I thought he'd better pull the beams out of his own eyes before giving me advice. We counted the rake teeth in our fists. Austin won, holding 174.

Later, our conversation returned to politics. "Scott's gaining by thousands daily. The Locos are leaving the sinking ship," exulted Austin. "Delaware and Florida have turned Whig!"

Oh God! I thought. I'd read some Whig boasting in the Mercury and it had troubled me ever since but I refused to reveal my worries. I said, "Scott may carry Vermont but Pierce will be a hundred thousand ahead in the popular vote."

"The New York *Tribune* pronounced Scott's election certain," said Austin. "Greeley says 'the Locofocos will be completely astonished at the immensity of their own defeat.' "

Of course his comments madded me. He didn't know anything about it.

We went back to the house where Austin got out his accordion and played. He announced his father was going to New York to buy him an aeolian and that he was going away to school in the fall. My politics were right, but oh, the differences between us! How great it would be to be thus! I would certainly have swapped homes with Austin and perhaps parents too, but I wouldn't swap selves. Austin was better off for flesh than I was, but not half so well off for muscle.

During dinner I saw how mannerly he was at the table. I supposed that I ate awfully mannerless — indeed Austin was amused! No matter, I thought. I meant to sit down and eat in peace. I didn't want anyone to keep sticking this or that in my face for I could find out what I wanted alone and get it too — and I liked to let other folks have the same privilege. Or if a person wanted me to hand them a thing, they could just speak and I'd do it gladly. That was my system.

Later Mother said that if she had any relations within 10 miles she wouldn't return to our house. I felt the same. Oh God! It was impossible to ever tell how shiftlessly Father conducted things.

No man in Vermont understood the strength of the parties as well as I did. The certain knowledge of defeat wouldn't be a fart in a whirlwind to being in doubt about it beforehand, so I sot down with pen and paper and reckoned my numbers again. I figured without New York or Pennsylvania or Ohio, Pierce MAY be elected and very likely would be. I might have erred about the strength of parties in Georgia since I didn't know exactly how strong Mr. Troupe was. I added up all the delegates of the likely states and they still pointed to a Pierce win.

Solomon, of course, continued to disagree. I was forced to spend the night before the election with him. We'd been carrying his father's hay cradle up to Father's mowing and it started to rain like fury. We took shelter under a big hemlock, arguing, as usual, about the strength of the Whigs versus Democrats. When we noticed that the rain was leaking down onto us unendurably, we put back to Solomon's house as fast as we could get along, though the bulky cradle hindered us mightily. I was never wetter in my life, with no dry clothes, mad at Solomon and in a Whig household on election eve. I couldn't get home for it carried on raining very hard till after dark. My own house wasn't so thorough a shelter from rain as Solomon's, but it was home and Democrat and consequently more comfortable.

I laid awake next to Solomon all night long, wondering why I was so painfully interested in politics. It would never make a cent's difference if Scott was elected but really, it would come hard.

The next day I watched Geo Grow, who wasn't even 21, going by and singing out that he was going to put Scott in. Old Grow followed. "It's my duty to vote for Scott. The *Mercury* told the town committee to get out all the Whig voters." Ed Willis drove by with old Morey to add another vote for Scott.

Election results started coming in by telegraph at noon the next day. By Friday we knew Pierce was elected president, carrying 27 states of the 31 and 240 of the 296 electoral votes! Glory to God!

Vermont voted for Scott, and Scott also won a decided victory in Woodstock. But Pierce was the winner and so Sol paid up his two cents.

I told myself I wouldn't be drawn into any more presidential elections only so far as to vote. They caused a summer of disquietude.

Chapter 15

Fiddling and My Great Book of Music

Frederick Cobb, Hiram's oldest boy, came down one day to show us his new 50-cent fiddle. It had been made by Warren Willis, who left soon after for the California gold diggings. When Mother asked what was going on at home, he answered honestly.

"Pa and Mam are quarreling in consequence of that rum he got on town meeting day," said Fred. Emeline Cobb had already told us the wonderful story about how Hiram, either by accident, design, or being crazy — or more probably because he didn't know enough to prevent it — had taken the road to Ches Raymonds' after town meeting, stayed there 'til nine o'clock, and abused Sarah the day after.

So intent were we on our game and our discussion that neither of us noticed Mother's kitten tearing Mr. Hartwell's Kossuth hat all to thunder, even though it lay not a foot away.

Fred said, "Pa kept scolding Mam and she cried. Pa swore he'd whip her and she struck his hand. She went upstairs to get some things to go away with and he followed her up and they both cried! Pa was the most to blame."

Mother gave him my old coat to wear home that day. It was just right for Fred, except a little too long and would answer a good purpose. I'd worn it when I had my daguerreotype taken in 1847. It was the neatest coat I ever had and was still good and whole, all save the sleeves.

Not long after that Mother sent me up the road to borrow some beans from Sarah. We had no food at home. I was beginning to realize how Mother struggled to feed our small family — I was an only child — and how ashamed she must have felt to beg for food from her sister-in-law. Hiram was abominable poor too, and had five children to support.

I turned into their dooryard, scattering a flock of chickens, and heard the scratchy sound of a fiddle inside the house. Inside smelled badly of pee, sour food and unwashed clothing. The baby cried and toddlers fought over bits of rags. Fred stood in the midst of it all dragging a small bow across his homemade fiddle. He sawed on those strings as intently as he followed his father doing chores. He was just 7 years old.

Frederick's raspy tones didn't resemble any tune I'd ever heard but still cast the terrible poverty of the room into the background. I became determined to get myself a fiddle. Father immediately went out and bought one of William King for $2 and fixed it up. I think he was eager to have me pursue something I might have an aptitude for. It was becoming clear I would never be a good farmer and certainly had no talent for singing.

Mr. Hartwell had paid me a dollar for hoeing his half-acre cornfield, and with that money I bought *Musician's Companion No. 1*. I practiced out of it about all the time. It contained over 300 pieces of music — marches, quick-steps, waltzes, hornpipes, contra dances, and tunes for singing — also 18 sets of cotillions arranged with figures.

At Mr. Hartwell's singing school in Andrew Thomas' parlor on the Flat, I paid more attention to how Andrew Taft played "Chorus Jig" than I did the singing, particularly since the singing was so poor. They bawled some psalm tunes, out of tune, in such a manner that the words could barely be detected by anyone other than those who had them before their eyes. It was a treat to hear the singing master sing some funny songs after such a monotonous and universal howling. But Mr. Hartwell quit the school about half way through, exasperated by how the boys trained.

I began studying theory of sound one night after an argument with Mr. Hartwell about the subject while playing checkers. We played about 25 games in Father's shop in the afternoon and I came off two ahead. This he didn't like and swore that if we played slow and took back no moves, he could beat me five times out of six. So we played three games as slow and sure as the Devil, but they didn't raise his self-sufficiency much for he came under twice and the second game was a draw.

So intent were we on our game and our discussion that neither of us noticed Mother's kitten tearing Mr. Hartwell's Kossuth hat all to thunder even though it lay not a foot away. I came off ahead, but my skull ached badly and Mr. Hartwell's hands trembled. The next morning I found lying on the table some lectures that Mr. Hartwell had delivered on the subject of sound. I rejoiced at their appearance and vowed to copy them. They were very good. I also studied harmony and chording in Charles Simon Catel's *Treatise on Harmony*, published for students at the Royal Conservatoire of Music in Paris.

I copied these documents into something I called my "Library and Journal of Studies" and later "Weekly Journal of Music." I planned to publish my journal at the rate of four pages a week or more, if convenient, commencing June 24, 1850. I was 14 then. I raised animosity enough to write off two pages, then a few more, until I'd copied the entire series. I never saw anything hang on so in my life.

I filled my trunk with musical writings. I discovered that I could hear a song once and write it down. Sometimes when I wrote a song down I supposed it to be original, but afterwards heard it played note for note, so no doubt I'd heard it sometime before I wrote it off. But sometimes my tunes were a little changed from how I'd heard them, to make them better.

I'd gotten other music books by then, Ole Bull's violin instruction book, Elias Howe's *Violin Without a Master*, and a preceptor for the clarionet. I'd studied them so much they'd fallen to pieces. Father then sewed them together into one large and first rate music book. I started carrying my fiddle 'round outdoors to sugarings and to the bee house where I could practice while watching for bees to swarm. I played for sings and parties, once earning $1.08 with which I bought a coat and vest.

Eventually Father arranged to have a book made to keep my musical writings in. He sold two boxes of honey on the Green in order to buy a skin of Ira Wood for the cover. I called it my "Great Book of Music". The book's magnificence, its thick white pages and heavy leather cover, appeared like a great Bible, but it was only a music book and nothing else — although the word "music" included poetry, vocal music, elements of music and instructions for various musical instruments.

Fred and I carried our fiddles everywhere. Henry said our tunes sounded like great violining from a distance. The music carried for a half mile over the hills and valleys, although, he said, it waxed smaller and smaller when he followed the music and found it was just us two playing.

The winter of 1850, I quit going to school in favor of fiddle lessons. Also I got provoked because Master Adams acted rather insulting to me, doubtless because I appeared rather unwarrantably green. Also I wasn't learning anything except geography. I took 10 lessons in fiddling from Leverett Lull who kept a singing school at the Flat. Mother was a very good singer, and I had gone there with her when I was younger. Lull also wrote songs and dedicated them to "big" people in Woodstock.

Father paid $5 for the lessons. I thought he should have spent the money more sensibly — on a large load of boards to build his barn or a warm coat for himself. His coat wasn't fit to carry guts to a bear in, nor were the vest and pantaloons. The outlines were rather irregular all around. I said he should have some admirer of colors inspect them and tell their colors. Were it not for his shirt he would not have presented an extremely modest figure.

Henry laughed at him and said, "It looks like someone was tempted to steal half your coat tail and made a frantic attempt to obtain your shirt tail as well."

I said, "I don't see what your object is in wearing such clothes."

"They're as good as I want," Father replied.

And so the $5 went to my fiddle lessons. At first Lull showed me how exceedingly inferior my performance was and that I practiced but little and was running down as fast as could be. But in reality, I was gaining, and soon could play much better than at any previous time. Yet I could not play any tune a thousandth part as well as I wished or knew it could be played.

*Facing page: Photo courtesy of
Woodstock History Center, Vermont*

Part Two

Chapter 16

Hill Farmers

Grandfather died soon after we moved onto Rum Street, leaving a most excellent and profitable farm of about 125 acres, several other farms, and notes from people he'd loaned money to, some of them quite old. Our grandmother had died a few years earlier.

His money and farms were divided among his five sons and one of his two daughters. Hannah Richmond, Grandfather's second wife, received a promise of $60 a year until her death and the town of Woodstock received $450 to support my aunt Betsey Cobb. Father and my uncles didn't realize the magnitude of these financial obligations.

Henry was to collect what notes of grandfather's that he could. He and Laura stayed on the good homestead farm, worth about $2,000 at least. Within a few years, he was better off than any of his brothers, selling $500 worth of produce to the community every year. He always had money and everything else. Sometimes I wondered if I would ever pocket a little of it, as they were childless, then dismissed that as a darned impudent, foolish, improbable story.

Hiram got a complete farm of 20 acres down the hill with a good house and barn. He could have gotten rich because he was a hard worker who wanted nothing more than to farm. But by 1849, he had a large family to support—five children all under the age of six and sometimes, his wife's sisters and parents, Granny and Granther Morey who came to Rum Street expecting to "be took care of." I called it the Morification of Rum Street.

The Moreys were somewhat too closely connected with us by marriage. The tribe were not very respectable people, neither were they dishonest or dishonorable people at all save that they could not live without a tongue conflict with themselves or their neighbors and no one of them would hesitate to lie. Granny Morey was very fat and healthy and very religious, though a curious sort of religion, for she played cards and delighted in quarrels. Said she could tell fortunes and thought she knew everything and frequently said so. None of them were ever worth a cent. Their living was always poor but it was honestly got.

My Aunt Almira was given 20 acres with an old ruin of a house on it. She'd married Chas Raymond by then. They lived on the Green and he had responsible positions at one place or another, including sometimes, the machine shop on the Flat. He farmed the land on Rum Street and did it well.

Uncles Norman and Hosea shared a large place in Bridgewater with a cabin and a decent log house that was worth about $450. But it was so mountainous that scarcely an acre was fit to plough and the mowing was so poor that they couldn't get more than half a ton of hay to the acre in 25 acres of mowing. And besides, it was miles from any human being and a place where the Devil wouldn't want to live.

Father, the eldest, got 80 acres called the Pierce Place and 20 acres of farmland near the family homestead. Neither had a house or barn. Father told the census taker his land was worth $1,000. He might have gotten that if he'd sold it, but instead he tried to farm, something he had no talent for. So we didn't get much from our piece of land as long as we held onto it.

Wool wasn't the lucrative venture it had been in Grandfather's day. So Grandfather's flock of 108 merino sheep, which had been divided among the brethren, was soon sold off. Without sheep, the highest part of Father's upper mowing that had been fenced off to pasture, was soon covered with raspberry briars that cost him $10 to cut.

Grandfather left two large debts. My Aunt Betsey had been a promising girl till 18 or 20 when she had the measles. After that her appetite knew no control. She did nothing during the day but carry provisions to bed and eat. Remonstrances were of no avail. Norman used to tell about her going down to Philemon Sampson's to Thanksgiving, eating her fill, going outdoors, gagging herself with her hand, throwing up, eating again, throwing up the second time, and again eating. About 1839, Grandfather shut her in her chamber and carried her meals regularly, determined to starve her to a cure. For a day or two she fasted entirely and at last made a rope out of the bed clothes, escaped out of the window, and never entered the house again.

THUNDERSTRUCK FIDDLE

Result, a constitution wrecked, a life thrown away, and a burden to the community. Verily, intemperance comes not of rum alone.

Father and my uncles gave the town of Woodstock $450 to pay for her care, foreseeing her inability to care for herself. When that was gone, Sam Wood, overseer of the poor, demanded payment for her care from Father. As the eldest brother, he was expected to see to it.

The second debt was to Granny Hannah Richmond. She gave up her share of the inheritance in exchange for a promise of $60 a year. At a time when cash was scarce and Father swapped for most of what he needed, these were ruinous debts.

For a day or two she fasted entirely and at last made a rope out of the bed clothes, escaped out of the window, and never entered the house again.

Chapter 17

The Abode of Satan's Poverty-Strickens

Isaac B. Hartwell owned an old house on Rum Street, and when his wife was confined to the Vermont Asylum for the Insane in Brattleboro, he let us stay there-in. Mother sang in Mr. Hartwell's singing group on the Flat. She did his washing, sewing, and cooking, and Father cared for his stock. Most of the time he came up only while he had farming chores to do, so we stayed there alone. During haying Mother cared for him and his hands.

- 64 - LESLIE ASKWITH

The house stood in bold relief on an elevation which slanted toward the west. It was a very pretty place. It was 28 feet square, solitary and alone, with no shed on either side. It contained the great chimney, 12 feet square and 3 fireplaces. A pair of bars served for a gate. The yard was the whole mowing and orchard of two acres. We cleaned the dooryard around the front door every spring.

All the roof wanted shingling and all the house wanted whitewashing very bad. Indoors, the whitewashing overhead was actually dropping down and looked abominable. I could sweep down a bushel.

Charles Cobb's drawing of his house, courtesy Woodstock History Center, Vermont.

The kitchen had a bed and table and a large fireplace with a stove just forward of it. Rain leaked through between the door and the stove before it had rained an hour. Its two kitchen windows were minus any glass, nor any cloth sewed on to block the weather. The kitchen ceiling was boards laid across the cross pieces, eight feet from the floor, thus making a garret where we spread butternuts and stored old boots, rags, glass iron, etc.

It was very cold in the kitchen in the winter, so about November, we moved into the square room and cooked and slept there until May. Nearly everyone on Rum Street did the same so as to not have to heat the entire house and thus save on wood.

 The square room was 14 feet by 14 feet in size and was our only decent room. Mother put up our old mantle clock with the face broken out and paper window curtains, which had been given us long before and were nearly torn all to pieces. She had an aversion to either Father or me being in the square room which I could not account for.

I had to be pretty still or else I molested her. If I sang while making pictures on a slate or if I got too many things 'round she'd say, "Your room is better than your company," and I had to take my cap and leave. That provoked me more than a

If I sang while making pictures on a slate or if I got too many things 'round she'd say, "Your room is better than your company," and I had to take my cap and leave. That provoked me more than a million times.

million times. If I wanted to write, I was obliged to build a fire upstairs in Father's shop, which contained his shoemaker's bench, a tool chest, and his desk.

Mr. Hartwell's room was also upstairs. It was decidedly the best in the house.

My bedroom was downstairs and had a fireplace and two windows. The ceiling leaked in the west corner after four hours of rain, causing me to move my bed. I never built a fire there or stayed, except nights. My furniture was a meal chest in the east corner and two chests in the north corner. There was also a light stand and two or three chairs. Below one of the windows was a bumblebees' nest. I took aim out of the window twice per night and when I let it down, the bees made a great outcry.

The real front entry, which we never used, had a table set against the door with a melodeon and books on it. Father bought the melodeon of Orlando Dunham in 1848, giving him a fiddle and $8, some tools at $8 and a note of $9. We took the melodeon and my fiddle to sings at the neighbors' houses during the winter. The entry was also used for a clothes closet, and having a large cupboard on the inner side it answered also for a buttery where we packed away old duds.

We had a cellar under the square room, which contained plenty of water, some boards to walk on, the pork barrel, and a lot of other empty old things sot 'round on benches to look at — boxes and cider barrels sometimes empty and sometimes not. The bottom of the cellar was three feet above the road and was equipped with a drain.

The chamber floor was covered with dirt, water if it chanced to rain, sawdust, old boxes, chests, barrels and the like. We tucked the sap tubs in the south corner and the corn was spread on the northwest side.

Father put a fire board in the square room to block the chimney. He also put in a stove which we bought a while ago of Chas Raymond. We paid its iron value, Chas having seen fit to throw it away and get a better one. Father worked most of the day on it, and then we could heat the room up to 200. That small stove looked real neat, but unfortunately it wobbled, having been raised onto blocks so Mother wouldn't have to bend over so far to lift the heavy iron tea kettle. Once the entire stove tipped over, raised hell with everything, and killed one of our seven cats outright.

It wasn't the very tightest or warmest house that ever was. The truth is that it was abominable, all rain, dirt and litter — like Tophet. The house looked from without like the abode of Satan's poverty-strickens.

The truth of our poor circumstances came upon me on October 19, 1848, when I was 12 years old. We were all out of wood and all out of victuals. It was an uncommonly scarce day. When Father and I got down from the hill with a load of wood, I found my friend Jane Osgood there with Mother. They had eaten no supper and had no fire, and it was not very warm, and nothing else. I saw this, then the house, then the clothes I had on, lastly those that Father had on. I never felt so dismally ashamed, so vexed and insignificant in my life. I never forgot it.

CHAPTER 18

THE FARM YEAR

SUGARING

I was 13 in 1850, the first year I sugared alone. I vowed to sugar most enthusiastically for I hoped to make $5 to pay for the fiddle lessons I'd taken from Leverett Lull that winter. Sometimes

I made out, after half freezing to death, to boil two pails full. Then I undertook to carry it down to Henry's through the snow with my neck yoke, and arrived there in anger and glory with almost one pail full. I never had such a walk in my life.

Father would come up to help, but he did things so insufficiently and was so cross that I hated to see him coming. That year Father tapped the trees, chopped a little four-foot beech wood to burn and made a miserable boiling place. My arch was little more than a limb stuck into forks in trees with my kettle hanging above the fire. He didn't even want to do that saying he knew I'd be too lazy to make any sugar.

But I found that I liked to sugar above all other labor. The weather was just right and there was something about the place — going back onto a hill and in the woods, where there was no one to disturb me and I had enough to do. The more I worked and the better I did, the more sugar I'd make, and so I was interested. And the more interested I was, the more I worked. I was never sick of it or tired. I preferred sugaring alone for when I worked with Father, I saw him do such abominable things that it seemed as though it was no use to work.

The following year I asked Father to build a stone arch. I picked a place for it on level ground in a grove of butternuts beside the upper mowing stone wall. When Henry came up with his horse and bobsled to draw logs — the snow crust was so hard, it bore the weight of the horse everywhere — he looked the sugar place all over, considering wood, stone, sap and weather and concluded that I had picked the best spot. I tried to shovel a place for the arch but the snow crust was harder than the shovel.

Father didn't take the place Henry and I had picked for the arch but another, further from the stone wall, so he had to draw stone thirty rods uphill. We worked all day, with a fire going to thaw out the ground around the arch, drawing stone and building the arch. I like to have starved to death and froze to death too. I criticized Father for forgetting to get some hooping timber to hoop the remainder of the tubs with and complained that I needed more "small tools" that year, a dipper, broom, hand sled, syrup keg, etc.

But my boiling apparatus was much improved.

This is a summary of my sugaring in 1850:

Day 1 ... I washed out the sap tubs and piled them in the kitchen for Father to take up on the hill. But he didn't do it, preferring to work on a trunk he was making. Nevertheless, I went up to my sugaring place which was on the very highest part of one of the highest hills in town. It was inexpressibly cold, windy and snowy. Ed Woodward and Owen Raymond came along — we were gumming for spruce gum — and we all concluded it was too cold on the hill to do anything so went to sliding, for they were armed with jumpers. We ended our slide at Lish's house and played checkers for an hour, I beating them every game and so went home, half starved, to find Father at work on a fiddle box. Thus was my first day of sugaring.

Day 2 ... Father hooped and soaked our tubs in the watering trough, tapped out sumac spiles and drew everything to the sugarbush up on the hill with the oxen and sled. The weather at our house was fair and warm but up on the hill was cloudy, windy and cold. We tapped about 36 trees, set up the arch which was rickety, and installed the kettle which was leaky.

Day 3, April 7, Sunday ... Sap didn't stop running on account of Sunday and I carried up my neck yoke, gathered sap and boiled it in.

Day 4, April 8, Monday ... Went up to the sugar place, tried for a fire with five matches and failed. Henry came along and he tried for a fire with six matches, and I am sorry to say, succeeded by almost a miracle. It was the last match he had, and it went out fairly enough, but somehow when he had lain it down and put the others top of it, it began to stew and presently burned. Father was up and made some bows for his two steer yearlings. I boiled all day.

Day 5, April 9... Tremendous cold and an awful wind. Father went up with me to syrup down. We like to have frozen to death. Father cut down two butternut trees, of which there was almost a forest northwest of the boiling place. We made a splendid fire out of dead limbs. He intended to make a fence of the remainder next summer. I read some *Christian Messengers* which I had borrowed from Laura. We made 20 gallons of syrup. Returned home and Soloman Wyman came and stayed till dark. We wrote, fiddled, played cards and checkers, read, and had an excellent time.

 Day 6, April 11, Thursday ... Ate too much breakfast and was so sick when I got up to the sugar place that I was obliged to go down to the calves' shanty and sleep two hours on the hay. Henry Willis came up with me and after training 'round two or three hours, trying to get me to quit, he declared I had stayed long enough and went to putting out the fire, which he declared he had built. I put it up three times and he hauled it away. I was vexed.

 "Depart thou," saith I unto him.

 "Depart thee thyself for I shall not," saith he unto me.

 Then saith I, sore in spirit, "Take thee to legs," and lo he did even so, for I helped him in a way he could not resist.

 "Vengeance is mine," he cried out, departing down the hill in great speed, threatening most awful things.

 The fellow was only 12 years old, but almost as large as I was.

 Day 7, April 12... Fast Day. The governor, in his recommendation, advised residents of our state to humiliate themselves and pray but he dropped the fasting part! I obeyed by feeling humiliated to see the sap run over and then I prayed that it wouldn't run the next day.

 George Bennett and Ed Woodward came up from the Flat in the morning, and we went to Lish's sugaring off and ate all we could. We — George, Ed, Owen, John and I — played tomfool an hour or two, always tomfooling Ed. We also had some awful snowball squabbles 'round the sugarhouse, running and jumping, John and I against the other three. I fell into a deep crevice behind a high snowdrift, and they had an awful time getting me out.

 Henry's had become almost a home to me. Laura sugared off my syrup, and every time I stopped in there on my way home at night, she'd set the table for me, and three times it was proposed that I stay all night so as not to have to come up again in the morning. Also Henry brought three loads of wood from Father's pile to my arch on his handsled and saw to my sap, collecting it, boiling a little, saving it from overflowing.

April 14 ... I stood at 108 pounds sugared off, and the equivalent of 4.5 pounds put into the big teapot for the bees. I wanted to make out 200 pounds.

Day 8, April 18 ... I hadn't been to the sugar place, though my presence there was almost absolutely necessary. On Wednesday towards night, the calves went away from the shed on the snow crust, which they found would bear. They chawed out five spouts and knocked down seven or eight tubs that hadn't been attached to the trees for want of nails.

Day 9, April 19 ... I went up and found the arch, kettle and all, almost entirely covered up with drift snow, and I could only get the kettle boiling at three o'clock. Twenty-eight trees caught sap. I made out, after half freezing to death, to boil two pails full. Then I undertook to carry it down to Henry's through the snow with my neck yoke, and arrived there in anger and glory with almost one pail full. I never had such a walk in my life. I vowed to be there the next day, spouts in hand, and gather and boil. I almost despaired of getting my fiddle up there.

Day 10, April 20, Saturday ... First rate sap day. Didn't wear my cap as usual when I was at work out of doors in warm weather. The effect of it was that I was as red as an Indian.

Day 11, April 21, Sunday morning ... I carried up the last *Saturday Evening Post* to Henry's as it had a portrait of Jenny Lind and arrived at the sugar place at 10 o'clock. Father came with me to cut some wood, though it was Sunday. Father never cared anything about Sunday and I observed it very little, for even if I actually believed every word of the Bible, I could see nothing in the book or the day that warranted resting on Sunday if anyone was willing to work. Built a fire and made it go pretty fast.

The day was clear, cloudless and warm, and the sap ran decently well. Things looked most glorious then, for cold winter was departing and summer taking its place. I feared that it would still freeze nights enough to make sugar weather, but if it did not I should not be saddened for in the extreme corner of my soul I was beginning to be a little sick of sugaring. I had not the least conveniences, and the hope of making much sugar in that situation had departed. Also, I had no company and I could not carry up my writing.

Ball playing had commenced at the Flat and I felt I must go down soon and play, for with the change of weather also came a change of business. It was the actual beginning of the year, and everyone felt gay and glorious. It was the time to fight battles.

Day 12, April 22, Monday... I made some remarks about sugaring on Sunday. Old Grow, supposing that sap would not dare to violate the Sabbath, left half of his tubs running over Saturday night and went to meeting to get his soul revived. Every tub he had, ran at least one and a half times full before Monday morning. I guess he had a good time in the rain on Monday, for his cries of dismay made everything down there look blue, the drowned Devil. From our hill we looked right down into his sugar bush which seemed to lie below our feet. I wrote no memoranda that evening, only to state that the run of sap after the late freeze was to be the last we had, despite the madness of the weather with its thundering, raining, and then being cold. The storm put my fire out and half froze me to death. I had almost enough of sugaring in that old apparatus. Henry had been helping, but Laura called him home by blowing the dinner horn. The machine shoppers were there and afterwards came up to examine my arch which Father built. They unanimously agreed that together with the kettle and everything else it was no more fit for boiling sap, than was hell for a powder horn.

I ought to have practiced at least a minute a week on my fiddle but I did not seem to do so. It was smart business to take $5 worth of lessons and then stop entirely. Something would have to be done.

Day 13, April 25, Thursday ... My time for writing was coming to the awful extremity of the little end of nothing, for sap seemed as though it would run well that day and forever after I feared, and as my work left no time but evenings for writing and fiddling, and even the evenings were decreased to almost nothing, I was indeed in a sad plight.

Day 14, April 30 ... Went up, syruped down, and took it down to Henry's. Found Laura a-sugaring off. Laura sugared off in the house every day. She'd sugared the first mess of syrup I made — 16 quarts made about 15 pounds of sugar. She said that if it had been as thick as Henry's it would have made 25 pounds at least.

Day 15 ... I molasses'd off the last mess of syrup and the settled settlings. Made about 25 pounds. Hosea brought my molasses down the next day with the neck yoke and two tubs.

Finished sugaring. Gathered my tubs. The frogs began to peep, creating a chorus in the swamp below our house, exactly as Henry predicted nine days before, for he said that Friday ruled the changes that year. On my last day I found it curious to stand on top of the hill and looking to the west see nothing but hills of snow while to the east there was nothing at all.

    I made 110 pounds of sugar in 1850, an amount that 'twould hardly recompense me for the grease used in greasing the sap in the kettle. The following year with my improved arch, I made about 93 pounds from 53 trees. In 1852 I made 151 ½ pounds from 45 trees. In 1853 I made out 218 pounds of sugar. Reckoning in the 55 pounds of store-tub sap and two tubs of settlings and skimmings, my complete total was not less than 300 pounds.

GRAFTING

All during sugaring, I fretted about not having time to write. When I was hard run for time, I found more time in which to write, even if I had to set up until 10 o'clock. When sugaring was over and I didn't have much to do, it might be supposed that I'd

My criticisms of Father proved to be short-sighted. Later, his apples paid for my future. Without them I'd probably have remained a hopelessly inferior farmer and miserable lazy cuss forever.

THUNDERSTRUCK FIDDLE

have plenty of time to write and would write more. But it was right the other way, for I had neither the inclination to write nor anything to write about. When I did nothing all day it seemed silly to set up to write in the evening. Also when I fully finished sugaring, it began to appear pretty evident to me that I should cease to write at all, for nothing interesting ever happened.

So I was perfectly willing to help farm and would be exceedingly delighted to have a good deal to do, for as I said, the busier a person was, the more leisure time he had.

So I urged Father to plow and, if that got done somehow, I'd urge him to plant. Mother told me I might as well be easy and not pester him, for if he did plant he wouldn't hoe, and if he hoed, he wouldn't gather. We were always behind. Grandfather said Father was good to work but needed a master. I wrote in my journal, "If Father isn't shiftless, what is?"

Father told me, "Set your business at rights. For we will be hard at work building fence and plowing soon."

"The Lord hasten the time," said I, thinking "and grant that the products of your farming be as great as your animation."

"You always represent things a dozen times worse than they are." Then he whipped 'round the oxen and plowed a little and perhaps as an apology for building fence put up a rod or two, but nowhere strong enough to discommode a calf. If the least shoot of corn sprang up it was immediately pastured down. But if by chance it survived that trial, it would be killed by the weeds.

Such was commonly the result of Father's blustering. He blustered, but delayed till the season was past, scolding severely anyone who dared to hurry him in the least. But when it was past hope, "and the last man was fairly hung," the very Devil was raised for a short time.

Father worked hard on things he was interested in. His mania for a few years was grafting, for he was invariably engaged in that which was most unprofitable to his business. He began by making grafting wax but didn't do it right. He put the comb in a bag, boiled the bag in a kettle of water, and got the wax out of the water! The correct way was to boil the comb in a kettle of water, put the whole in the bag, and squeeze the wax out of the bag but he hadn't the necessary things.

Nevertheless, I sometimes helped Father in grafting.

When he was grafting for Henry, I helped by pulling the grafting wax, carrying away the brush, looking on, sleeping, and once, trying to make a butternut willow whistle, but found I hadn't mechanical skill enough. Then I picked stones for Henry, earning 50 cents in doing so.

That spring Father worked at grafting for about 75 cents a day, sometimes with Mosely Thomas. They'd set 485 grafts for Hathaway and he grafted for Chas Raymond, $10 worth towards the old house Father was buying from him.

For himself, he'd grafted Northern Spies, Roxbury Russets, Mass Baldwins, Lemon Pippins, New York Pippins, Fall Pippins, Pumpkin Sweets, Blue Pearmains, Harveys, Sweet Russets, Morgan's Winter Sweets, Morgan's Early Sweets, Golden Sweets, Rhode Island Greenings, Summer Sweetings, Henpeckeds, and others.

My criticisms of Father proved to be short-sighted. Later, his apples paid for my future. Without them I'd probably have remained a hopelessly inferior farmer and miserable lazy cuss forever.

FIXING FENCE

We built new fences in the spring and repaired them almost year around since our farm animals were always looking for better food or a mate on the other side of their fences. They knew about our orchards, fields of oats and buckwheat, patches of corn, potatoes, and beans, and vegetable gardens, and they found gaps to get out of the pastures and other gaps to get into the mowings or plantings.

We stopped up gaps with top poles and brush and built new pitch and board fence with ash and butternut posts or stone. We used the old dry fence for firewood. I'd been learning about fixing fence for a fair number of years and thought I knew all about it until I read that stakes should be driven top end into the ground because they would, in that position, remain sound six times longer than if the butt ends were in the ground. Much astonished, I spoke to Father about it, and was more astonished to find that he had known the fact and acted accordingly for years. Wood conveys moisture upwards while alive and so it does afterwards if it stands butt down, but if top down it can't,

After a long chase we got the steer and oxen back into our pasture.

explained Father. I guessed I didn't know everything yet.

When we built stone walls however, they were expected to stay. I helped Mr. Hartwell build his wall by getting the stones. I used Hiram's oxen, the best around, because rain and snow sailing about in the atmosphere did not discomfit them at all. Mr. Hartwell, Norman, Father, old Morey, and I threw stone. Hiram lifted and placed each stone into its place. That wall was still there, smothered by brush and covered with moss and lichens, years after the barns had collapsed or been taken away.

Much energy was spent arguing about whether fences were high enough, in the right place, and who should fix them — the landowner who should have fenced to keep the animals out or the animal owner who should have fenced to keep the animal in. If a dispute was serious enough, a fence viewer was called in to settle it.

Even if we kept our stock corralled by mending our fence strong enough to stop the Devil — Father called it "stopping up the gaps" — it didn't always stop the neighbors' stock. Henry's colt got into our mowing so many times I figured he'd have to pay us for the colt's keeping. And Chas Raymond claimed our hens had eaten and tangled his oats 50 cents worth, although his oats would have scarcely been worth a damn after Grow's turkeys had been in them most of the summer. Chas killed one and warned Grow that next time he'd kill another one and then they would be about even.

One of the times Chas Raymond's steers got out, Father had to track them, Chas being two miles away at his house at the Green. He followed them more than half a mile to the Bridgewater road and along that until he found them in a man's barn. The man offered him supper, which he accepted, and so didn't get home until night.

Another time Lish Raymond came up in a big sweat to where Father and I were haying in the orchard. "Who owns the horses Hiram uses?" he asked. "They were in my corn this morning and I've yarded 'em up. I'm going to advertise 'em and charge for keeping and damages and make the owners — whoever they are — pay $15 or $20 costs! I won't stand it ANY longer. It's impossible to fence against the Devils!" He said they'd been in his mowings, corn, and oats, or else in the road and 'round his house, about every other night for six months and deprived him of a good share of his sleep.

We owned the mare and Hosea owned Old Bill, but Hiram used them. Hiram could better afford to go to California than to build $300 worth of fence to stop those horses. Later that day, when he wanted his horses for getting in the hay, he went onto Lish's land, although Lish had forbid it, got his horses, and that was the last we heard of it.

Here's another example. It was August 1, 1851. I was walking up the road to find Father who was on the hill with the oxen cutting spruce poles for rafters for our barn. He'd just broken his axe off in the eye when I arrived. The axe had been cracked, riveted, and breaking for some time. As he was complaining about the axe, the oxen noticed our old dun cow that had escaped her pasture to go "bullin" 'round. The oxen set off in chase. Father followed the oxen and I followed Father, carrying the broken axe. By the time we caught up with the oxen, they'd broken the yoke in two, which hurt the off ox some. We drove the oxen into Bradford's pasture and the dun cow followed as we'd hoped. We borrowed a yoke of Henry and yoked the oxen, I got another axe, and we began cutting poles again. (One dollar and a half minus for our time and the axe.)

Meanwhile, Gibbs' devilish steer and bull, which he'd

been keeping in our pasture, had escaped and were in the road and followed the cow into Bradford's pasture. Again we noticed the escape and after a long chase we got the steer and oxen back into our pasture. We then returned to cutting rafters. When the cow got enough, Father, descrying from the top of the hill, came down and helped me get her into our pasture and turned the bull into the road.

It being one o'clock, I walked home to eat dinner and carry Father's dinner up to him. I saw our horses in Bradford's pasture. I told Father about the horses and he told me to stay and watch the oxen and not leave for anything while he went and got 'em. He got the horses by leading the old mare and the horses following, but it took him two hours.

When he got back on the hill, he found I had lost the driving stick, although I'd gotten a better one. Upon learning this, the axe that he had broken earlier and the yoke sunk into insignificance. A great outbrawl followed and I had to look up the stick. We managed to get down one more rafter, two small logs for home, and some more logs for our new neighbor, Jo Dodge, and his wife, Hannah, who was another of the Morey sisters. They'd moved into Hiram's house (which was the beginning of another kind of trouble). We got done at nearly dark.

FIXING THE ROAD

Folks stuck to sleighs in the spring like the old Harry, just as they did to wagons in the fall. On March 6 one year, Bailey from down on the Flat looked outdoors and saw that the road was dry and clear of snow. Everyone was using wheels. He removed the runners from his wagon and put on wheels and a bell and drove up to Rum Street where he had a hard time keeping even one wheel out of the snow. By the time he reached Henry's house at the top of the hill, he found the snow drift in the upper mowing (where corners of the towns of Bridgewater, Sherburne, and Barnard were crowded into six square rods), was probably 10 or 12 feet deep if not 50 or 60 feet. He got out, tied up his horse and went afoot from then on.

We had to wait until June to fix the ruts, pits, and caved bridges on our road. I called the little bridge near Mr. Hartwell's

Sometimes I was given the job of driving the oxen and fetching the scraper, plough, iron bar, and stone boat. I complied, grumbling of course, attending each excursion.

house the toll bridge because everyone had to stop there and proceed cautiously, it being nothing but a general hole with slabs stuck over it to aggravate the misery.

On road-fixing day, I helped work out Father's tax, for we were each assessed a road tax based on our ability to pay. We could pay it off in labor, so that's what nearly everyone on Rum Street did. This created a problem since some cash was needed, so five prosperous taxpayers from the Green, who paid their tax in cash, were added to our district. The family of Old Maids who ran their own farm on Rum Street, worked out their debt by loaning us their oxen.

Most of the folks working on the road didn't do 25 cents' worth of work in a day, and what was done, wasn't done right. Geo Grow was one of those. He was always an extremely inferior worker and didn't do but a cussed little work, but he sang so many cunning songs that I thought he plenteously did his part.

Sometimes I was given the job of driving the oxen and fetching the scraper, plough, iron bar, and stone boat. I complied, grumbling of course, attending each excursion. I also hoed water courses beside the road as instructed and hauled that dirt into the road, which I thought was worth no more than a fart in a gale because water was still left to run down the middle of the road.

Father was voted to the office of highway surveyor four years in succession before giving up the position. I figured

Father's final highway bill and found he had just enough cash to cover our tax but had a credit of $19.08, which was partly swallowed and partly swapped for logs and help on his barn. Thus Father retired from office even.

HOEING

I knew little about farming. I could not ride, could barely drive oxen, or chop very much. I couldn't even swim and I lamented that more than all the rest. Mother and the neighbors called me lazy. I wasn't lazy, but Father never had anything for me to do. And if I undertook to do something, he opposed it. But I could hoe and had once earned a dollar by hoeing Mr. Hartwell's half acre of corn.

Folks, such as Geo Grow, talked of hoeing an acre a day, but I was shocked and astonished to see how abominably he did the work. A quarter of an acre a week was my stent, and still I could hoe as well as any mortal and pretty near as fast. It was in the disposition and patience and not in the hoeing. Put me at work with another person and I couldn't be beat. I could hoe like thunder because my mind was not on my work. But all alone, the time used to pass horrible slow because I wanted it to be gone.

So by July 5 of 1851, I saw that the weeds in the corn field had come to a crisis and I knew they must be looked to. I reckoned I could do that myself. I started a little before sunrise and hoed till all was blue. If I worked, I could not think so I worked and imagined what I hoed to be at war with what I hadn't. I killed the sorel and brake here, and then their enemies, the mullen and grass there, back and forth. Weeds died as the war raged, my Braman hoe the

I didn't want to stop because when I stood still, I started thinking, and that seemed kind of lonesome.

weapon. I didn't want to stop because when I stood still, I started thinking, and that seemed kind of lonesome.

Our cornfield was near Henry's house and at 10 o'clock I heard Laura's dinner bell ring. Being half starved, I went to eat, then read *The Rangers or The Tory's Daughter, A Tale Illustrative of the Revolutionary History of Vermont, and the Northern Campaign of 1777*. The Revolutionary War battles there-in inspired me to resume my own war in the cornfield. "There old men and boys, with others who, like them, had come unarmed and as spectators of the battle, would spring forward after some retreating band, seize the muskets of the slain, and engage, muzzle to muzzle, with the hated foe."

At three o'clock I came in again and had dinner, then slept until seven o'clock, when I rose and went out and hoed by moonlight. When it began to sprinkle a little, I quit, not wishing to show any unwillingness to have it rain. Half of our corn was beginning to curl up from the drought. Having quit work, it stopped raining, and I went out and worked for another two hours. This may be stretched a little.

I carried down a pint of grubs for the hens — Old Dovey, Granny Texas, Abolitionist, and Isaac — who gobbled them enthusiastically. I'd gotten my shoulders well-rounded hoeing that day.

I had asked Father to get a cultivator but he said he "expised" such improvements in agriculture. I'd used Lish Raymond's once, but it was chained together so clumsily that it kept getting out of rig, and the Old Maid's horse was abominably mean and contrary and kept backing onto the cultivator until I resorted to whipping her. I did a shameful and inferior job.

That year I wrote, "We shan't have enough corn to hat a chicken." What with Lish Raymond's oxen and Old Grow's turkeys getting into the corn, and the mice and squirrels eating it while it dried up on the great beams in the barn, I figured it would amount to a few bushels of sprouted, mouse-eaten, squirrel-eaten, turkey-eaten, misery-struck ears of corn good only to give the chickens. I was right. We made out but four or five bushels by the time it was shelled. Father and Hiram had to buy corn to feed the cattle, 894 pounds at one cent a pound from Mr. Hartwell.

WATCHING BEES

I was glad when it was time to watch bees. The bee house was beside a brook and, getting comfortably seated, I could sleep, read, and write in my music book and my "Vermont Collections" about all the time. I'd stayed there in the swarming season and watched the bees every year since I was 8 years old.

When I was young, the bees used to swarm from May 15 to July 15, but later, they didn't swarm until June 15 to August 5. It seemed so with every other thing — it was later in the season than formerly.

When the bees swarmed I got Father so he could hive them. He put new swarms into hives he'd made out of strips of elm bark. Sometimes he sold the swarms, delivering them, hive and all, tied up in a piece of cloth. They were valuable — worth about $5, the equivalent of five cords of wood, ten music lessons, or about half a ton of hay. Once Father let Barzilla Richmond have a swarm of bees for four calves. If he found a late swarm that he considered worthless, he'd store it in some way such as sticking it up an old cabin chimney and selling it cheaply. Reuben Daniels once bought one for one dollar and a half.

When George Bailey lived on our road, he liked to watch with me. George, age 10, had fits and was not very well, ever. I had work to convince George that the inside of the great bee

In 1851, I was hoeing with Henry when a swarm of bees flew into us. We thought we should easily keep up with them as they were flying by, they not being close together, but pretty soon they all got by and then we found that they were going darn'd fast and what was worse, right over the top of the hill. We clawed up the hill with all our might, but when we got to the top, they were out of sight.

LESLIE ASKWITH

house was not full of bees and that he could safely enter it.

In 1851, I was hoeing with Henry when a swarm of bees flew into us. We supposed that they had come out of the bee house it being so near, though the direction didn't come from that way. When they first came up on us we might have stopped them by throwing dirt in the air, but we didn't know anything about it. We thought we should easily keep up with them as they were flying by, they not being close together, but pretty soon they all got by and then we found that they were going darn'd fast and what was worse, right over the top of the hill. We clawed up the hill with all our might, but when we got to the top, they were out of sight.

We went on as fast as we could over into Perkins' woods. We heard what turned out to be them, so we marked a tree and came home.

Father was taking windows out of the old house nearby and boarding up the holes when I told him about the bees. He looked in the bee house and said there weren't any gone and then said they were Henry T. Marsh's bees from the Green, for he had a swarm fly to the mountain the night before but one. But it was found that they came further to the north east. Father said he could find them in a little while if he knew the direction they took, so Henry and I started off again. At the top of the hill we thought we found them, but after we looked at them a little while, Henry said they were nothing but flies and called them the "will of the wisp," for they sounded off in any direction we were of a mind to have them. But an hour after, we saw they were bees flying into a tree trunk. Father got leave of Perkins to cut the tree, and Henry and I carried the piece of the tree that held the bees down to Henry's to sot up back of the house with a shelter over them. They were worth altogether $10, according to Father, half of which was mine.

Father's honey was his most lucrative farm product. He sold it for cash ($1.55 or so for a box weighing about four and a half pounds) or traded it — to get his horse shod for example. But when neighbors stopped by, Father set honey on the table where it was eaten at a great rate.

In 1851, we had 13 swarms in the bee house and since Chas Raymond had planted more than four acres of buckwheat nearby, we got an abundance of buckwheat honey. The next year, we had 22 hives. I helped Father load his honey boxes onto the wagon for the county fair in White River Junction. The day held squizzly at times but faired off just before we left. I figured Father's honey production at 1,309 pounds total. He beat Pierce of Barnard, and got first premium, $2, for the greatest amount of honey raised on one farm and second premium, one dollar, on best specimen of honey.

Many years later, the *Spirit of the Age* wrote, "There is no man in this country that understands the habits of the little busy bee any better than Mr. Cobb."

HAYING

Between the weather and Father's ability to be distracted by odd jobs, haying progressed as shiftlessly as all of our farming operations. The hay grew to peak condition, passed that point and began to age. It was a constant aggravation, standing around everywhere, withering and turning brown. We felt guilty as hell. Father got mad at the hay and everybody else. He hated to be reminded of work that needed to be done.

As I said, our haying commenced slowly every year. One year we started on August 6. I helped Father put away the cart body, change tongues, draw the wheels up to the barn, fix up the old hay-body, put the body onto the wheels, and clear a road to the barn. Then, claiming to be in an awful hurry, Father took two hours improving a turned pitchfork handle and then took another hour to grind out the tines that had a little broken off them although that was done well enough in 10 minutes. Then he ground four scythes.

I'd turned grindstone for one scythe for Mr. Hartwell and turned it about 2119 times — I always counted when I turned — and he said the scythe wasn't half finished.

The following day was rather cloudy so I stayed indoors sewing together a collection of old papers. It was a mighty job to keep 'em all even, drawn tight, etc.

At 10 o'clock I mowed the barnyard and read *Uncle Tom's Cabin* until noon. After dinner I went up to the little mowing with my scythe, although there were still a great many light clouds overhead. It rained so I stopped a spell under an apple tree, and when it stopped, mowed three times across the field, spread out the hay and came home to find Father. He was mending his boots and jawing Mother about going to sings with Mr. Hartwell, which she'd done several years ago. She was so mad she refused to get him any supper.

Old Grow and Granther Morey came up the next day just as I was sitting down to breakfast. They carried with them six scythes they wanted to grind. Just as they were ready to begin, Grow's hogs got out at home and he had to leave forthwith, so put his nose against the window and told me he wanted I should turn for Mr. Morey till he got back. I told him I was damned if I was going to turn stone for six scythes. I'd turned grindstone for one scythe for Mr. Hartwell and turned it about 2,119 times — I always counted when I turned — and he said the scythe wasn't half finished.

That day, all the hay that was down got perfectly dry. I went up with Father and piled up three or four little heaps when it began to pour down hard so I went off to read *Uncle Tom's Cabin*. I was impressed by George Harris who "talked so fluently, held himself so erect, looked so handsome and manly, that his master began to feel an uneasy consciousness of inferiority." I thought it was an awful pity I hadn't a little George Harris slave blood in me!

I'd had a tremendous jaw with Father during mowing two or three years before. Father had seen fit to hire hands that year and they were all present. It was my first year with a scythe. I mowed a swath, struck at nothing, and watched 40 stones roll downhill. If I cut low enough to get any grass, every blow dislodged those stones. I dulled the scythe so that I had to spend more time grinding it than mowing. I called our mowing "digging stones." Father heard me and called me lazy and ignorant. I called him a shiftless hog and left the field, weeping. I swore he wouldn't make me appear an abominable fool again.

Since then I studied the art of self-defense and had more chances to do that than the study deserved. When he jawed at me about my manners, I said the house was cold and that there wasn't a stick of wood at the door. He jawed at me because I couldn't yoke the oxen — they were afraid of me — and I, about his inability to answer a civil question. So by the time I was 16, I thought of myself as having a pretty considerable share of coolness, cunning, and presence of mind.

One afternoon I pulled the handle off the gudgeon rake while tumbling the hay. Father got mad and scolded. I didn't speak loud or angrily. I didn't point out that the rake was rotten. With another rake, I continued working as fast as I could, minding my work and saying nothing about it. He raked after me, aiming to get me behind, he being dissatisfied with himself and me. I took it easy, or that is, didn't work any harder for it, and did get behind.

Then said he, "A boy 6 years old can rake after a cart but you can't."

"What you say implies at least two lies, and hints at another," I said.

He said he guessed I had better work for somebody else. He didn't want such a cuss around. He'd hire Geo. Grow, etc. etc.

But I continued raking, unflinchingly, and avoided shedding any tears. I think he looked rather sheepish.

I'd been working two hours and the rain had stopped some time earlier when Jim Cobb and Owen Raymond came up. We set off to find Father who'd gone off mending fence between the pasture and orchard. The off ox had escaped the pasture and gotten into the orchard again and eaten up a mess of apples along with a lot of the beans I'd hoed. Father was indignant when he saw me — too mad to tell me to rake the hay. So I thought I'd just as lief let the hay be, seeing he didn't want it raked, and we three went to the barn to get weighed. We lifted weights — Jim and I could lift 216 pounds — and we played cards for three hours. They stayed the night although it was rather uncomfortable sleeping three deep.

Our haying limped shiftlessly along. We mowed a little when it was fair and hot and stopped as soon as the weather began to growl and mutter. Father made an axle for Royal Smith and feeding boxes for Pierce. The hay continued to deteriorate. I did a little scything along the road and Mother said it was best I not hay alone so I went to find Father who was hovering about the barn.

I'd always thought of myself as determined to work, hindered only by Father's lack of instructions. But I found myself as distracted as Father. That surprised me. Somehow I didn't want to follow his orders and found endless excuses. The less I worked, the more Father and I jawed, and the more we jawed, the more excuses I found not to work.

Seeing how desolate our prospects for haying were, Father finally hired some hands. We started haying in earnest a month later than usual. The day was cold as Tophet. I had to button. A great and respectable company assembled up at Henry's to grind scythes. Oramel Churchill ground, then Geo Grow, and then another and another. Everyone who was finished sot down to wait until all were done. I thought they ought to have gone to mowing but John Raymond kept everyone entertained with a long string of talk. "It isn't worthwhile to work all the time. I'm a'going to have a'goings in with Cynthia after haying about $3 worth. I must go somewhere on a bust," and so on. This went on until 8:30 am.

Everyone mowed fast when they got at it, although none too well. Geo Grow had held on his own scythe and ground it ridiculously bad and couldn't make it cut any. He had bragged so, and mowed so hard, that everybody got to making sport of him. He quit at nine o'clock in the am, went off and was gone an hour, and then came back and went to spreading and tumbling with me. We got out the team and began to draw at nine-thirty. Oramel pitched on and Alden laid the load and pitched it off. They kept it going till after seven o'clock. We drew in nine loads.

At noon, Father brought pails of beans, potatoes, green corn, herrings, crackers, bread, and cheese for dinner. There were 10 of us and only knives and forks for eight, which caused a short-lived crisis that was passed over (until the next year). The meal didn't last but 10 minutes. I was given a drink of water, molasses, and vinegar mixed together, and told of its refreshing properties, but it sickened me so that I couldn't work for an hour.

After dinner, we helped Henry and Laura get in a lot of hay. Laura raked, wearing her newly adopted breeches costume, the first woman on the road to do so. Henry and I argued about the effect of labor-saving machinery. He said " 'Tis a curse to the laborers," and I said "It's raised laborers' wages and lessened their work." He paid us with a barrel of cider. He wouldn't part with less than 20 gallons since he was liable to be fined $10 for selling a single jug of cider.

The hands carried the barrel to our orchard and continued mowing, much cheered. The cider, showing its effect, caused John to train Geo like the Devil. He began by informing him, "You don't know so much as Balaam's touch-hole."

Then later John asked Geo if he'd married Mrs. Gates yet. Mrs. Gates was an old lady, 30 years older than Geo. "I saw your names published in *The Spirit of the Age*." We all knew that nobody, even the Reverend Kidder, would marry them.

Then later still, John said, "I hear the boys on the Green followed you and Mrs. Gates home," this occurring on the day they'd gone down to be married, and "heard they got your hat," and so on.

It was a ridiculously ludicrous scene for us spectators.

Then John raked Geo's heels and Geo returned the insult. John struck Geo over the head with Father's old stout rake, teeth down, with force enough to break the rake head off and then beat the handle up about him. It made a cut in his head two inches long and much deeper than I should have thought possible on account of the skull, plus several minor gashes. Geo tried to smash his rake on John, but it broke, being new and extremely weak. Everybody blamed John for striking Geo, and they settled it by Alden's agreeing to mow for the Grows, thus relieving Geo of half a day's work.

By nightfall, we'd got all the hay into the barn, only tipping over one load, and none of it wet. It was a great success. We gave three cheers. The hands ate supper at Father's house with the exception of Oramel and Ches, who were cidered so badly that they didn't come down from the barn.

HERDSGRASS, OATS AND BEANS

Most years we grew oats, barley, corn, hay, potatoes, and beans. Our crops were often meagre but I couldn't blame it all on Father's shiftlessness. We could do little about the weather and any number of critters wanted our crops as much as we did — chickens, mice, grasshoppers, steers, sheep, horses, turkeys, crows, hawks.

They raked in such a slovenly fashion and bound so poorly that our hens benefitted and ate oats half the afternoon.

Oats were particularly well liked. Here is what became of Chas Raymond's oats one year. Chas came up to gather his oat shocks one afternoon but got to playing checkers with me and we played until night, so he paid Lish Raymond's boys to stack the rest of his oats. They raked in such a slovenly fashion and bound so poorly that our hens benefitted and ate oats half the afternoon. We put a stop to that by shutting the hens up in the barn. Mother and I clipped their wings after they went to roost, so they couldn't fly out and get at the oats again.

Chas Raymond put the rest of his oats into our barn floor where they were discovered by Hiram's — really ours and Hiram's — two horses that had gotten out of their pasture again and came up the road. They pulled off about 60 bundles and chawed up 30 of them. The damage was at least 25 cents.

I prided myself in the quality of my oat stacks. I bound the oats tight and laid the bundles into stacks so well that no binding pole was needed to keep them on. When I'd got up high enough to begin to draw in, I laid all the bundles till I got them almost arched clear over at the top and completed the arch in such a way to keep the whole hopelessly in place.

We used Jerome Cox's threshing machine to separate the oats from the straw, then borrowed a winning mill to clean the oats. I cleaned fifteen bushels on a Sunday. Henry Darling, a man of 25 and good fellow, was down where I worked and we had a long talk about violating the Sabbath and being an infidel. He died of consumption not long after.

The mill was a poor thing. When I saw how it wasted oats I declared I'd do the whole pile over again but by the time I finished I was rather too tired. Instead I got together to play with some boys who'd gathered in the orchard where we threw apples at each other.

We also raised beans. One year I earned $1.25 pulling and stacking 125 rows for Chas Raymond. Mordecai threshed them and got 10 bushels. I thought 15 bushels wouldn't have paid for the seed, plowing, planting, plastering, hoeing, pulling, stacking, getting in, threshing, cleaning, fencing, and taxes to say nothing of the use of the land and muck drawed on last fall.

This was particularly true for Father who delayed planting and then planted little. In 1850 Father finally planted six quarts of beans. I neglected the weeding except in the bee yard. Then Mr. Kent's sheep got out of Father's pasture and into the bee yard and cleared the beans off so clean I thought they'd been harvested. The few beans left were spoiled by being left out through too many frosts. We had to borrow beans of Hiram that winter. He let us have a peck to pay for reading our *Saturday Evening Posts*.

The following year, we had so many beans that they were the only crop that wintered us out. We bought corn before January and potatoes before April 20. We ate beans with vinegar, stewed with corn, or baked with or without pork, almost every day. I admired them above all things. They never hurt me and cured me when my other victuals made me sick.

We grew Timothy for hay and one year we hoped to harvest the herdsgrass seed from it, which Henry said, would make us a devilish sight of money–$7 from two bushels of herdsgrass seed. At that rate Father might have collected $100 worth of herdsgrass seed easily. I thought it was a splendid idea.

But it wasn't as easy as it had seemed. When it came time to cradle the herdsgrass and clean the seed, Henry found that the blow from the seed poisoned him, setting off his asthma. I think it was true, for I could hear his sneeze three miles off. Oramel Cox thought he cradled enough herdsgrass to yield two and a half bushels but instead he only got three-quarters of a bushel.

Father tied his best herdsgrass into 69 bundles and put them on the great beams of the barn. But he left it there too long and when time came to thrash, he found the mice and chickens got nearly the whole of them. He saved enough to sell a peddler four quarts for 42 cents.

The prospect of farming in Vermont was hard and unpromising. That was true for all my uncles, yet I increasingly realized Father was a particularly poor farmer. In the end he made about nothing.

ELISHA RAYMOND'S MILL

Elisha Raymond had a mill at the bottom of the steep road that led up to our farm. If Lish or his son, Lute Raymond, needed water to power the mill, they opened a gate at a reservoir up on the hill. Lute Raymond was almost a giant. If he had been like Ed Woodward he would have been a smasher, but he was a first rate fellow.

One day I found him sitting outside the door of the mill eating bread and milk with two great rags on his hand and the blood running. He said he'd cut two fingers almost off about 10 minutes before with an axe, probably on account of attempting to work on Sunday. But the gash on either finger would almost have severed any common-sized man's wrist. He was turning wheel hubs from slippery elm hub timber, holding stick on the floor with his left hand and holding his axe near the helve. The axe handle swung behind him and struck a grindstone. The edges of the gashes lapped open about half an inch. And to prevent them from bleeding he filled them up

He said he'd cut two fingers almost off about 10 minutes before with an axe, probably on account of attempting to work on Sunday.

with soot. Father came along soon after, stripped off his coat and went about sewing them together. I asked Lute why he didn't go to a doctor. He said he guessed it would do well enough to cut off one and let t'other grow. The accident he sustained would have been rather bad for a fiddler.

In the fall they let the mill out to the neighbors for making cider. It didn't grind enough to kill a snail hardly. Abominable press too — the middle board squashed in and cider ran out behind like Satan before we got it squeezed hard enough.

In 1852, thanks to Father's grafting, the orchard bore more apples than ever before. Father shook the trees and I picked, and then we spread them out on the barn floor to season. The snow flew considerable. 'Twas so cold I could hardly stand it to do anything. I put on three vests and two neck-handkerchiefs. I wore my summer breeches over my best ones. I'd mended my old mittens more than 20 times. Granny Morey gave them to me in April 1850.

We had use of the mill for only three days, for Lish wanted the cider tub to scald his hog in. Father had to hoop and scour the cider barrels and then couldn't yoke the oxen and it cost him a whole day to instruct them. When we finally began on November 20, Geo Grow and Oramel Churchill shoveled apples into the press and looked on encouragingly as we crushed. The next day was equally cold. We lost a good deal of cider on account of the cheese being frozen and cider being frozen onto every piece of apple skin.

Father left all but one of the barrels in Hiram's cellar as there was no way to get them down cellar at our house without tearing out some of the wall and rolling them down a board from without. That's the way he had always done it before, but that year he chose to set the barrel on a bench outdoors, soaking it morn and night for a fortnight. He ought to have drawed it off then, so that he could have put it down cellar, but he let it be till it had frozen once or twice and had to be drawed out in the house. We put it up on two chairs, set a half barrel before it with a small tunnel in it, and I kept the hole clear so it would run into the tunnel.

We'd picked 372 bushels total, 210 of them cider apples, from which we made 20 barrels including half a barrel of water cider. We sold 14 ½ barrels at $1 a barrel. I thought it didn't pay enough for the making to be worthwhile.

WORK AND PLAY

When I laid about the house, I was uneasy. It seemed that I ought to be at work producing something. But work interfered with fiddling and writing, which seemed like play. When I fiddled for the fun of it, I didn't produce anything. If I fiddled for money, I was producing something and therefore it was not play. Yet in playing by fiddling, I was learning, which was of as much consequence as producing something.

I have got so snarled up that I know I am speaking nonsense. Yet I will continue.

The product of writing was altogether different than the product of working. In writing my journal, I was playing, yet I was also learning to write and it seemed that it was of as much consequence as learning to fiddle. I was satisfied however, that writing a journal simply for the sake of writing it, wasn't worth anything. I knew full well that not more than one man in a million did any such thing. Yet I continued those pages and vowed to do so, in some form, until the day of my death.

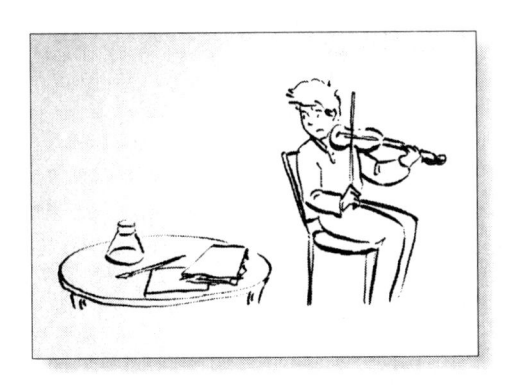

To write or fiddle or work — that was my dilemma.

I have always been unusually given to writing. I liked to write better than I liked to fiddle and practiced it ten to one. To write or fiddle or work — that was my life-long dilemma.

Chapter 19

Norman Cobb Leaves Woodstock

My uncle Norman Cobb was great to endure hard work, even when it was cold enough to kill. But that isn't what enriched a man after all. What enriched a man was a good farm, few debts, a contented helpful wife, prosperous in-laws, helpful brothers-in-law and healthy children — at least some of them boys to help with the farming. Norman had none of these, in fact just the opposite.

He inherited a farm so remote and on such a poor road that it was impossible to draw home a load of 500 pounds with a two-horse wagon. So Norman corrected it by selling the land and buying the Bradford farm near the family homestead, paying $240 down and agreeing to pay $35 a year in work for four years.

His wife had given him two sons and a daughter but died when she was just 26. Not long after, Norman married Emeline Morey. Emeline had been caring for Norman's baby and while others noticed how poorly she treated little Mary Elizabeth, Norman didn't notice or didn't care. He married her on Thanksgiving Day of 1843. It wasn't a day of thanksgiving that year, for Emeline immediately sent Norman's three children away, keeping her own two daughters.

Norman's children were my cousins and James and Eddie Cobb were about my age. We walked to school together, played in the hills and helped our uncles with their popple coalpits, sometimes staying all night while they tended the making of the coal. We'd picked spruce gum, and swum in the reservoir. We'd grown up together, and I was mad when Emeline split up the family. Eddie was sent to New Hampshire and James to a family down on the Flat. Baby Mary Elizabeth was sent to Aaron Whitney's family, also on the Flat.

That's why I wrote in my journal, "She is a dishonest, sneaking thankless devilish old rip, looked at from one side. From t'other side, if there is any, I never got a view."

Emeline's parents, Andrew and Lydia Morey, followed her to Rum Street. Granny Morey told me, "There isn't another woman so good-souled and full of religion on the face of the airth," referring to herself. "I can tell at a glance the character of any stranger I see," and had quickly concluded her daughters' husbands, my uncles, were drunkards and "poor unconverted devilish inferdevils."

One morning I came upon a fearful hot-water tragedy at Morey's. I was passing by their house when I heard Granny yelling and bawling. I looked and saw her out back of the barn putting for the woods, shouting, hollering yelling, bawling, jawing, hooting, swearing, and making every describable motion and some indescribable ones. She was headed for Old Morey who was going out to hoe his corn. But it so happened that on t'other side of the fence and 50 rods off, one of the old maids was going in the same direction with a halter under her arm to catch her horse. All this Granny Morey beheld and misinterpreted, assuming a meeting between the two.

Granther Morey's drunkenness couldn't be wondered at, considering what a rip old Granny was. Never did a man have more to bear than did he. He brought up some 15 children, did a great deal of hard work, been a poor man all his days, and was knocked 'round enough to kill 10 men.

The next Morey to arrive on Rum Street was another of Emeline's and Sarah's sisters, Mrs. Jim Willis. She brought with her, three children, scamps who stole from George Scales' peddling cart and Stearns' store and borrowed my accordion, taking it off to Bridgewater and leaving it somewhere thereabouts. Her husband had gone off to work in Rutland, leaving Mrs. Willis with Emeline, adding several mouths for Norman to feed.

The town had given her money enough to last a short while and told her that when that ran out, her next stop would be the poorhouse. Determined to avoid that fate, she resolved to stay with Norman, especially after a new thing came to light, hitherto unknown, which was that she was about to "be sick" — have a baby. Upon learning that, Emeline and Granny Morey were more determined still, that she not be so shockingly disgraced as to go to the poorhouse.

Norman was a poor gone critter — so cussed poor he couldn't half live. So one Saturday night in May of 1851, he left Vermont. He'd heard about cheap, level land in Four Mile Grove in La Salle County, Illinois, from others from Woodstock who'd gone there. They praised the rich soil and hospitable climate.

As it turned out, he didn't just run away in the night as I'd first thought. He'd prepared to leave and had Father's help. Father bought Norman's 13 sheep and a yearling calf for $20 in cash, and some old augers and scythes for another dollar. Norman owed Father an old debt which he paid up with a pretty poor wagon, a lumber-wagon body, a decent sleigh, 64 sap tubs, a harness, a cracked cauldron kettle, a miserable old white mare, two buffaloes and an old harness, a grindstone, and a harrow. He conveyed all these up into the bee house and gave Father a bill of sale.

After Norman left, Father and I did his accounting. Norman owed Hiram considerable, so we needed to settle that debt.

We learned that the sheep didn't exactly belong to Norman but had been promised to George B. Warren to pay old debts. So Father hid the sheep and calf in the barn until he could swap them with Mr. Gibbs for a pair of steers worth at least $30.

Norman's other treasures had been secured to Bradford to pay for the farm. Father stored them up at the bee house until he could sell them at auction. The only people who knew of the auction were Father and his brothers so Father was able to buy everything save the sap tubs for $22.75. Henry bid off the tubs for six and a half cents apiece. They were first rate ones and had cost Norman 25 cents apiece. The total netted was about $30. Father turned all of that over to Hiram.

Then we figured Norman still owed $420 for the Bradford place, which he only gave $380 for, and wasn't worth more than $280. Hosea came in and took a deed of it, so then Hosea owned it and Norman owed Bradford $140 in labor for it. Curious operations.

Norman hadn't intended to leave his own family, only his wife's relations. He sent a letter to Father telling him to send Emeline to join him.

"Gaius P. Cobb i got here last tuesday, i am wall, i had a good time going out, I went from Whitehall to Saratoga to Senecda, to Bufalow and Detroit and new bufalow and then to

Chicago. Gaius, don't never build a house in that Cold Country Come out here & see this Country — here is thousands of acres lays to common — good land. Corn is 20 cents a bushel and wheat is 40 cents — tell hosea to let his land go out there and come out here for one dollar and twenty cents acer.

"Tell Emeline that I will sent the money within six weeks if she will come out here — I have got $13 left. Gaius, I want you should write to me how Emeline gets along — i am to work for Mr. aldridge — tell emeline that she can come alone jest as well as though i was with her, and tell her she needn't feel bad about leaving her friends for she has better wones out here. Norman M. Cobb."

Father wrote back.

"Mr. N.M Cobb, Sir, I received your letter last evening. Henry brought it from the Green (postage only ten cents). Charles copied it off and I carried it immediately to Emeline. She appears to be very willing and anxious to go to you, and thinks she can raise from her effects in the house, and what the town owes her for keeping Mrs. Willis (which is about $6), a part of the $30. I have seen and talked with Henry about what method to take to raise the money to send your family there, and we have not yet concluded. As soon as we conclude on something I will write again. Gaius P. Cobb."

Father carried the letter up the road for others to add to. Laura wrote that she hoped Norman would be blessed with health and that he might procure a comfortable and pleasant home for his family. Father wrote more that I didn't see. I enveloped and directed the letter and Father mailed it in the afternoon.

Left behind on Rum Street, Emeline and her daughters became Father's obligation, he being the oldest of the brothers. He enlisted Henry's help and they enlisted the help of Ovid Thompson, Overseer of the Poor of Bridgewater, Mrs. Willis being from Bridgewater.

Mrs. Willis had been staying with Emeline from the time she was "taken sick." Mr. Thompson had given Emeline $3 a week for her care and Henry was entrusted with $5 to buy her provisions. "That is all the town will pay," he told her, showing that he didn't know but a darned little about war.

Mrs. Dodge came down one night wanting Mother to go to Emeline's house because Mrs. Willis was SICK. Mother was always asked to assist at the births on Rum Street. That night there was parade enough for two babies. Every woman was sent after from Dan to Beersheba. Old Morey got drunk, Whitney got drunk, and had the Delirium Tremens — he was a fallen Son of Temperance and a gone goose. Old Morey went to the Green after a doctor but couldn't get anybody because they knew they'd lose their labor. So he drove to Bridgewater for Dr. Furber who made a business of doctoring for that town's poor. The baby was stillborn and Mrs. Willis was so sick that moving her would result in "instant death," according to the Moreys.

All Moreydom was in complete sizzle. They'd got it into their heads that the town owed them $20 and pay for all the provisions they asked for until Mrs. Willis recuperated. Moreys from all 'round came and made enquiries of Henry. The way they stretched the story was laughable. Going home that night I heard Granny Morey swearing exceedingly and uncommonly bad, and ever since, whether going or coming by, I delighted to stop a moment to listen to her outcry.

Finally Mr. Thompson agreed to continue paying $3 a week to whoever cared for Mrs. Willis. Norman was gone. Mrs. Willis and Emeline were arguing, for Morey sisters couldn't live together for very long without fighting. So Mrs. Willis moved in with her sister, Hannah Dodge, surviving the half-mile trip.

Still, Father needed money to send Emeline off to Illinois. He approached Sam Wood, overseer of the poor in Woodstock. "It's the cheapest and only way that you can get rid of her," said Father. "If you don't help her off and let Norman take care of her, the town will have to."

Sam Wood reluctantly handed Father $10 with the grave stipulation that if Emeline didn't get away for good, Father, Henry and Chas Raymond were to pay the $10 back to Woodstock.

With Emeline about to start, a general fix was in order. Laura and Mother sewed new clothes. The men rejoiced in doing other things. Father made boxes to carry her things. Hosea bought her furniture. Old Morey took her dog. Laura gave her a small trunk and Father gave Laura a larger trunk to replace it. Laura bought $3 worth of stuff for Emeline, for which Laura was to be paid in things that Emeline had already sold to Hosea and Hosea wouldn't give up, thus creating a rift between Laura and Hosea which wasn't realized until Emeline was long gone.

Father paid Emeline $2 for some debt she claimed he owed. Sarah paid her for some other things. Chas Raymond paid her for improvements made in his garden. The brothers-in-law figured Emeline had $40 on starting, though she said that it wasn't anywhere near that much.

Hiram left June 27, taking Emeline and the girls as far as Rutland. He had firm instructions to see her started for Chicago, thinking she might yet change her mind and go off somewhere else with the money. The heads of the families had taken considerable pains to have her gone. The last sentiment that Emeline expressed to the inhabitants of this region was, "Gaius and Henry had got all the property and that was all they cared for. I never should get a damn cent of it."

Emeline arrived at Four Mile Grove eight days later. Norman sent two letters that I took out of the post office — one for Hiram and one for Henry (postage due, five cents). Mother ran up to Hiram's with his letter and read it aloud. Norman wanted everybody to quit farming in Vermont and go out there. All the neighbors were Woodstock folks. Emeline was well, happy, contented, hearty as the Devil. They kept house — boarded an old bachelor — had the use of the house — two cows, and 50 cents a week to pay for it. Norman had 40 acres of land and thought he could save enough by next spring to pay for it. I was glad.

Hiram left June 27, taking Emeline and the girls as far as Rutland. He had firm instructions to see her started for Chicago, thinking she might yet change her mind and go off somewhere else with the money. The heads of the families had taken considerable pains to have her gone.

THUNDERSTRUCK FIDDLE

Chapter 20

Fiddle Mania

He made a dozen bridges, finally concentrating all his skill in a final bridge. I offended him by declaring that it was not as good as the one originally on, but was obliged to partially retract my statement.

As I've said before, Father was subject to manias, and when he got into one he neglected all else on his farm. In April of 1850, Father got the fiddle mania.

He studied the treatise about the construction and improvement of violins in my fiddling book, the *American Violinist*, until all was blue. He examined Dr. Tom Powers' fiddle when Mother was sick and he went down to the Green with the best wagon to get 80 cents' worth of physic. Dr. Powers' fiddle was valued at $100 and was labeled De Cremona, although it was probably not made by any of the celebrated Cremona makers. "It's made on pure scientific principles, laid down in the book," said Father. He strove to emulate them. He worked in his shop all day and late into the evening, demanding me to hold the lantern for him to work by.

We had one red and one dun fiddle. The red fiddle was a very handsome color and was as good looking a fiddle as any fiddle I ever saw. The dun was a dark color, meant to look old, but it was handsome in my eyes and bright when looked at closely.

But if the sound of the dun fiddle was like thunder, the red fiddle sounded like a fart. There were few in the diggings so tremendous loud and yet so soft and mellow as the dun fiddle. Anything could be played on it with as much expression as could be wished. It sounded just as the player felt. It made an ocean of noise, and though the sound was very clear and beautiful, the least fault in fingering or bowing could be heard as loud as thunder. Still, it seemed to give the tune independent of the player and I wasn't afraid to do my best. Leverett Lull agreed the dun fiddle was worth a cartload of the red fiddle.

Father tried to improve the red fiddle by changing the bridge. He made a dozen bridges, finally concentrating all his skill in a final bridge. I offended him by declaring that it was not as good as the one originally on, but was obliged to partially retract my statement.

Father sold the red fiddle and immediately went to putting a top onto another old fiddle which he'd traded for a jackknife worth 62 1/2 cents. The top had been smashed in, but the back, sides, and upper end of the neck were good. Father thought he could make a good fiddle of it. I called it the thunderstruck fiddle. When he finished, it was a handsome fiddle and played with less weight of bow. I thought it was powerful and well-toned and I immediately began to practice on it.

Then Father started making fiddle boxes. I had two fiddles and two boxes and that was more than enough. I wished he'd put his energies into something that would enable him to buy me a coat, which I needed far more than fiddle boxes. My only coat worth a damn was a little thin thing unsuitable for winter wear. My old winter coat wouldn't button, was holey and minus the lining. I'd seen a coarse but warm one I wanted down at Anderson's on the Green. It cost $5.

The first box Father made was lined with green baize and was good enough. Then he made a second lined with red morocco which did not keep the cold out but everyone said it was as neat a one as they ever saw. Then he made another box and covered it with black kid, creating the most handsome box of the three. It had a round back end and three-sided front with a ridge raised up in the middle but only held one bow whereas the others held two.

Father's fiddle mania interfered with farm work so much that Mother said she was going to do it if nobody else did, which of course made him mad and resulted in another day's work lost.

I fretted over our inactivity. Mother said it was no use. "Father can't plant or mend fence in the spring because he didn't get up any wood in the winter and must do it now. He can't hoe in June because he needs to plant. He can't hay in July because he needs to hoe. We are always behind," she said. It would unquestionably have been better for Father to leave his farming, fiddle repairs, and fiddle boxes to work down on the Flat at 75 or even 40 cents a day.

One day it held squizzly and cool and Father had been reading novels all afternoon. In the evening he lit the lamp. Mother, thinking he was going to continue reading, protested that it wasn't lamp-lighting time yet, and that furthermore, we were out of victuals. This drew down an awful shower of wrath. He called her a damned fool hog, expensive to keep and good for nothing, said she lost so much in cooking that she cost 10 times as much as she came to! Father had intended to use the lamp to mend my boots but instead sot down and spent the rest of the evening chewing tobacco and scolding.

My boots needed repair devilishly. My feet were wet all day in school and I couldn't go up onto the hill to chop wood. I called it a great evil, further infuriating Father. Even with my wet boots, I'd run two or three races that day and could beat any boy at school. But as a result of the running and the wet boots, I had the lames and was too powerless to go up on the hill to get wood even if I'd had decent boots. Mother said it was rheumatism caused by cold instead of exercise and the shop being warm, I made myself perfectly comfortable in it and accomplished nothing.

The next morning Mother scraped together a meagre breakfast which Father scolded about. She said supper would be a darned sight scantier. So he had to go to the Green through the snow, which had begun flying lustily, with Mother. She was crying when they arrived at home, at four o'clock.

Mr. Hartwell was home when they returned, at work in his room making a parallel ruler and repairing his compass. Mother stopped crying because she was very careful never to weep or complain in Mr. Hartwell's presence. In fact, she never told anybody of Father's meanness, however much she had to endure. At dinner that night, Father flung out a few abominable jokes about how Mother was so lazy she couldn't get dinner on time. Still, Mother didn't defend herself. She didn't comment on how she'd just then gotten enough food to even cook for Mr. Hartwell, how I'd had to borrow pork of Hiram to bake with the beans, ours being all eaten up, how the week before we'd had some sausages and cheese but Father ate them mostly himself.

I hated Father when he told his hired hands during haying that they ought to come down here to dinner, but his wife was so lazy that she couldn't get any! Or when he'd agreed Mother could visit someone, yet when the day arrived, refused to let her have the team. I knew her to sit down and weep when she saw company approaching because she had no victuals in the house.

I struggled to tell the truth in my journals, including these stories about Father and Mother. How hard it was to put down The Truth the Whole Truth and NOTHING BUT THE TRUTH. I thought I described their quarrels to an exactity but in reading them later, I realized I favored Mother's side, making Father's side to be most awful. I was consumed by the injustice of Father's behavior, furious at how he applied his power, but Father was not mad and unreasonable all the time.

And Mother was not of weak mind, although at times her excuses were insufficient for they were really falsehoods. I don't know whether it was through fear or through a noble motive that she did not justify herself even if she'd been doing something entirely for the good. She never told Father that she'd not been at home because she was doing for Granny Morey who was "sick unto death," or helping Sarah when Hiram was sick with the phthisic. One January evening, she went down to neighbor McClay's house to help when his baby died of a cold — and then was scolded at by Father for going away. She was too foolish to tell outright where she had been, and thus justify herself, till after a great jaw. She gained nothing by it but fresh torment applied more boldly. Mighty heavens! I vowed I would conceal nothing through fear.

Chapter 21

Mother's Sickness

It was this frame of mind that made me vow to help Mother prepare for a sing we were to have at our house. We were to have an uncommon amount of company — 18 people. And not everybody was from Rum Street. Some were from the Flat, and even some from the Green, so Mother wanted to make a good impression. She prepared for a week.

I didn't wish that women could vote, or anything one thousandth part so ultra as that. All I asked for is that they be allowed the right of enjoying life!

On wash day I carried in buckets of water from Mr. Hartwell's hogshead and built a fire in the kitchen fireplace to heat it. I went down to buy a gallon of soap from Mrs. Leach. Mother had been telling Father to set up a leach so we could make our own soap for some time, but he hadn't done it. He had however, made her a washboard. Mother scrubbed clothes, rinsed them, and laid everything on racks to dry. I left her alone during this work because the house was in arms all day and I couldn't concentrate on anything.

The next day I carried more water from the brook, then went

into Father's shop to fiddle and found to my astonishment that I could play slow music as well as ever. Mother cleaned lamp chimneys and washed up the floor and did the ironing. I went to bed early so she could have the oil lamp to sew me a shirt by, so I'd have something decent to wear. I woke at one o'clock in the am and the lamp was still lit. She kept her movements quiet so as not to awaken me or Father.

The day before the sing, she prepared milk emptyings bread. The house smelled badly of ripe cheese as it worked.

The day of the sing she got me out of bed to search for eggs laid by our hens, and bring in some firewood after. She spent the day baking the bread, a veal pot pie, a cake and a custard pie.

The next day she had such a severe sick headache that she ought not to have moved at all but still Father expected her to get up and cook for us. I wrote in my journal, "Women are worse than slaves! Down with the abolitionists and let a party be raised in women's stead that will look nearer home." I didn't wish that women could vote, or anything one thousandth part so ultra as that. All I asked for is that they be allowed the right of enjoying life!

Mother was not the only woman who suffered at the hands of her husband. The women on Rum Street owned nothing and if they wanted anything they had to pay for it themselves. If they made any butter or sugar and sold it, their husbands took the money.

On the day of Mother's bad headache, Father agreed to take Mother down to see Dr. Tom Powers. I was greatly surprised when Father, instead of scolding like the Devil, merely asked how she intended to pay for the medicine.

Dr. Powers told her to take 20 grains of quinine to warm and strengthen her and 80 cents' worth of physic, also to eat only half as much as usual. Mother ate scarcely enough to sustain life and with these new instructions I thought she would starve to death. Both the physic and the quinine did her good, but they made her rather weak.

A few days after that, she consulted with Mrs. Chase, a celebrated root and herb doctoress on the Flat! Mrs. Chase had saved my life 11 years earlier when I was but 3 years old. She told Mother to go through another course of physic and gave her some medicine that cost a dollar. Mother was to mix it with three pints of gin. She called it bitters. She also said to get one pound of dandelion roots and tops, boil them, and add the juice to a pint of gin and a pint of the best West India molasses. The physic brought her quite low, but the treatments revived her enough to make plans to leave Father and me.

    She said she had to get away from the work. Not only did she take care of us, but she did all of Mr. Hartwell's wash and cooked for his hands during haying. I'd seen her even scald his bed to kill the bedbugs when she knew he was about to arrive.

    She intended to stay with her sister, Polly Woodruff, in Lewis, New York. Father said, "So, you're going a-vagabonding? Why do you suppose they'll want a sick old woman coming to live upon them?"

    "Although I'm an old sick woman," she said, "I've worked hard for you for 20 years, and if I stay, I'll have to work as hard for 20 more and at the end of that time, when I can't work anymore, I'll have to go a-vagabonding just the same for all of it!"

    He asked her to wait until haying was over. She refused.

    I wasn't positive that she intended to return or even if she'd get better. Perhaps Father would do better, I thought, and if Mother gets better, I'd do better too. I hoped we'd all live together in Father's house again sometime.

    After she left, Father hired Solomon's sister, Clara Wyman, to keep house. Mrs. Hoisington wanted to do it, but Father didn't like that she sot down plates and basins for the dog and cats to eat from.

    He spent 50 cents fixing the broken clock face that had bothered Mother so, and he replaced a great heavy iron teakettle that Mother declared she had killed herself by lifting. Then he traded away her butter churn worth $5 and two swarms of bees worth $20 and got in exchange, an anchor escapement watch, 12 holes jeweled, made by John Harrison of Liverpool. He gave me the watch. Had I known of his intentions, I'd have opposed it, as true as I live. I always said I didn't want such a watch until I knew enough to have it. When Mr. Hartwell found out about it, he said it was astonishing how much some folks could have! Father's profuseness was entirely the wrong way. If he were determined to lay out so much for me, he should have laid it out to much better purpose. I couldn't account for the fact that he bought unnecessary articles and wouldn't get those which were necessary.

Father and Mother corresponded by letter. Father noted in his diary each time he "wrote a letter to Mrs. L.E. Cobb," and how much money he sent her.

She stayed away three months. On November 16, toward night, Father went to the Green and brought her home. According to his diary "Mrs. L.E. Cobb started from Lewis with $5.50 and brought home $1.70."

Father helped with the housework for a while, and Mother told Mr. Hartwell that he should board with Mr. Leach's folks during haying.

I asked her if coming back had been doubtful. She replied that she didn't know if she would live to come back.

I wrote out why Mother was unhappy as well as I could.

First, Father didn't carry on his land half decent and hired help at that. In fact, he wasn't much of a farmer.

Second, he was slow about getting victuals, firewood, etc. She had to tell him again and again and get him provoked before he would do it.

Thirdly, he didn't like her to get clothes and if she wanted a gown or a bonnet he would scold and call her the most expensive woman in town when she really was one of the most saving.

CHAPTER 22

HOPELESS

As a boy I'd go off down the road for a walk, singing along and imagining some great thing I should sometime do. I thought I could maybe be an editor or a clerk. I thought I could write considerable of a piece. I dreamt of being President.

In my old coat over t'other, hair a foot long, face and hands unwashed six weeks, and tanned like thunder, I looked bad enough to scare crows.

At 11 years of age, I was actually handsome, judging by a daguerreotype of Mother and me. In 1848 when I was 12, I'd been a pretty fair looking specimen of a boy, according to glimpses of my reflection in the reservoir.

By the age of 15, however, I was losing confidence. I saw that Mrs. Jaquith, Laura Cobb's sister, thought Jim Cobb knew a good deal more than me when we saw her at Henry's. When Laura tucked something into my pocket as a present, which, as soon as I got out of sight, I found on inspection to be a hair brush with a looking glass in the back, I got a good look at myself and immediately knew why she thought I needed it. In my old coat over t'other, hair a foot long, face and hands unwashed six weeks, and tanned like thunder, I looked bad enough to scare crows. My nose was one-sided — caused by John Daniels who knocked it so at school. And my shoulders were getting forward distressingly. I was poor as a scarecrow, my breath stank, and my teeth were overlaid with tartar unless I rubbed 'em all the time.

I'd grown to 5 feet, 11 inches in height and weighed 136 pounds, with four pounds of lead in my pocket. People said I was consumptive. When I struck the left side of my ribs, there came a sound hollow as a tub compared with the sound that came from t'other side. Jim Cobb said it was the most abominable of diseases and claimed to know several people who'd died of slow consumption in full possession of their faculties.

People who didn't know me, took me for a fool because of my unimpressive appearance.

One Saturday in May, Father and I were carrying a load of pomace that was rotting and stinking like the devil, talking spitefully to each other about the plowing, harrowing, and furrowing that badly needed doing. So I gratefully abandoned Father when Sol Wyman came along with Jim Clapp.

Jim Clapp was a little runt of a cuss and mighty self-conceited and didn't know much. He was one of the boys from the Green who used to pick on me, trying to get me fighting when I frequented town meetings. He announced he'd been at work at Nashua, New Hampshire, for four years, showed me his gold watch and spoke eloquently of his vest and breeches. He said he wouldn't live in Woodstock for the best farm there, remarked how green Vermonters were, hit me about the holes in my hat, and asked about the girls, particularly Cynthia, wondering if she was still public.

Even so, I was having a good time 'till he said, "I hope I didn't hurt your feelings."

"None that you can hurt by allusions to holes in my hat or talking of greenies when it's plain you meant me," I said. I wished I'd told him I didn't care a damn what his intentions were.

But I did care. I resolved to fix my appearance. I thought my nose might be slanted to one side because I always wiped it with my right hand. So I invariably began to employ my left. I tried to straighten my shoulders by sleeping flat on my back with my head between the pillows so it was as low as the rest of me. During the day I wore a pair of shoulder braces Mother made. They crossed in back and pinned together in front. If I stooped forward, I got my shoulders pulled back but also got my lungs or guts squeezed. They cut under my arms rather severely.

I didn't care what I looked like on Rum Street. I didn't think I was inferior to anyone there, but even if I improved my appearance, I knew I'd still be seen as a fool elsewhere — down on the Green particularly. For I didn't dare look strangers in the face or, if asked a question, I jabbered, stuttered, couldn't think of any word to speak, got confused, and finally couldn't say anything but nonsense from all points of view. I would have preferred to write down what I wanted to say and hand over the paper.

I didn't know why it was so. Was ever anybody like me?

I didn't believe that others would turn out of the road and go across empty lots to avoid meeting two or three people. Nor would they hesitate to go even into a village.

Oh God! I concluded I'd be a miserable cuss forever. I'd given up my thoughts that I'd have a chance to educate myself or do great things in the work line. I had no mechanical skill about me. I couldn't nail two pieces of wood together! I would always be poor, never would earn enough money to keep me alive.

Even my writing seemed less than I'd thought it was. In reading over some of my old writings, I found it a curious and discouraging fact that I hadn't got so much meaning into a piece, oftentimes, as I'd intended to. In fact, I sometimes couldn't find a single idea where I'd expected to find a dozen.

My independent treasury amounted to $2.06 in silver and coppers, earned by cutting beech logs, picking stone heaps, cutting up yellow dock with a stub hoe for Henry, and drawing twenty large loads of manure out into the little mowing with the oxen. That was a hard day's work for even a stout man.

I began doing nothing all day until I was almost sick from being idle. I was so far gone by the time evening arrived, that I couldn't even read. I developed such a cold sore in one corner of my mouth that I could barely eat. I couldn't even write in my journal. I thought maybe I'd better go down and see Cynthia. It was true that her character was so established that it was beyond all comment or question, but I'd grown up with her. We'd played cards and checkers and I'd eaten my first popped corn with her. I didn't go.

But then something new turned up. Laura's brother, Hezekiah Smith, asked Father if I could go to Boston with him to tend his furniture shop. Hezekiah was a professional mechanic and inventor and used to discuss inventions with Henry until daylight. It seemed that Hez took furniture in exchange for sashes and blinds he made with machinery he had a patent on. He said he would watch, take care of, board and clothe me, and pay my expenses, and I needn't stay a day unless I was willing — but he couldn't afford to pay me any wages.

I was thunder-struck and terror-struck. Me, who didn't dare to speak a piece before the school assembly, go to Boston? I was sick to my stomach. I took courage in the knowledge that my folks wouldn't hear of it.

But they did hear of it. Father remarked that for a year back I hadn't done enough to pay for my board and clothes, so he thought he should gain instead of losing if I went off. Mother told Sarah of the going-to-Boston affair and though Sarah was sick, all heaven soon heard about it.

I knew I should be a shame to myself in Boston, an object of pity to all who knew me, and of ridicule to everybody else, even if I had good clothes which I hadn't. I wondered if this dread of folks was good sense or foolishness? I wrote in my journal. "Oh misery! What should I ever amount to?"

But then, what did I care about other folks' observations of me, "that greenhorn," as long as they used me decent? I would have an opportunity to improve.

Nobody in Boston would take the trouble to kill, scare, or bother me to death, and I could come home whenever I wished. Furthermore, I was not quite so bashful as I thought. Others may have thought I was a fool, but I decided it didn't do any good to make a bad matter worse by concluding I was a fool too! I was not so bad looking, either, as I was in 1850. I was a little round shouldered but I held my head straight, not for the looks of it (for anyone who knew me would say I never cared a damn how I looked) but because I should live longer. My forehead sloped, but was high enough and very broad and full over the eyes. However foolish I may have acted I didn't believe I looked like a fool. I was not stout, but healthy, full chested, and never sick.

I could see plainly that Father wanted me to go, sink or swim. By mighty, I thought, I would go! I wished to stay home no longer. There wasn't a boy in 10 towns that would be likely to appear better.

But first I needed some decent clothes. If I could have a Kossuth hat and a pocket pistol, a good pair of pantaloons, a good vest, and a black summer coat, I could go to Boston with delight. Once outfitted thus, I could shift for myself.

Father agreed. I washed myself in the reservoir and we went down to Munger and Daman's clothing store on the Green. Father bought me $13 worth of new clothes, promising to pay for them later. The clerk said he never saw such a critter to fit, I was so long, slim, and mighty hollow-backed. He told me to hold my head up straighter and to wear my shoulder braces always.

Hez came up onto Rum Street often, saying he would

need me in Boston shortly. One morning I fixed up to go down to Hez's house on the Green with Henry and Laura, Hez being home then. He desired me to bring my thunderstruck fiddle. All morning I practiced on "Ostinelli's Hornpipe" for I knew Hez was trying to learn it and would ask me to play it. I was right. I was glad I'd practiced it, for fiddler Horace Dunham was there and also Mr. and Mrs. Briggs and other guests. Hez gave me a set of violin strings and told me authoritatively and solemnly that I was not holding my fiddle correctly. We had some oysters for supper–positively the first I ever guzzled.

But then, a few days later, Hez appeared at our house, claiming that if he had a boy he'd sooner cut his throat than let him go to Boston and clerk in a store. So my new clothes were for nothing, I once again had nothing to do, and Father was deeper in debt. It was the first of many times I learned that Hez's promises often came to naught.

Facing page: Photo courtesy of Woodstock History Center, Vermont

Part Three

Chapter 23

A Celebrated Musician

I had to go home afoot with the boxes in hand, arriving at midnight. Father had sneaked off and left me because I let Perkins play on my fiddle.

Even though I was a greeny from the hills, folks on the Flat and Rum Street knew me as a musician. Mr. Shaw even thought of me as celebrated and wanted to know if I had gone to New York to take lessons in fiddling! He had heard it so! I'd wallowed through the snow to visit Benoni Shaw, my rival in spelling contests, one winter evening and while there, I fiddled some old tunes for his parents. Mr. Shaw was considerably affected which I took as a compliment to my playing. When Benoni and I played "Rosa Lee" and "Bonaparte's March" together, they were in ecstasies. The tunes went grand, better than I expected, for Benoni couldn't play anything quite decent. Mrs. Shaw said we'd better play together at the exhibition at the North Bridgewater

School the next Saturday night. All of that made me think rather well of myself.

The Shaws were not handsome, but they were good folks and their way of living contrasted very strikingly with ours. They had everything right, lived in a good house and thrived, while we lived in an old ruin and grew poor. I didn't want to disappoint them. But Benoni couldn't play much of anything and I hated the thought of playing with him in public, my first public performance other than parties and dances. Also, my clothes weren't decent, for I hadn't but one suit. I hoped I would find an excuse for staying away.

I almost found one in the form of a tooth-ache — the first real tooth-ache I ever had even though I knew my teeth were rotting, a personal defect that was worse than any of the old ones. The honey I'd eaten that winter had advanced the rotting business greatly. Were I a person of importance I would have gone down to Dr. Chase and got those holes filled up. But alas! I was scarcely worth what 'twould cost. Mother never had a tooth fixed for the same reason. But as my teeth continued to ache, I vowed I'd have 'em filled before I ever laid out a cent for any other purpose, even if there was no hope of obtaining a cent for six months.

But Benoni wouldn't hear of me not coming. He even offered to pay me but I wouldn't take anything. The exhibition came off as I expected. About 130 were present—men, women and children.

Jo Pratt spoke two pieces alone with great gusto. Jo had the St. Vitus Dance in his left arm, so couldn't hold his arm still. He took care to have his arms folded, but it was plain enough. It spoiled his learning to fiddle, of course.

N. Carlos Thompson read Satan's "Address to the Devil" by Robert Burns and a chap named Chas Emerson with one eye, spoke some comic pieces, as he supposed, very cunningly, but it struck me that he was, strictly speaking, a damned fool. Everyone else laughed. There was a puppet show and some theatrical dancing but what interested me was when Nathan Ladd showed magic. Mr. Ladd got up Geo Cobb, my cousin, to "assist" him in his tricks and made a good deal of fun at his expense. He pulled a lot of old brass out of Geo's nose, sot him to holding a potato on his nose in the middle of the floor on his knees and with one hand held up. He then went behind the curtain and stayed a spell, the audience expecting to see the potato conjured away, but it wasn't, and when he reappeared he started on seeing Geo and told him he'd forgot all about him. He did some astonishing things, or that would have been most almighty astonishing if they were really done. But he admitted 'twas all deception beforehand. He put three dishes on the table, each one covering a ball, then conjured all under one or all away from under any of 'em. He took eight apparently solid rings and in plain sight put 'em all together and then took 'em all apart again, and other tricks.

Father hadn't wanted Benoni playing any of our good fiddles, so finished off an old one and we fiddled some tunes together. I could have made much better music alone, Benoni's tones being all flat.

That was my first exhibition. As my ability as a musician became more widely known, I was asked to play at others. In 1853 I played at an exhibition at the English Mills Schoolhouse. By then I'd acquired a horn. I thought I could play basses to "Old Zip Coon," "Money Musk" and other similar tunes quite handsomely, and thought I'd like the opportunity to try.

Fiddler Perkins agreed to accompany me. But again, there was trouble with the fiddle. Father didn't want even Fiddler Perkins playing ours because he thought getting bad tones would ruin them. Mr. Perkins often came to Father's shop to hear me fiddle although Mr. Hartwell claimed it was to get some cider. But he was convinced to the contrary when Perkins continued to visit even after Father drew off all his cider to avoid being fined for giving it to known drunkards.

I walked to the exhibition, picking up Geo Grow along the way. He'd whittled out some castanets to shake while I fiddled. By five-thirty the school-house was already jammed full. They put me up behind the curtain and so high I was visible over it. For a spell I fiddled well and Geo Grow rattled away to kill. A load of Pomfret chaps almost raised a row.

At eight o'clock Henry Perkins got along but without any fiddle! He came with a fellow named Harvey Vaughan who brought a melodeon and the two sang songs and played. They were heartily welcomed and told that "we hadn't any music until then," which made me mad.

Contrary to Father's instructions, I gave Perkins my fiddle which wasn't in tune with my horn by a full semitone. Perkins played miserably and I could hear folks whispering about that "d-d old tin-horn." We played two or three tunes that were more satisfactory, but just as I got ready to take back the fiddle, the E string broke and had to be dispensed with for the last and longest half of the exhibition. Geo Grow had gone home and I played alone and not very well either. I got no thanks.

Seeing my folks there, I declined two offers to stay till morning. I waited half an hour for our team to come 'round, but it had gone home! Father had sneaked off and left me because I let Perkins play on my fiddle. I had to go home afoot with the boxes in hand, arriving at midnight. The next day Father seemed ashamed. He certainly should have been.

I saw Lewis Taft some time later when I went over to borrow his old spy-glass. He spoke at large of his own musical talents, then spoke of my playing at the exhibition, remarking only that I didn't do very well. So much for the exhibition. I satisfied no one, including myself.

CHAPTER 24

FIDDLING AND DANCING DOWN TEW HELL

Father got track of a dancing school at the Green and was determined that I should go. He made me a pair of pumps to wear. I didn't want to go. I thought I would cut a most ridiculous and awkward figure, kicking up and jumping 'round, so I told Father he needn't spend three dollars so that I could learn to dance when I never intended to do anything but fiddle.

Then Father declared I must go to Mr. Cheney's singing

Nothing out of the way was seen or done at these dances, but afterwards the Morey sisters and the Raymonds, being quarrelsome, got mad and lied so much about each other and the horrible things that happened at the dances that any person who was not there would believe them all to be mean as tophet.

school on the Green. Mr. Cheney was a great singer but I told Father that my voice had just changed and I couldn't sing. So I avoided that school as well.

I kept to fiddling. The winter of 1851 I fiddled for six dances in our neighborhood. Nothing out of the way was seen or done at these dances, but afterwards the Morey sisters and the Raymonds, being quarrelsome, got mad and lied so much about each other and the horrible things that happened at the dances that any person who was not there would believe them all to be mean as tophet.

Our dance was held on Friday, January 31. Mother began cooking on Tuesday. Father made pumps for the dancers, turned the stove around so as to make more room, and fixed other things in the square room to get ready. I gave out invitations as far as the Flat and borrowed some plates of Sarah.

The night was very cold. Trees froze and the cracking sounded like gunshots across the valley. The moon was bright enough that people could stay on the road and avoid tipping over in the soft snow along the sides, which was such a common occurrence that women were advised to cling to each other like a bag of wool when traveling by sleigh.

We'd invited the Raymonds and others on our road, many of whom were not over-respectable. Some mean folks from out of our neighborhood came too — the Scales, Mrs. Willis, the Woodwards and John Bravard, the stagecoach driver, also Miles who'd been in state prison for three years. Chas Raymond was the only respectable person there. We had a full house, about 40 folks in all.

Our dance wasn't as elaborate as the great dance at Shattucks' on Biscuit Hill earlier that winter. They had an oyster supper. We had cider and apples continually, and at about 11 o'clock Mother passed victuals around. People stayed and danced until four o'clock in the morning.

About half-way through the winter of 1851, some folks stopped going to the dances. Our Orthodox Christian neighbors had convinced them that dancing was a path straight to hell. Old Grow came to our house and lectured Mother on the evils of dancing. Mrs. Dodge told Mother she heard the fiddles saying "nothing but down tew hell, down tew hell."

Two of the more vocal opponents were sisters, Mrs. Thomas and Mrs. Holmes. They were painfully pious and horribly opposed to cards and company, but especially to fiddles. They observed the Sabbath very strictly and abominated and despised all the "horrible critters" they called infidels.

After I started playing the fiddle, Mrs. Holmes lectured me. "Playing the fiddle for money shows a great lack of principle on your part. And besides, nothing but a contemptible saw can be played on it."

I thought Mrs. Holmes had never heard a person play decently but I didn't say anything.

"Dancing makes people spend their money and leads them to desperation," she said.

"It's little money I ever spent on dancing, ever got by it, or ever expect to get by it," I said.

"Milton and Alden went to dances and spent their inheritances in the prime of their days," she said, speaking of her nephews. "Now they'll have a hard time getting work."

It was true that Milton and Alden, her brother's sons, who'd been raised very strict and Lordacious, wasted their inheritances on dancing and gambling. Milton still lazed 'round but he was honest and generous and could sing and was suited to the company of girls. I liked him. Alden was a spendthrift and profane swearer but the best informed of the three.

The third Thomas—Mosely—was also brought up in the nurture and admonition of the Lord, but he had a good knack at the getting and saving of money. He had the double chin that was evidence of being economical.

Once Henry had accused Mosely of being a "poor mower." I reminded him that Mosely "won't work a particle till he's sure of getting the cash for it."

Mrs. Holmes didn't mention her own son Byron. He ate largely and continuously and as a result had incurable fits. When Byron rebuked me for fiddling at dances, I said, "Intemperance in eating is worse than in drinking or dancing, as much an abomination in the sight of the Lord, as lying lips."

In the spring of 1851, just as the dance season ended and sugar season began, a terrible event occurred in Hiram Cobb's family, an event that vindicated some folks who'd criticized the dances.

"The Lord is raising Tophet with all rascals," said Mrs. Thomas. Said Granny Morey "God Almighty sent upon Hiram and Sarah a dreadful curse to pay them for dancing so like the Devil".

Chapter 25

Tremendous Bad Times

My uncle, Hiram Cobb married 19-year-old Sarah Morey December 6, 1842. A year later, in January of 1844, Fredrick Carlton Cobb was born. Then came along Caroline and three more sons, John Andrew, Henry Eugene and Orlando. Their house was filled with the activity of five children, all younger than 7 years old.

Hiram and Sarah were so destitute, they borrowed money against their farm. After that Hiram's hopes for his farm lay in his sons' success. "When my boys do well," he often began, "we'll get our land back," or "we'll fix this house," or "I'll pay you." When Frederick was old enough to go to the Cox District School, Hiram kept him home. "There'll soon be children enough to build a school on this side of the hill," he'd say, listing his own children and those of the Dodges and Emeline.

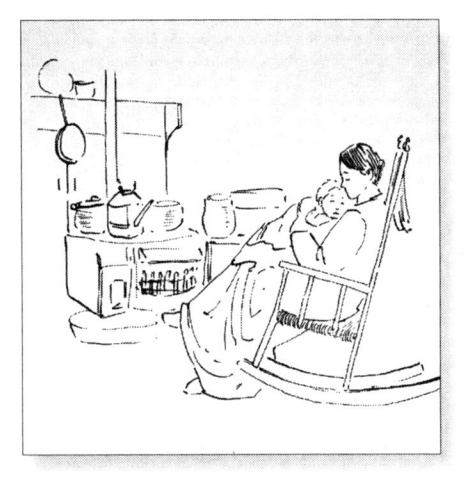

The local doctor told them "You needn't worry. It's no more catching than a broken bone."

March 23, 1851, was most gloriously fair and warm. Sap began to run even though it was a Sunday. I hadn't commenced sugaring an hour too soon. Father and I went up on the hill and tapped 30 trees, cleaned the kettles, got sap in and boiled some. I carried up my neck yoke so as to carry the syrup down to Laura's to be sugared off. Father drew a load of wood to my arch and another load home. He said he'd hoop more sap tubs and make spouts, for we had used them all, and he'd make me a skimmer. It was my second year sugaring alone and I'd proved my reliability. I liked to sugar above all other work.

I stopped at Hiram's on my way home that night and found Mother and Granther Morey there. Caroline and Henry were sick.

Granther Morey was saying, "They've got the real, reglar cussed old spotted fever. They had it down in Putney jist 40 years ago."

Mother wasn't so sure. It happened that Dr. Hazen came in just then for Father had gotten him. He dug into his pocket for a handkerchief to block the smell in the room. I'd always thought Hiram's house had a bad smell, even when they were all well.

The house was dim and crowded with everything seven people needed to live for a winter. Sarah gestured toward two small children lying on an iron bed against a wall. "They're starting to look bloated up," she said. The children lay with their eyes closed, breathing heavily. Dr. Hazen felt their necks and pushed his fingers into their mouths, peering at their tongues.

"Canker rash." He sighed heavily. "It's badly about in Bridgewater and Plymouth."

Hiram had taken Almeida Foster home to Plymouth earlier in the week. Sarah and two of the babies went, not knowing about the canker rash until someone asked if they were not afraid of the children's catching it. The local doctor told them "You needn't worry. It's no more catching than a broken bone."

The door to the next room in Hiram's house was ajar with two children gawking in, taking observations. They were Jo Dodge's children. He and his wife and their four children lived in that room. I saw Mrs. Dodge's arm jerk the children away and slam the door.

"My sister," said Sarah, looking at the door. "She and Ma say God sent the sickness — because of the dancing."

"It would be full as well for you and the children if your mother and Mrs. Dodge would make themselves scarce," Dr. Hazen said. I knew there was no fear of that since Mrs. Dodge had never offered an instant of help.

"Ma's wise above all account," said Sarah. "That's what she says."

"Dancing isn't the trouble here," said Dr. Hazen, looking around at the dirt and disorder. He still held a handkerchief to his nose.

"Tell Gaius to arrange a general cleaning," he said to Mother. "Get some oil of vitriol and chloride. Burn something to purify the air in here."

He confided to Father later that Hiram's house was about the filthiest he'd ever seen. I thought the children would have gotten well if they'd had decent air to breathe.

"Dr. Hazen don't know nuthin'," said Granther, the instant the doctor left.

The weather was misty and smoky for the next few days. Father and I tapped more trees, 53 altogether, and drawed a load of fencing stuff and limbs to the boiling place. We struggled to get two mill logs onto the sled, and after a good deal of slipping off, we drawed them down to Hiram's. I didn't protest as I usually did when seeing Father's shiftless way of doing things.

Mother watched up to Hiram's most nights. By then, all the children had the canker rash. Five children sick in the same room was as much a killing idea as it was a killing fact. I stayed away, for although the doctors claimed it wasn't catching, Mother and everyone knew the doctors were badly mistaken. However, they knew from the news coming from Plymouth and Bridgewater, that adults didn't catch it.

John Andrew died on a Sunday at six o'clock in the morning. He would have been 5 years old if he'd lived a few days longer. It made me mad, for I'd seen him up at Norman's sugarplace not long before, with a bad cold and feet as wet as water. He'd been eating frozen apples that had hung on the trees all winter and puked them all up. I thought his death could have been avoided if any sensible person, like Laura Cobb, had been caring for him.

Father set aside his work on the log sled and made a coffin and a box to put it in. Mother sewed the burial robes. Laura cooked an apple pie, loaves of bread, and nut cakes for Sarah.

The funeral was on a warm, dull, mean sort of day. Old Morey borrowed some breeches of Henry for Hiram to wear to the funeral. Granny Morey and Mrs. Grow stayed with the children. I hoped to stay home, for I despised funerals and thought I'd show the most respect by staying away. But then Jim Cobb came along so I dressed up and went with him. Father took the box down to the burying ground between Wyman's and Shaw's. Mr. Hartwell and another man from the machine shop carried the box and Ed Whitney carried the coffin. Sarah, Father and Mother, Norman, and Granther Morey were all the mourners. Everyone else was too afraid of the disease to come. Mr. Kidder made a prayer. Hiram appeared perfectly composed, but I don't think he felt so. Sarah didn't by a great sight.

Afterwards I went up to the sugar place, but I didn't feel very smart. I stopped all along and then stayed at Henry's till afternoon when he and I went up on the hill together.

On Sunday I began to chop up the logs but it started to rain, convincing me that it was a sin to break such a Sabbath, so I got out my Great Book and wrote and fiddled all day. Hosea was here and read till four o'clock. Mr. Hartwell put four new lights of glass in the windows. Father stewed out beeswax all day in the old kitchen and got pretty near enough to pay for his labor.

By then, three of the Dodge children had come down with the canker rash. Dodge's folks were mad at Hiram and Sarah, blaming them for dancing and bringing the disease down on them all. I wondered if they thought repenting of the dances half-way through the season hadn't been enough, that lo and behold, God Almighty was reminding them of their sins by punishing them with the canker rash too. A terrible thought.

The Dodges moved into the shed outside Hiram's house. Hiram and Jo Dodge came down and took the big stove from our kitchen to set up for heating and cooking. But alas, it was too late.

On March 31, I awoke in the night with a fever and listened to the rain pounding on the roof, as if the windows of Heaven were wide open. I laid still until midnight, my bones aching to the fiddle tunes I'd played in the evening. When Father learned that I had a fever, he ran up to Hiram's where Mother was watching. They tried to make me take a lot of miserable stuff called physic so that I'd puke. Instead I picked over some beans which always cured me. I was scared that I had canker rash and didn't know but what I was fated to die with it. Dr. Hazen had told Mother that since I'd had the canker and the rash separate in the past, and almost died with each, I'd survive. But Mother didn't have much faith in Dr. Hazen.

Baby Orlando died next. His funeral was a day late because "nobody didn't do nothing, and so nothing was done," according to Father. So Father took over. He built, stained, and varnished the coffin, got the coffin box on the lumber wagon without sides and went to the graveyard where he ordered a grave dug next to young John Andrew's. Then he went to the Green for the coffin-trimmings. Chas Raymond, Ed Whitney, and Mr. Leach helped trim the coffin.

Again, the day of the funeral was rainy, dark and foggy, a comfortless time. The entire month had seemed so. The disease was so fatal that everyone feared it and nobody would volunteer to carry the coffin. So Chas Raymond got Jasper Raymond and Francis Churchill who were working in the machine shop, to be bearers.

At about that time, Mrs. Lish Raymond died too, probably

from dropsy as near as I could find out. In the afternoon after Orlando's funeral, Dr. Hazen, Professor Clark, and another doctor opened her up. About all who went to the funeral went over to the "examination" including Carlos Pratt and his wife and Mrs. Shaw. Her funeral was the next day at 1 o'clock in the afternoon.

I went to the examination too and couldn't sleep that night, thinking about it. Finally, I made Mother swap beds with me so I could sleep with Father.

That canker rash was the worst sort ever seen in our area. Little William Dodge died. The neighbors took turn watching at Hiram's and Dodges' houses. Laura went round on the other side of the hill begging for the two families. She got provisions of all kinds, including a bundle of old shirts, giving most of them to the Dodges who were the most needy. Dodge's folks were all out of anything to eat. Folks came from the Flat, brought over a lot of eatables, and they all cried.

It was tremendous bad, the times were. I didn't care anything about anybody's children except Hiram's. Henry had got a cold and bloated up again. Then Frederick showed signs of being sick. I felt about as gloomy and mad as could be.

April 7 the frogs in Mr. Hartwell's swamp began to sing and I cussed 'em for it. I wanted to go down to the swamp that night and by dint of war, stop the music. I would have certainly stoned a frog if I saw him sing out.

The neighborhood had come to doubt Dr. Hazen's skills, so Old Grow went down and got Dr. Chase to see the children. He expressed considerable contempt for Dr. Hazen's management but didn't do anything.

Meanwhile the sap didn't stop running. Most of mine was lost through neglect. My sap soured, buckets filled with rain, and the wind blew away six of my tubs. I stayed at Henry's house reading *Ivanhoe* — "We are like the herb which flourisheth most when trampled upon," a sentiment I agreed with under the circumstances. Henry and I diverted ourselves with talk about whether a ball shot from a gun would fall just as fast as it would if it were not in motion or whether a plug driven into a sealed barrel of air would press on the air within and smash it sky high. It was better than talking about the neighbors. Laura gave me a long coat to wear in the steady rain we'd been having. She said it had been "fabricated for my Grandfather." I was the tallest Cobb by then, almost as tall as Grandfather, so it fit me well.

Dr. Hazen continued to insist the disease was not catching. We heard about its comparison to a broken bone again. Nevertheless, Chas Raymond carried it home to his own children. Emeline helped Sarah some and took it home to her daughters. Mrs. Willis brought her daughter to visit and the girl soon caught it. Even Dr. Hazen found out that the "impossible" could happen for he carried it home too. He employed two or three professors from the Medical College to doctor his girl, but she died. Funerals were thick for a spell.

I was at home writing music in my Great Book when I learned that Frederick had taken a turn for the worse. He'd developed a great sore on his neck, couldn't eat and was troubled for breath. Three-year-old Henry Eugene was also not well. Father went to the Green again and saw Dr. Palmer and Dr. Pierce who told him the boys would live if they could be sweated. He took the advice up to Hiram but couldn't stay long, claiming that listening to the children's hoarse breathing and smelling the air made him sick.

"Hiram and Sarah have given up on both of them," he said.

"Then they're darned fools," I said and went outdoors, determined to see Frederick even though I was afraid to.

Earlier in the season, before the canker rash, Frederick had come up to the sugar place with me. We stopped at Henry's house to borrow his firebox with embers to start a fire. We got the fire going fast and Frederick helped me empty the sap into the boiling kettle. It leaked in a way which, I must confess, made me swear some.

The fire and sun felt hot on our faces and the air was sweet with clouds of sticky steam and spring stirrings of plants and soil. It was a first rate sugar day.

We'd talked about how much sugar we'd make — enough to do something great we hoped. Frederick wanted a music book like mine or lessons from Lull or a bigger jackknife, maybe even another fiddle. He still played the fifty cent fiddle Ed Willis had made. He'd tried to get one by swapping for Geo Grow's.

"Geo says it's a Stradivarious," said Frederick. I laughed which made him look sober.

"What did you swap for it?"

"Father's shotgun."

I knew the gun. Geo had been trying to get it from Hiram, who'd said, "I wouldn't give it to you for another just like it, all the clothes you're wearing, and a year's worth of your labor."

I also knew what the consequences would be if Hiram were to discover how he'd cheated Frederick so took the fiddle up to Geo's house and got the swap unmade.

"I guess I need a new coat more than anything else," Frederick finally said, holding up his arms to show how the sleeves of his coat were ripped wide open. He'd envied a fine coat he'd seen on a boy at Solomon's house when we'd fiddled there.

We both had our fiddles that day so we could practice while the sap boiled.

"Has your Granny Morey given up on makin' you put away your fiddle?" I'd asked.

"No," said Frederick. "I don't play when she's 'round."

We'd been practicing "Roslin Castle," a glorious melancholy tune about the coming of spring. Frederick preferred more cheery tunes — hornpipes and jigs like "Beaux of Oak Hill," "Haymakers" and "Dog and Gun."

"You need to know slow tunes," I'd said. "To mix in with quick ones."

We were on the highest hill around, and as we played and dusk arrived we could see the windows below us begin to glow as our neighbors lit their oil lamps and candles — the Grows, Moreys, Raymonds and Cobbs. Smudges of smoke rose from hills around where men worked at their sugar places.

I went to see Frederick when I heard he'd been taken sick. He had a great sore on his neck. We went out back behind his Father's house and sot on stones near the brook. Frederick tried to play his fiddle but couldn't for long. His coat provided little warmth and he was weak.

He died April 16. I was at home writing music in my Great Book when Mother returned home from watching, her long skirt muddy from walking along the road. It was all sposh under the snow. "Frederick died," she said. "Your father was with him. He swapped that small jackknife he carried for your father's big one just before he died. Your father said you should have it." I recognized Father's big black jackknife. Frederick had made a good swap.

Then it was the same as before. Father got nails, screws and lining for the coffin and plank for the box. I helped Father by keeping up his fires and doing odd chores — took away the banking around the house, buried the frozen-footed rooster — the poor cuss. Then I looked on at the coffin-making, which was called helping. My standing and looking was so indispensable that I couldn't leave a minute. Mrs. Leach and Mother made the robe. Father didn't get the coffin trimmed a minute too soon for the funeral.

They wanted to have Frederick's funeral at the Flat but folks were still too badly afraid. So it was at the house and just like all the rest. I put on my fine shirt, best coat and new breeches and stopped at the funeral a minute or two, as I happened to get there just before they started off for the burying ground. It was darn'd cold.

Early the next morning, Father went down to get Dr. Tom Powers to prescribe for Henry. I hoped he wouldn't die, for a boy and a girl was five times as much of a family as one girl and Henry was unquestionably the smartest boy there was — so everyone thought.

Henry got better. One of Jo Dodge's three children lived. Both of Chas and Almira's children survived as did Norman's daughter and Mrs. Willis' girl.

Frederick was the last to die of canker rash. In early May, Hiram moved his family into Ed Whitney's house. Henry was well enough to take a ride down as far as our house and back. Mr. Morey got a jug of cider for the movers — he, Hiram and Dodge. The name "Rum Street" was becoming so thoroughly true that the only Son of Temperance on the road, neighbor Whitney, had been getting drunk and had trouble from Delirium Tremens (Devils troubles). Quite a startling event that. I guessed the Sons would "dispel" him.

With the deaths of most of my cousins, few of us young Cobbs remained. Grandfather's descendants had been reduced to four boys, only two on Rum Street and one, Jim Cobb, in another family's home in Woodstock and another, Eddie, somewhere in New Hampshire. There were only two girls, both young, but promising to be credits to the Cobb family.

I went back up onto the hill to see to the last of my sap but it was a sad business. I hated being alone.

Granny Morey was the first to say aloud that the canker rash was the result of the dances. But others said it too and even more decidedly. Mrs. Holmes knew it to a moral certainty. "I know for a FACT that dancing was the SOLE CAUSE of the deaths of Hiram's and Jo Dodge's children," she said.

Chapter 26

Leaving Woodstock

It was the first car-ride I ever had and the first time I ever boarded away from home.

In March of 1851 George Scales began talking about studying with the great music teacher, Abram Pushee, in Lebanon, New Hampshire. He proposed that I go with him. I was 15 years old and had never been further from home than Plymouth, Vermont, a distance of 14 miles and then only once, with Uncle Hiram to go fishing. Lebanon was 20 miles distant and in another state. Nevertheless, Father wanted me to go even though George Scales, although few years older than me, wasn't a reliable chaperone. Also, I didn't like his company very well. Mother ridiculed the notion. She said it would be better to spend $30 on a pair of steers or to pay Stearns part of our store bill.

I think Father saw music as a way for me to make my living. He raised the $30 for room and board and Pushee's charges by selling a good part of his land, the hill we called the Pierce Place. When Albert McClay paid $50 on the land, the trip seemed certain, provided I was accepted.

I struggled with great fears, doubts, and hopes about whether I'd be taken for a fool and decided if people bothered me, I'd consider myself some other person whom I cared nothing about.

Father, George, and I set out on a rainy day in Father's new green wagon, stopping for a haircut by a barber at Hatch's grocery store on the Green. We paid 12 1/2 cents, the first time I had ever paid for barbering in my life.

At the audition, I played "Katy's Rambles," a spirited tune that showed off my technique, but was barely able to look Pushee in the face. It was better than George's performance of "Dunkin House." Father examined Pushee's fiddle long and intently, intending I think, to alter the bridge of my thunderstruck fiddle again. I don't think Pushee had a very exalted opinion of any of us. He had no reason to.

We ate dinner at the tavern and got the horse fed, which cost 50 cents. Father bought an umbrella for 92 cents, for it had been raining all day and he'd left the one Mother made at home. We could have avoided paying the toll at Lyman's Bridge over the Connecticut River, since the toll-taker was nowhere to be seen, but Father walked some distance in the rain to find him and paid 35 cents each way.

Our ride home in the rain was mighty slow. I held the umbrella while Father tried to hurry the horse, clucking and shaking the reins without effect and finally letting him stop entirely on a hill. I, being cold, got out to walk a piece. I got way ahead and it was growing dark so I continued walking, thinking I'd be overtaken by the wagon on the hill down into Taftsville.

The road was muddy and the surroundings darker than the very Devil which moved me so that I dared not stop. I walked helter-skelter all the way home, a distance of almost 10 miles and arrived 40 minutes before Father. "I never had such a walk before in my life," I wrote in my journal that night. "We got our new wagon almighty wet."

Father's getting the wagon soaked through was a freak of divine justice. At sundry other times he'd scolded Mother and me severely for getting it a mite wet. Once coming home from the Green, we stopped an hour under the covered bridge to let a storm pass over. Still we got a scolding. I hoped that in the future I'd be allowed to take it out without such an outcry.

Pushee accepted both me and George. We were to stay three weeks. In the days leading up to the departure, Father made me new thin calfskin boots and a box to hold my things. Mother bought two pairs of stockings and three handkerchiefs and cloth for a vest. She sewed until midnight the day before we left.

On the morning of our departure, Father and I found George Scales in a kind of stand-off with Mrs. Holmes and Mrs. Thomas, his wife's aunts. Mrs. Scales held her month-old infant while a wobbly toddler hung onto her skirt, a scene of domestic vulnerability that could have been planned by the aunts to enhance the wickedness of George's leaving. The women were questioning George about how he intended to support his wife and small sons, since he obviously meant to leave them behind in Woodstock while he wasted his time in Lebanon.

George was just 22, the oldest of six children and felt responsibilities wrapping around him like a boa constrictor. His father's stock had recently been attached for non-payment of debts and was, at that very moment, in Mrs. Thomas' barn while his creditors argued amongst themselves over who had rights to the cattle.

The aunts had always opposed the marriage. George's father, William, drank excessively and his brother, Earl, had been detected in stealing Lemux's wool in Bridgewater. Also George's family was far meaner than their own. Being correct in their assessment of George, at least in their own minds, made them more self-righteous than ever.

Mrs. Thomas stood, her backbone as rigid as her strict and indisputable beliefs. "It seems you're to be an exceedingly great violinist," she said. The idea seemed ridiculous to all of us, in light of her scorn. "I thought you meant to be a lawyer. And what happened to your peddling cart?" Her glare revealed what nonsense it was to abandon his family, particularly to learn to play the fiddle. She wasn't alone in considering it a profane and carnal instrument that should be held in tremendous hate and abomination.

"And what of your promise to cut my hay in return for living in my house?" She glanced around at the small shabby room. That she was a good Christian was indisputable in her own mind for she would render assistance to any suffering person for money, but without it, alas! He would be told to call on the neighbor. She'd laid up her treasures in heaven and the next thing was to scrape together what she could on earth.

Mrs. Thomas' sister, Mrs. Holmes, was also well-to-do, a widow who'd returned from Whitehall, New York, with two sons and her dead husband's money. She owned land and four houses on the Flat and was not afraid to maintain her rights or to assert her personal certainty about what was good. She was in the midst of her latest battle with Mr. Daniels to keep the Flat from laying out a road through her land to a proposed new school, which Mr. Daniels wanted built on his own land. Most people knew of their feuds and loudly condemned Mr. Daniels, thinking his object was to injure Mrs. Holmes. The widow, however, maintained her vigilance. She was not dropping the matter. That spring a flood of ice had descended on Daniels' shop and fixed it so that it wouldn't run for a fortnight. Mrs. Holmes considered that proof that God was on her side.

"As long as you have a family to support and nothing beforehand, I think you're in rather poor circumstances to be going away to learn to fiddle," she said. She then produced an arsenal of evidence that the fiddle led straight to hell, which seemed not to be so much the fiddling, but the dancing that arose as a result. "Brother Eben spent his money in that way and stole to keep up appearances and got into state's prison," she said. "Jo and Roena Leonard go to dances and people mistake their house for our pig pen."

I could see George's arguments for leaving swarming through his head. He sidled over the door and began to push it open. "This is my chance," he'd told Father and me earlier. "I've straightened out my old man's affairs," although his own were so crooked that the neighbors carried in stuff for his wife. "A man owes my father money and I mean to collect it." And finally, "I'm not doing anything great right now, so I can go."

Father and I turned to leave as well. We needed to get to the train.

I longed to express the eloquent arguments that filled my head. I wanted to tell Mrs. Holmes that her idea of God must be immense to think he would take a part in her quarrels with Mr. Daniels. I wanted to say that abominating unbelievers or avoiding card-playing, fiddling, and dancing did not make a true Christian. Furthermore, I never made more than $2 at a dance and unfortunately, probably never would make more. I was unlikely to get into trouble on the account of too much money.

But George meant to get a living by fiddling and was doing his best to learn. Privately, I doubted that George would be successful. He couldn't play nearly as well as I could. What tunes he could play, he couldn't play in another key while I could play them in immediate succession on every note it could be pitched on. But enough of those thoughts. In order for me to go, I had to have George along as a kind of chaperone.

I kept silent because I knew from experience that if I tried to speak when angry, and often when not, my words came out as a nervous stammer, a garbled series of words that made me appear a fool.

Then Mrs. Holmes went too far. "It's a moral fact that dancing caused the death of Hiram Cobb's and Jo Dodge's children."

"You know no more about it than Balaam's ass," I said. Father was at that moment, hurrying me out the door so the effect of my statement was diminished. Father didn't want to alienate the widows and create a war unworthy of their ignorant opinions. They were Mother's friends and good people and in some way related to her. He knew others had the same thoughts, although few people stated them as firmly or loudly as these women. And it was better to avoid an argument there was no chance of winning.

We all scrambled into the wagon and Father drove to the Woodstock train depot in a great hurry, going afoot up the hills with the stage just in our rear, which we more than kept forward of. He got $11 in Woodstock bank bills at the Green to add to the 50 cents I carried in my pocket. I paid 20 cents for the car ride and bought three sheets of music paper for six cents. It was the first car-ride I ever had and the first time I ever boarded away from home. I found a seat next to the window and looked out at Father who waited a moment before turning away to take the wagon and team back home.

He probably knew he wouldn't be able to provide me with a good farm to make my living on. He sent me off in hopes that I'd do well with the great Abram Pushee, celebrated throughout Vermont and New Hampshire as a violinist, teacher of dancing, High Priest of the Masons, organizer of the annual Musicians' Ball. I was somewhat of a prodigy back home, or so the neighbors thought, but Pushee would expect much more of me.

I was equally apprehensive, insecure about my abilities and aware I'd be competing with fiddlers from all around New England. I was 15 years old, a greeny from the hills, irascible, touchy, and withdrawn among strangers. I'd gotten an impression about musicians from the book, *Life and Adventures of Valentine Vox, the Ventriloquist,* by Henry Cockton, who wrote, "As men, musicians were indolent and dishonourable; as husbands, they were faithless; as fathers, they were heartless; as friends, they were envious and insincere." Was that the group I was about to enter?

The great locomotive pulled out in a cloud of steam and a squeal of scraping metal that echoed the anxiety in my heart.

Chapter 27

Studies With Pushee

The window of my room at the Lafayette Hotel in Lebanon, was above a grocery. It looked out onto the street to the park on the other side where the boys played ball in the evening. I didn't dare join them, knowing exactly what would happen—I would never hit the ball.

George and I ate in the tavern, a source of great humiliation for me and humor for surrounding tables. I realized I was awful mannerless. I told myself that others laughing at me meant nothing. I wanted only to get through my time in Lebanon without being molested. I practiced in my room at night, going to bed by nine o'clock while the boys gathered in the great hall and sang and played guitar and fiddled until much later.

I discovered that Pushee's playing wasn't as far beyond my comprehension as I thought it would be. Also I learned that Pushee swore considerable and that he was an infidel, although neither of these made me think any less of him. They only confirmed my suspicion that all great men pretended to be very religious.

Since I stayed in the same room with George Scales, we couldn't both

I joined them in games of whist in their rooms, contrary to Father's advice. "Don't play cards with anyone in the rooms, but in the barroom if anywhere and not there unless others do so!" he'd said.

practice unless we played together, or we'd be at odds with each other's tunes. This got to be a darned nuisance because George only wanted to practice what he already knew, not what he didn't. At first we practiced major and minor scales and a few psalm tunes, then common contra-dance tunes like "College Hornpipe" and "Money Musk." Pushee wrote off "Hull's Victory" for us, and I played it well right away — while George Scales put near a day's work into it. We played our tunes out of all existence, and I, so vigorously, that I lamed my fingers like thunder. However, I learned how to use my wrist to play each note.

    I asked to borrow some music of Pushee, for I expected to write off a lot in my Great Book. He only gave me one book of Old Cotillions written off in such a bungle that they were hardly good for anything. I copied off 50 of them.

    George started acting kind of mean so I acted mean back at him. But when I was even with a person, conscience would never let me go any further, and I wanted to do them a favor. George had been looking for a letter every day, saying he expected one with $30 in it that was owed to his old man and he meant to have it. It seemed he had just enough money laid up to pay Pushee for lessons and Trescott for room and board. But it turned out that the debtor had moved west to Four Mile Grove, Illinois, where Norman and others from Woodstock had settled. I had to give Geo Scales 37 cents or he couldn't have returned home. On the other hand, Geo Scales said he was going to take dancing schools next winter and I disinterestedly noticed that in speaking on the subject, he kind of said or implied "WE."

    Pushee had a favorite student, a Canadian chap, whom he praised almightily. That student could play off a dancing tune pretty smart, but I thought he played it devilishly out of tune. He had the mistaken impression that I didn't know anything. But I knew I could beat him all to the Devil and vowed to do so. The proof of my superior playing came when Hezekiah Smith visited Pushee, a devilishly unexpected event. We all went into the great hall—the Canadian chap, George, some other boys, Hez, Pushee, and I. At first we all played a few immortal tunes. George, by everlasting and murderous practice, had got so he could play them tolerably correct. Then I took out some new contra dance tunes and struck up. The contrast among us was indeed great. I played them a good deal better than the Canadian chap and

George couldn't touch the tunes at all. Even Hez couldn't keep up with me. Pushee took my thunderstruck fiddle and put in a rough Italian E string, the kind used by the best fiddlers in Boston, and my fiddle sounded slicker than ever.

Before long I played the fiddle with the boys in the hall. I had been so afraid of acting like a fool in their eyes that I acted like a fool, whether I was one or not. I started feeling comfortable though and after another week, I joined them in games of whist in their rooms, contrary to Father's advice. "Don't play cards with anyone in the rooms, but in the barroom if anywhere and not there unless others do so!" he'd said. I figured that soon enough I'd be playing ball with them and wanting to stay longer if I'd had the money.

After about 10 days, George and I hired a horse and wagon for $2.50 and went home for a visit. At Lyman's bridge George waited a minute or two for the toll taker, then drove on, rejoicing at having saved 35 cents. In the same situation, Father had walked ten rods in the rain to pay the toll.

I returned to Lebanon with improved confidence. My fiddle was sounding darn'd familiar and I felt a good deal more "real." I got along very well with the people there.

My final week, I took short excursions away—once to the iron foundry to watch the hands pour in melted iron and take out pieces of stoves. We went to Hanover to see Dartmouth College. Boys not much older than me walked confidently among green lawns and magnificent buildings. I thought how great it would be to wear good clothes and study with well-educated teachers! I was glad to have seen it, but to have done well with the boys studying with Pushee, was enough for the time being.

Pushee played considerable with us on the Wednesday before leaving. He played more with me than George, which I took as confirmation that I had greater talent. But whatever I thought about it, Pushee told us that we had both made "most remarkable improvement." I guess, on the whole, that I had improved well. To my surprise, Father came to get us, thinking I might not have enough money. I told him I guessed my playing wasn't as inferior as I'd thought it was, which was almost as important as learning that I was not as green as I'd thought I was.

Chapter 28

Father's Miserable State of Affairs

So Father sold his oxen. He'd been hoping for $85, but their weight was less than he'd supposed, so he got $75. Without the oxen we could no longer plow, draw dung or distribute muck. We couldn't haul logs for burning or building, draw stones from the fields or tubs up for sugaring. Furthermore, Father's oxen had been in demand and their loss meant we couldn't use them as a source of income.

That summer I realized just how miserable Father's affairs were. Our flour barrel was empty, he had a mountain of debt and not a cent to pay with. Fortunately, Mr. McClay came by with more money he owed for the Pierce Place. With that, our being out of flour was divested of its terrors and Father paid some of his debts—$20 at Stearns store on the Green for cloth, nails, food, shot and other things, $3 to Southgate for meat long since devoured, $7 for taxes to Gaius Perkins and a $21 bank note from the Woodstock Bank which he mailed to Norman out in Illinois.

But when he returned home with $70 remaining, he found Mr. Hartwell there with a writ for $60 and interest from W.H. Scott. I hadn't known that Father had mortgaged the Pierce Place long ago in order to help Hiram avoid losing his house and all his possessions. And still, Father and Henry had to pay the town $75 for Betsey's keep and $60 to Granny Richmond.

When Father got his land in 1846, Henry said that it would be a curse to him, and it was, a most abominable curse, for it prevented him from working at anything else. And yet, he might have succeeded if it had not been for those debts. As it was, it would unquestionably have been better for him to leave it and work at 75 or even 40 cents a day.

So Father sold his oxen. He'd been hoping for $85, but their weight was less than he'd supposed, so he got $75. Without the oxen we could no longer plow, draw dung or distribute muck. We couldn't haul logs for burning or building, draw stones from the fields or tubs up for sugaring. Furthermore, Father's oxen had been in demand and their loss meant we couldn't use them as a source of income.

Father's next hope was to collect on some of Grandfather's outstanding notes. When Grandfather died, Henry had taken about $500 worth of notes to collect but through negligence and foolishness, didn't do so. It seemed that most of the notes were lost.

Father called a meeting of the brothers–I called it a meeting of brotherly love–to see what could be done. Hiram and Chas Raymond came and played checkers while Henry and Mosely Thomas, who came anyway although he wasn't an heir, jawed politics. Hosea and Father kept still.

Losing hope that the brothers would accomplish anything, Mr. Hartwell and I studied the notes and concluded that one debtor had failed, another had sold his farm because of his own debts and a third had gone to Canada. Another had gone crazy when his business failed and went to the asylum at Brattleborough. Mr. Hartwell said he'd try to collect $30 from the Atwoods, who were the only ones likely to be capable of paying. He said he'd sell the other notes for whatever he could get.

So it went 'till midnight when the meeting adjourned.

The next day Henry and I got together to figure how much each brother was still owed from the estate and concluded, unfortunately for Father, that in the end, he would get nothing and still owed the brothers $6.81.

We were increasingly poverty-stricken and destitute.

I tried to help by fiddling for a dance at Seth Taylor's on the Flat but it was a miserable experience, all hands drunk. I earned one dollar.

Then I agreed to play with George Scales for a dance in Lempster, New Hampshire. He promised me food, lodging and pay. Only 12 couples danced, each paying 50 cents so George claimed he lost money and refused to pay me. He gave me seven or eight crackers for dinner at Merritt's Tavern at Three Corners in Hartland and that was only because I caught him sneaking his own dinner and insisted. The next stop, at Nichol's tavern, also produced no food, although George had plenty to drink and leaned on me the rest of the trip home. That night I drank one swallow of gin, but afterwards regretted it. My pay, including the crackers, amounted to 12 cents. I thought I ought to be revenged on George Scales, for using me so damned mean. Father sued Scales for $5 plus expenses, but George had nothing to pay with and then left town so we got nothing.

I should hate to have left town after the precise model Mr. Scales set, with everybody rejoicing because I had gone. He next appeared in Canada where we heard that he'd written to his wife, telling her he'd lost his best suit of clothes. Then we heard he'd been tarred and feathered and ridden out on a rail because he'd been found somewhere he shouldn't have been. I can't be certain of any of this because we heard it from Emeline Cobb and it was impossible for Emeline to live in a neighborhood long with anyone without lying about them.

The last news was that he'd gone to Four Mile Grove, Illinois, probably after the debtor he claimed owed his father money. Emeline saw him there. She said he was with two women, one of them dressed as a man and one of them, another man's wife. He started a dancing school, got drunk and kicked out and so on. I felt a small amount of satisfaction.

I decided I would be foolish to attempt to get a living wholly by fiddling.

CHAPTER 29

THE RISE AND FALL OF SPIRITUALIZM ON RUM STREET

But one night I'd been reading about luminous manifestations of spirits, and about 10 o'clock I was astonished to see a light moving around on the wall over my bed. I began to sweat in full expectation of seeing a specter.

Mr. Hartwell surprised us all when he said, "I have good news. There is certainly and truly life beyond the grave." We couldn't have been more surprised. The respectable Mr. Hartwell, who was trusted to write deeds, administer estates, serve as Honorable Referee at court hearings, was suddenly convinced he could talk with the dead. He read the *Spiritual Philosopher* and *Celestial Telegraph* every spare moment.

"Mr. Horace Wood established a channel of communication with Mr. Samual Wood," he said. I knew Mr. Horace Wood. He was a teacher at the English Mills School who'd likely lose his work if people learned that he was conducting secret rapping sessions where he talked to people who'd been long dead. He ran a finger down a written alphabet and the spirit knocked out his message. No one saw the alphabet, not even Horace Wood himself sometimes. He didn't know anything about what was coming."

He pulled a paper from his pocket. "Here's the message. I want you to write it off."

I armed myself with my gold pen and paper.

"Communication from Samual C. Wood, deceased to Elijah Wood, Horace Wood, and I.B. Hartwell. Question 'How are the spirits permitted and enabled at this time and in this manner, to communicate to us?' Answer 'In the year 1843 a change was made in the world of spirits, and the immortal principle of man was enabled to so far break from the inertness of their condition as to come to the earth and communicate through electrical agency, a subtle agent, but sufficient for the purpose. For agents or mediums we take nervous people because they are possessed of more nervo-vital fluid, which is a better conductor of electricity being more purely electrical in its nature, physicians' theories to the contrary notwithstanding. How glorious for those who have had no faith in God to be assured that there is a life beyond the valley of the shadow of death.' "

Mr. Hartwell sank back in his chair, his eyes alight. He seemed almost taken away. He set about writing a piece about the rappings and mailed it to *The New York Tribune.* People said Editor Horace Greeley praised it considerably. He persuaded Father to make a rapping machine. It had 36 keys for the letters and numbers. The spirits could easily have communicated by tapping the keys. Aaron Whitney, highly respected foreman of the machine shop on the Flat, took the machine down to two respected Boston mediums, Mr. La Roy Sunderland and Mrs. Cooper. "The spirits won't tolerate it," he said, handing it back to Mr. Hartwell upon his return to the Flat.

Mr. Hartwell's enthusiasm seemed to be diminishing. "An Ann Hartwell of Dover, New Hampshire, has thrust herself upon me as my guardian spirit," he said a few nights later. "She told me she died seven years ago at the age of 9. Her father's name was Almon Hartwell, but he's dead too" He seemed troubled.

"I rather mistrust her. I think she may be a lying spirit." He wrote a letter to a relative of the same name living in Dover to ascertain if she or the folks she told of ever existed 'round there. "If she exists, I shall make myself heard through the *New York Tribune*," he said.

Nothing came of his inquiries and Mr. Hartwell lost all confidence in rappings.

Henry agreed with Mr. Hartwell, saying "It's all a sham." Laura was more open-minded. "I won't go where there are raps but if they came here, I'll cheerfully investigate them. I've always believed spirits to be 'round."

Of course Mrs. Holmes hated the spirits and found a passage in the holy Bible where it said something like, "'And in the last days Hell shall come and get the very elect.' I'll be darn'd if they'll ever get me. And that is all I have to say about it."

But the rappings, or Rochester knockings as they were called, because they started when two sisters in Rochester, New York, began to regularly communicate with the spirits in front of large audiences, had taken hold of some people in Woodstock. Spiritual circles met regularly lead by local people who claimed to be mediums.

Horace Wood wrote about the spiritualists' conferences in Woodstock to *The Spiritual Telegraph*, a New York City newspaper that reported news of spiritual phenomena. The meetings are "attended by a more numerous and intelligent audience than any other religious meeting in town," he wrote. The editor of the *Woodstock Mercury*, wrote "the most charitable excuse which could be made for Wood is that he's crazy."

In early July of 1851, the Rochester Knockings that started it all, came to town. I'm not sure of what happened but heard rumors of them performing in Barnard or at Mr. Randall's house on the Flat or at John D. Powers' house and that the folks on the Green thought of raising a mob or did raise a mob, but succeeded in scaring them out of town. I wished I could have witnessed them.

At first I was bitterly opposed to all of it. Then Solomon Wyman said he'd begun getting raps four days earlier although nobody else knew of it. He suggested conducting a rapping session at his house. His stepmother, who was a strict Congregationalist, objected, and requested that rappings not occur in her home.

But Solomon and his sisters and some others of us wore her down and won her over. We gathered around the big table in her square room. (Things were on rather of a better looking foundation over there than they were at my house—such things as eatables, woodpile, clothes etc.)

Mrs. Wyman's father, Old Square Damon, was in the room all the while. Old Square prayed night and morning and asked a blessing before every meal. But he was almost deaf and not very sharp sighted, so didn't realize what was going on, or the Devil might have been to pay.

Amid a good deal of scolding and fretting at the spirits, Solomon claimed to have contacted his own dead mother. She had a message for Solomon's sister, Clara. "Turn your course or you'll be sorry. Dr. Barrows is studying your character." Dr. Albert Barrows had been paying Clara some attention.

She said to Mary Ann Wyman, "Leave off your acquaintance with Jane Ann Woodbury." Jane Ann was a troublemaker who went to school with Mary Ann.

Neither Clara nor Mary Ann were confident that the raps came from their mother.

The spirits addressed Julia on general theological subjects. "The Lord is preparing mansions for all the human race etc."

His own guardian spirit, Mary Sabin, told Solomon, "Glory and fame await you."

"You know what all RESPECTABLE PEOPLE think of that business," said Mrs. Wyman who'd come into the room. So far, I hadn't seen anything very bad about it. I thought the spirits' advice had been rather unremarkable.

At the end of our session, Solomon said he was hearing from a Caroline Ainsworth who claimed to be my guardian spirit. Her message was "I am ever with you." I thought her message wasn't very profound, considering that she was speaking from beyond the grave. Many more interesting things could have been said.

Then Solomon said to me, "The spirits predict that you will be a medium in eight days." I greatly hoped it would prove true, although I was afraid the spirits wouldn't heed their promise. Still, I thought they ought to.

Solomon warned me not to tell anyone about the raps. I

agreed but went home and immediately told Mother who was taking quite an interest in the rappings. She had apparently decided that the spirits might help her locate a lost deed that would prove that her father had never been paid for land he'd sold. If she could find it, part of the land might still be hers. She'd pinned her hopes of leaving and going out to join her brother in Michigan where she could "enjoy her life," on getting that money.

In hopes of becoming a medium, I took more interest in the rappings. I began reading *The Spiritual Telegraph* at bedtime. Most nights, nothing but a strong dose of Morse's sleeping tonic would have been better for my sleep. But one night I'd been reading about luminous manifestations of spirits, and about 10 o'clock, I was astonished to see a light moving around on the wall over my bed. I began to sweat in full expectation of seeing a specter. Afterwards I satisfied myself that the coals in the stove caused the light. It's hard for one who doesn't sleep alone to get an idea of the effect of any such thing on one who does. It had seemed impossible that there were such things as disembodied spirits, ghosts, spectres, but I began to have doubts.

I tried receiving raps, but upon strict investigation always discovered that I'd somehow caused them. It was almost impossible to lay one's hands and ear on a table, light stand or otherwise and not cause raps. I couldn't even lie still without breathing at all without making them. Occasionally I did hear knocks that I knew I didn't make, and they scared me considerably. But on the eighth day, having almost no success, I concluded that I was no medium.

Mother tried to receive raps too and supposed she was receiving them even when her finger joints snapped a little. When she heard that Mrs. Dodge had certainly become a medium, she went up to investigate. "It was the table-leaf making the raps," she said. "Mrs. Dodge isn't a medium."

While most of us hoped we could become mediums, we all doubted that the common noises around the house were messages from the dead. Not surprisingly, Geo Grow was more easily convinced. One night, Owen Raymond, Geo and I were playing cards at our house when Mother got us to rapping. At first Geo said he got raps, but nobody else could hear them. We all pounded on the table, laughing a good deal. But by and by we began to hear raps that we hadn't made. We fell to asking questions. Geo correctly answered them.

Geo had been adopted by Mr. and Mrs. Grow when his father died, so the first message he claimed to receive, came from his dead father. "I lie beneath the clods of the valley in a lonely graveyard in Holland, Vermont, awaiting the resurrection morn," he said. Then he moved the table enough to tip down a slate set up sideways on it. We had quite a demonstration.

Owen was so scared that he didn't dare to go home. All three of us slept in my bed. We laid plenty thick enough.

News of our session got out. Geo Grow's sudden emergence as a medium encouraged his long-held opinion that he was a wonderful man and awful smart. When he entered a trance, he closed his eyes and nodded his head until it nearly rested on the paper on which he wrote the spirits' words. "I am ever with you. I am your father that watched over you in childhood. Remember me, and so on. " Geo completed each communication with an X on the paper and said "There it is. I don't know what it is or what it's about."

I thought Geo's messages were old and worn out and could have been written by anyone. When people asked him specific questions, the "spirits" rebuked them as persons of little faith. Geo reported them as saying, "Why do you ask that question?" or "I will not now answer your question."

I remained fairly certain rappings were all a cheat until I witnessed Ed Willis' performance. Nearly all of Rum Street was there. Even Henry came, determined to ridicule it all. Geo arrived determined to reveal Ed as an imposter. I was ready to denounce Ed as an untrustworthy fraud, although that may have been because he'd borrowed my accordion and never returned or paid for it. Hiram came to see if it was all humbug.

Even Granny Morey came. "I can tell whether the very fust knock I hearn was made by Spirits or not," she announced at the door. She didn't believe that the spirits were alive and knocking round. "Moses says the spirits sleep till the Great Resurracktion Day, and then, if they're fit, they descent to Heaven and, if they hain't, they go tew Hell."

Ed wore a broad-rimmed hat. He looked tremendous. The room was dark but for an oil lamp turned down low that reflected on our circle of faces. At first we sot still and quiet.

Ed acted kind of bashful and decent. Then he began to shake and his hands trembled in a way that no live man could come up to under ordinary circumstances. He closed his eyes and his countenance changed as though he'd just given up the ghost. He drew his hands off the table and made passes, first out, and then in, before his eyes. Then he was ready for action and made three mighty graceful bows, using his hands. He always ended in the same way too, by making three bows.

Each spirit that arrived wrote their name. I know Ed didn't see them. He answered questions by tapping on the table with his hand, one, two, or three times. When anyone made sport of it, laughed, or thought something he didn't relish, he slammed on the table with his hand, looked toward 'em with his eyes closed, and pointed at 'em. He sent Granny Morey out of the room. Once he opened his eyes, and they looked horribly. I knew it wasn't Ed sitting there. He was mesmerized and senseless. It was clear that some other mind, not among us, acted through him.

Ed acted out the death of Vernon Knight, one of Granny Morey's sons-in-law who died in a fit. He fell down and jerked about so much I didn't know but what he would die.

Frederick came and spoke to Hiram. Ed kept putting his hand up to his neck where Frederick had the sore that killed him.

But one thing I didn't like. Ed got me to fiddling on Morey's miserable old thing of a fiddle when General George Washington came over him and made him dance.

When that was done he said that Charles Osgood was a medium, and straightway Charles Osgood began to twitch and jump in a most marvelous manner, keeping it up the rest of the evening and all night. He said he couldn't help it. The session lasted until midnight.

Neither Ed nor Charles Osgood pursued mediumship although they would have perhaps been better at it than Geo. Austin Simmons, a locally prominent medium, took Geo on to work with him and the two sat in as mediums at important rapping societies in town like the Mt. Tom Spiritual Circle and in people's homes.

Simmons endeavored to make a man out of Geo, and I hoped he would succeed. Geo claimed they were soon going to hold public meetings and in three years would have a meeting house on the Green. He told Mother that a medium could walk in the air, read any person's thoughts and find anything lost. He'd also started claiming that he could make any person become a medium for $12 dollars—and it would cost one dollar to attend a meeting. He said he was debt-free, that he'd spent $36 and still had $30 in his possession. He showed everyone a gold ring he claimed to have paid a dollar for, or $1.25. The figure varied with each telling. He showed off his $11 worth of new clothes including a sort of a black felt broad-brimmed Kossuth hat that cost one dollar. Geo actually strained on such occasions.

Not long after, I came across Geo picking stones into the cart with old Grow and thought it strange that he, the prophet of the Lord, with three suits of clothes and a rifle, should condescend to pick stones in the rain. I wondered how long it would be before he gave up lying.

However, seeing Geo boast made me wish I had some decent clothes and a pocket pistol and that my finances were in a less embarrassed condition. His hat in particular, struck my fancy as being the thing for me. Even so, the Lord knew I couldn't bring myself to envy him, even if he possessed the whole planet.

Geo did great things at Shaw's one evening, during which the spirits rapped out a message most terrible loud, telling him not to rap on Sundays. He was telling this to his mother, Mrs. Grow, and attempted to imitate the raps by banging on the stove with the tongs. This pleased her. She believed in the spirits a little, but was firm about observance of Sundays. "If the spirits rap through you, will it make you better?" she asked and he answered, "It will," which pleased her even further.

After this promise, that he was indeed a better person, Geo and I thought we'd better not risk sliding downhill because it was a Sunday. But by and by, he put on his cap and called me out and we went to get the sled, only to find that old Grow had tied the clothes line 'round it so that he could tell if it was used. So we desisted.

Interest in spiritualism grew and believers tried to find larger places to host their sessions. Austin tried to use the schoolhouse on the Flat but the master and scholars locked and barred the door and nailed down the windows. Nevertheless, a staunch spiritualist burst in and Simmons gave a lecture that night to a crowded house. They were also der the Woodstock Town Hall. Town fathers claimed that destroyed by fire, the insurance would be lost. Dr.] Randall from the South Village pointed out that he'd religious meetings of all descriptions there and the onl spiritualists were being denied, was because the father ... the town didn't like their faith.

To hear Geo tell of it, his role as a medium was increasing. He and Austin had received a list of 40 people to be admitted to an important spiritual meeting. The list included NO FOOLS. At first he said my name was on the list but when I tried to enter he said I wouldn't be admitted without a fuss because the list given to Simmons by none other than GEORGE WASHINGTON did not include me. Geo had always been famous for lying and being a simpleton and I wondered how long it would before Simmons tired of him.

As I'd predicted, soon Geo and Austin found themselves at odds. Their disagreements became more heated until Austin read a communication from the spirits ordering him never to admit Geo Grow into the circle or into his house again. "He isn't fit!" said the spirits. Asked why Geo had been a medium for so long, the spirits said "God intended to confound the wise with the base and foolish."

Geo claimed he'd decided to leave the group to expose its humbug. He said one of the mediums in town had been expelled by the spirits for putting it to Cynthia. But shortly after, he appeared at a circle as much of a medium as ever. Geo explained that away by saying the medium had repented.

The Grows, who'd always disliked spiritualists, encouraged Geo to demolish the whole movement. "They're the work of Devils and damned spirits," said Old Grow. "They're nothing new–they were known in Bible times to give rise to witchcraft," said Mrs. Grow. "Mediums will obtain the curses of God for their pains," said Granny Morey.

Christians began to come down on the rappings with a vengeance. Austin Simmons lost his office as district clerk. As he returned home after the meeting where he was dismissed, boys pursued him, precipitating stale hen's eggs. He returned such politeness with stones!

With the expulsion of Geo Grow rapping sessions died

out on Rum Street. I returned to my original opinion that they were the damnedest nonsense that could be thought of–until Geo's final display.

Geo conducted his last rapping session at my house. He whispered a word to Father. I had the alphabet in my hand and ran my pen down it and Geo got a rap from the spirits when the correct letter was reached. He couldn't see the letters or my hand. The letters were all correct. Geo said he willed that the raps come when I pointed at a letter and they did–that was all he knew about it. And he told the truth. He told us all of a sentence he would rap out and did so without seeing the alphabet pointed at. So there was still mystery about Geo's raps, but alas! I think few spirits had anything to do with the matter.

CHAPTER 30

FROM THE WOMEN'S PERSPECTIVE, HELL RIGHT HERE ON EARTH

(This story is from the women's point of view. Although there were certainly many quiltings on Rum Street, none were described in detail in Charles' journals. The situation here was invented. Opinions and anecdotes were real, taken from Charles' journals; Lucia Cobb's memorandum; the diaries of Emma Graves who was a single young woman who lived in English Mills during the same time period; from the book, Woman in Her Various Relations *by Mrs. L. G. Abell, published in New York by William Holdredge in 1851 as a fireside series containing practical rules for American females; from the story "Hearts of Iron, Hearts of*

"Cousin George is raising a mustache," she said. "I told him I didn't like it, it loomed up so. He said it must make him look old for he met General Nathaniel P. Banks on the street and the general bowed to him for the first time in his life. It is said that General Banks takes a good deal of notice of voters."

Gold, and Hearts of Steel" by Mary F. W. Gibson from Woodstock who wrote under the pen name Winnie Woodfern (published in 1854); research done by Daniel Cohen on Mary Gibson as an early woman story writer, and other sources.*

Laura's house was crowded with women for the quilting. Some had even come from English Mills, a mile and a half to the north by road. I was in the room reading or pretending to read William Cowper's *Task*, a glorious poem about God and nature. But I could hear the women and even see them as well as if I was quilting too and in truth it was a wonderful thing to hear women talk.

      Laura had arranged the quilting for Hosea. Her brother-in-law was unmarried and a poor sewer. She'd seen him do a miserable job of trying to mend a shirt. She held the quilting even though she had a grudge against him for refusing to relinquish small items Emeline Cobb sold him and then sold to Laura. I don't know who had the greater rights but I thought Laura should have been mad at Emeline, not Hosea. I didn't understand Laura's tolerance for her sister-in-law, who turned the most ordinary events into scandals and began quarrels that lasted long after she'd gone a thousand miles away to Illinois. But Laura, generous as always, felt it was her duty to help Hosea. I thought he should get married.

    I was pleased to see Mary Gibson come in with Laura Churchill. They were sisters by adoption. Laura Churchill's father adopted Mary when her own parents died. Mary's life had become rather of an interesting spectacle. Joseph Churchill sent her as a student to the private Thetford Academy, but she got kicked out for smoking and other misdemeanors. Then she left home and went to Lowell, Massachusetts, to get work, but soon left there for Boston, where she married a 68-year-old poet and architect and published stories about adventurous girls who made their own lives rather than living in the reflections of their husbands. The Boston story papers were full of such tales. I understood why. Mary was barely older than I was and had seen the unhappy plight of the older women, the women like my aunts and mother. The last time I'd seen Mary, we'd gone up to the old house Father was tearing apart to build his barn. We ransacked it and built a fire in the shop. I played my fiddle, which she liked to hear. She told me she'd left her husband.

    I saw Laura Churchill often. She walked up onto Rum Street, often without a bonnet and bare-footed, or if it was raining, she carried a parasol. She liked to botanize and dig roots. She pretended to eat only a little. The neighbors considered her a little deranged but I thought she was just weak-minded and a little odd, wanting in common sense. I also thought she imagined herself to be very high-minded, coming up to mix with the inferior classes. Laura Churchill sometimes stayed with Laura Cobb for a month at a time, but after she ran off with a towel and bread and sugar, Henry complained that she was worse than a hired man to keep.

    The women bent their heads to the cloth, their fingers flying along the rows of stitching with the exception of Mary and Laura Churchill who hadn't as much quilting experience as the others. The women talked like a flock of birds, their voices rising and falling, everyone talking over everyone else.

    Emma Graves, a girl from English Mills who walked with a limp, told of how her Uncle Emeroy had been thrown from a load of hay. "He fell some 15 feet or more off a high bridge and into the water—struck his head. He couldn't move himself at all afterwards except his legs and arms. He got quite a cough too. I fear he's run down."

Her older sister, Mary Graves, who I thought was the handsomest girl in town, had been visited by a cousin from Boston. "Cousin George is raising a mustache," she said. "I told him I didn't like it, it loomed up so. He said it must make him look old for he met General Nathaniel P. Banks on the street and the general bowed to him for the first time in his life. It is said that General Banks takes a good deal of notice of voters."

Mrs. English and Almira shared stories of their sicknesses. "I went down to have my teeth out," said Mrs. English. "I took ether and had three partly extracted. I came home nearly distracted. I've been sick abed with teethache for the past six days. It wasn't until Tuesday I felt myself getting quite smart."

Almira said, "Dr. Hazen visited me when I was taken sick with cramp colic, which I am subject to. My usual remedies utterly failed. He gave me a dose that I supposed was largely morphine. It relieved the terrible pain after a short time, but I was so unstrung that I couldn't do anything for several days."

And so it went until Old Maid Priscilla Raymond spoke up. She'd been peering closely at her work, having lost her eyesight over her nearly three generations of sewing. She been living on Rum Street for at least 50 years and was 86 years old. I think she must have made enough bed quilts to cover all of her family and neighbors several times over. But still, stitches flowed perfectly from her needle.

"Mary," she said, "that story in the Boston paper–folks say it's about us."

Nearly everyone stopped talking except for Mrs. Pilcher who was hard of hearing and shouting to Laura Cobb, "Each day bears us onward to the great mysterious unknown." Laura tried to ignore her and remain mannerly at the same time.

Mother spoke up. "'Hearts of Iron, Hearts of Gold, and Hearts of Steel'–that was the title. I read it in *True Flag*."

Mary blushed. She'd known these women all her life. Their opinions meant something even though she tried to pretend otherwise. "Yes–well–maybe. Hilda Siler was an orphan, like I am. She lived in the mountains of Vermont. That's true."

THUNDERSTRUCK FIDDLE

"You say she lived a wild life—dwelled in a wild home," said Priscilla. "Susan, isn't that what it said?" She patted her granddaughter's arm. "Susan's been reading your story to us evenings."

Susan nodded. "Yes, that's exactly what it said." She didn't look up from the quilt. Susan ran the farm that supported her grandmother, mother and sisters, one of whom was blind and deaf. She was often in mortal strife with her uncle Elisha Raymond who lived next door. Elisha used them plaguey mean. He argued with them about their shared property line, who owned the log-chains they both used, and how much of the barn they each owned. Elisha had been tearing it down lately, and Susan had been building it right back up in his wake. Susan wasn't about to admit defeat. When Father was road surveyor, she jawed so much about the credit she thought she was due for the use of her oxen to fix the road that he got the town to give her $1.64.

"Do you think our homes are wild?" said Priscilla. "They seem domestic to me. When Lucius heard that, he wondered where you'd find anything wild. The biggest thing wild we have around is a squirrel." Priscilla chuckled. "He blames Geo Grow for it—always with his gun shooting one thing or t'other. There's nothing left to shoot."

"It's a story," said Mary. "It's not supposed to be exactly true. It's exaggerated for dramatic effect. Although some would say it's more wild up here than down in the valley."

"It sounds like you should be a story-writer, Sarah," said Priscilla, laughing again. "You make up stories and tell 'em instead of writing 'em." Perhaps she was trying to make Sarah laugh. Everyone knew that Sarah made up little incidents of no consequence at all and told them as the truth, but everyone else was careful about what they said considering the recent terrible loss of her children.

Old Maid Priscilla squinted as though trying to remember. "'We never live till we shake off our bondage and stand forth free and responsible human beings.' I think that's what you wrote, Mary. There's been a lot of talk about women's suffrage lately. Are you talking about that?"

Granny Morey looked up, gray hair poking from her white cap like stiff wire. Her old fingers seemed to know what to do without her watching them. Like Old Maid Priscilla, she'd worked on enough quilts to keep everyone on Rum Street warm through the coldest nights. Her face was wrinkled by a lifetime of harsh judgements, for she disapproved of almost everything. "She means women have their hell right here on airth and are all saved," she said.

"Hilda Siler has her own ideas that aren't bounded by four walls. She has higher goals than simply a quiet home," Mary said, gaining courage.

Mrs. Pilcher from English Mills straightened her already stiff back. "A quiet home is a most worthy goal," she said. "A smile, kind feelings, serene affection, gentle tones—that's what ensures happiness in the home."

She went on, although I could see some of the women smiling slightly. "I cultivate four goals: patience, cheerfulness, amiability, and gentleness."

"Does not your husband ever bruise your spirit?" asked Mary.

"Remember that a meek and quiet spirit is the female standard," Mrs. Pilcher said, casting her eyes modestly down. "We must remember that a good woman will be loved and treated well if she brings happiness, contentment, good cheer, and beauty to her home."

"It sounds like you've been reading Mrs. Abel's practical rules for American females," said Susan Raymond, looking straight at Mrs. Pilcher. "Those rules may work for you. Your husband has a good farm and is an industrious provider. You live in comfortable circumstances. Any woman who's ever had to depend on herself, would do well to ignore those rules."

I thought of Laura Cobb. She was a thorough housekeeper, helpmate to her husband, and sensible neighbor. She baked, scrubbed, sewed, dug potatoes, and raked hay. But her efforts didn't stop Henry from telling her once, while I was there, to "shut up and go to bed," whereupon she burst into a flood of tears and went off weeping. Henry accused her of ailing in her mind. I thought of Mother who hid the fact that she'd bought cloth for a new dress to avoid being called a "hog." And that was even though she and I peeled, sliced, and dried more than a thousand apples to pay for it.

Did Mrs. Pilcher think they could prevent being treated so badly by being even more submissive? Father behaved like the perfect model of a good-natured husband when others were around. But, in truth, he gave Mother mad and unreasonable curtain lectures at least once every week. Although anyone who ever could hear him scold her and knew the truth, would be tempted to kick him, yet he and Mother kept his actions secret. And I had no doubt that one half of the husbands in our neighborhood, probably the town, used their wives as badly as Father did. But the wives never complained to anyone.

Except for Granny Morey. "Old Morey'll go tew hell for sartin" she said. "But you can't find no instance in the Bible of no woman's ever goin' tew Hell." Granny's philosophy allowed her to jaw at her husband without guilt. Anyone passing by might think all hell had been let loose.

"If circumstances became simply too trying, recall that God would not give a woman more than she can stand. He will help her forbear," said Mrs. Pilcher.

The women were unsettled. Sarah Cobb had lost three children and suffered more than any person should be expected to. Laura lost her only child too, a few years earlier and had been searching for comfort ever since. She mothered all the children in the neighborhood, including me.

Mary said, "Perhaps I would be content if I had dared everything I wished for. If an unfaltering love, a happy home, and freedom to write poetry was offered to me, well and good. I should settle down." She put down her needle, stretched her hands. "But my spirit may be too lively to be restricted by a husband."

Mrs. Pilcher's eyes rose abruptly. "Perhaps your—um—spirit—would be satisfied if you devoted your artistry to music, drawing, embroidery and reading aloud, particularly religious papers, to provide contentment to your family." She looked at Mary's stitches in disdain. Even I could see they were uneven. Laura would probably do them all over.

Mother looked like she had a sick headache coming on. Laura announced it was time for sweet cake. We waited through Mrs. Pilcher's lengthy prayer. "My heart cannot but fill with emotion as I remember the deceased who have preceded me, but it is a beautiful thought to think that at some future day I will be gathered together with them, in a more glorious and a brighter world than this, where we are never to be separated, but shall dwell together in one family. Thank you Lord for this food …"

and on and on.

We left together. Mother accompanied Susan and Old Maid Priscilla down the hill. I could hear the old lady tell Mother, "I've lived right here in Vermont for 75 years and expect to die here too. Most of the time has passed pleasantly although there are always some clouds to obscure the fairest sky."

I carried Mrs. Pilcher home with Henry's rig and wished I could plug my ears. "This day has almost gone with hosts of others," she shouted, "And we do not realize that there are hosts yet to come in the future. The Lord is preparing mansions for all the human race but most especially for those indisputable Christians who observe the Sabbath very strictly and abominate those who fiddle and play cards. This taken all together makes a properly good and true Christian!"

How I wished I had Mary Gibson's courage in speaking. I didn't have words adequate to combat the relentless force of Mrs. Pilcher's convictions.

CHAPTER 31

GOLD

Father and Henry talked endlessly of going to the gold diggings in California. They both, but particularly Father, perceived that they were going to wreck and ruin in Vermont.

"Wages at California are from $75 to $200 per month—last winter $250 to $325 dollars," wrote Warren Willis in a letter home—postage due on the letter, 45 cents.

"Warren is worth now $50,000, sent $1,000 home and is going to take his relations there," said his brother Ed Willis.

"He expects and promises great things," said Ed. "He said all who are in great want of money to get home with are ones

Lucius Raymond gave Henry some specimens of gold and loaned us the glass he'd bought for a dollar. Father, Henry and I headed out to the hills searching for gold.

who have just gambled away a fortune."

His mother told a different story. "Any person might find out what hard times are by going to California. Warren sleeps in the fields every night with nothing but a blanket to cover him."

Mr. Stewart, Jane Richardson's husband, went to California almost as soon as anybody and stayed there two years. We'd heard that he hadn't got much of anything, and if he could get $500 over and above the expense of his passage home, he was going to start for home immediately. Next thing, he'd returned with—some said—$6,000 and some $11,000 more at the mint in Philadelphia, considerable gold in doubloons and eagles, samples of all kinds of dust, and dresses and other things bought at New York, enough to make $2,000 more. That was what people said.

Then Oramel Churchill gave us the true story. The stage driver, who might have been drunk, said the check on the mint was a lie. He had $1,200 in gold dust, some ore, and another bag of dust of a different quality or different in some respect—I'm cussed if I can say what it was. Besides all that, he had a lot of doubloons, a lot of eagles, things which he bought at New York, such as dresses and a watch worth $175! Mr. Richardson (his wife's father) thought the whole amounted to nearly $6,000!

It would seem that he got his money by making coffins and made it all in only a month or two. I thought he should have discovered the potential in making coffins sooner.

Lyman Cobb, my cousin who lived over in English Mills, had gone too. His father, also named Lyman, said his son sometimes sent home $500. He was saving it to buy a farm. Young Lyman had a brother named Charles Cobb, the same as me, who wanted to go but young Lyman told him not to come, and their father offered him $100 to stay at home. Yet he went.

I felt cheered by the possibility. Perhaps Father would go. He was healthy. He could fight, dig, shoemake, work on wood or iron. He could do as well as anybody in California.

We discussed the fare. Charles Briggs and seven or eight others from our neighborhood had paid $50 to $125 from New York, via the Isthmus of Panama.

Henry said he could raise $1,400. Father said he could barely get $500. Henry asked me how much I could raise, and I told him 23 cents! Henry said he'd go, even if alone!

Then we heard about Orlando Dunham. He'd boarded a ship bound for San Francisco but the ship never arrived. He was about 25 years old and a decent fiddler and respectful person. I hoped he would come to light again.

Then Osmore Thomas died in California and Dean Fairbanks died on the Isthmus of Darien. He'd been left on the Isthmus and couldn't go any further because the ship that was to take them was wrecked, I think. He'd been a saucy little cuss just like some other boys raised on the green, but he'd grown into an intelligent quiet peaceable man.

We grew discouraged and it seemed safer to stay at home. Then, on December 19, 1852 we learned that a Mr. Kennedy had melted nearly pure gold out of rock in Bridgewater, only a few miles from our land. I didn't know if what he found was pure gold but get out the rubbish and 'twould be.

Rumors abounded. The Taggart quartz vein on the Thompson farm, a mile west of Bridgewater Center, yielded $32 in gold to the ton. Norman shouldn't have sold his land in Bridgewater! People waded the Quechee River and found bits of gold in the gravel, eroded, they figured, from rich veins in the creeks that emptied into the river. Someone found $75 worth of gold in three shovels full of dirt up in Sharon! Thousands of dollars' worth of gold had been found down in Plymouth.

I expected that people would come from Australia!

Lucius Raymond gave Henry some specimens of gold and loaned us the glass he'd bought for a dollar. Father, Henry and I headed out to the hills searching for gold. We scraped moss from stone walls and pushed aside grass from boulders in the fields, closely examining bits of shiny stone. Father's pockets were filled with stones when he came home from his land. He found what looked like iron ore. Henry held it next to his magnet with no result.

Henry carried a stone down to the Green for examination. Laura waited up with Mother until 11:30 at night before walking home alone in the dark. The assayer said twasn't anything but mica.

Men reduced veins of quartz to rubble. Hopes rose with each new bit of real gold but most of the crystals and flaking layers of yellow turned out to be worthless galena or mica schist. Soon the hills west and southwest of our hill in Bridgewater were pocked with shallow caves.

Matthew Kennedy's ore was found in the Taggart vein about five miles west of Rum Street in Dailey Hollow and, while some rich pockets were found, the gold was unevenly distributed.

Like with bees, silkworms, and grafted apples, our hopes for quick riches faded and we went back to the day to day tedium of farming.

CHAPTER 32

FISHING FOR HORNED POUTS

About eight o'clock, we were out in the middle of the pond with the moon and sky overhead reflecting on the water. Our shadows, tremendously dark and deep underneath, looked so bad that I had to keep my eyes shut.

We still had gold on our minds when Hiram, Geo Grow and I decided to go fishing in Plymouth, a purpose disguising our hopes of seeing some of the gold diggings there. It was darn'd cold the morning we set out in Hiram's wagon. I wore the new green breeches Mother had finished at a cost of 67 cents. I put my cap on and an apple pie and cookies in my pocket. I had 27 cents of my own and $1.50 borrowed of Mother. I forgot my hooks and lines.

Old Bill struggled to pull the wagon up the steep hills

of Plymouth so we got out and footed it, reached Plymouth Notch at noon. We found Plymouth Cave and crawled in. From a description I'd read of it, I expected to travel underground for about 609 rods, crawling half of the way and being in rooms that would take in a meeting house, with t'other half hung with stalactites and so on. And we did crawl half of the way, maybe three rods or six or eight. It was impossible to judge distances. We found ourselves in some of the damndest holes imaginable. With ever so much looking and crawling, we couldn't find the same holes again and in the scrape got our clothes abominable dirty and didn't know for certain that we should find the way out again, there being several crooks, turns and different ways. Our voices bounced and echoed in the jagged passages, sounding garbled as though spoken under water. The candle burned so short that it burned Hiram's fingers, but he held on. When we got into an uncommonly mean hole, cold and still, we found it covered with names, one of which was dated 1819. I was mightily relieved when we were in the light of day again.

Cave Number Two wasn't much. It was for ore diggings and reached about five rods underground. A few drops of water falling from the ceiling made a most deafening and continual splash.

At two o'clock we went down to Ludlow Pond, rowed to the upper end, and went to setting eel-poles and pouting. Our boat was a devilish leaky thing and we bailed nearly continuously. Hiram got three eels and two horned pouts right off. I caught two eels but couldn't get them into the boat without losing them-so that amounted to nothing. I could have done it the next time and shall do it.

It was a dark night. About eight o'clock, we were out in the middle of the pond with the moon and sky overhead, reflecting on the water. Our shadows, tremendously dark and deep underneath, looked so bad that I had to keep my eyes shut. I'd felt awfully once before, looking from the top of a very high hill, but that sky underneath and overhead, beat all that.

Nearby was another fisherman singing "The Ballad of James Bird" to the tune of "Good Shepherd." I listened to his deep voice drift across the water telling his story of heroism, *"... I'll stand by you, gallant captain, Til we conquer, lest we die. Still he fought, though faint and bleeding, Till our Stars and*

Stripes arose." He did it up well.

I thought of how much Frederick would have liked the song and fishing and of how much he'd never experienced, of how he'd been courageous enough to play the fiddle even though it jeopardized his soul. I carried his jackknife in my pocket.

Geo and I fished for horned-cocks patiently till 11 o'clock, when we gave up. Then at one o'clock in the morning the eels left us and the horned pouts came. Hiram hauled in two right off but Geo Grow, the ignorant cuss, had thrown out all the worms and there we were. Being sleepy, we roused up and started for home, took lodgings on Mr. Priest's haymow and stayed till morning. I'd seen enough that I never saw before to satisfy me. At the end of it all, I thought I'd go out and try that fishing over again, but with worms, to see what I could do.

CHAPTER 33

THE OLD HOUSE

Ever since Father inherited his land, he'd been threatening to build a barn and house, in that order. He walked the mile from our house to his land at least twice a day to see to his stock. "Old Grow says I wasted $40 a year walking 800 miles up to my land and back," Father said. "I'll do great things in farming when I build our house." Heretofore his farming had been astonishingly miserable, and I feared it always would be, under any circumstances.

I predicted we'd move into an old house Father had bought from Chas Raymond with the intention of using it for materials to build his barn. As I watched the floor in the kitchen torn up for boards, wrought nails, and spikes, and the windows moved to the stable for the horses to look out of, I wondered what

Mother was fully aware that our house looked like the very Devil and hoped to have a better one soon.

would be left when we moved in. It would no doubt be even worse than Mr. Hartwell's house.

For Mr. Hartwell's house hadn't been improved in all the years we'd lived there, and it had never been very good. I'd stopped noticing the lack of whitewash, the buttery that was a most abominable dirty hole full of all kinds of stuff, or the back door that wouldn't shut on account of the snow. Then Jerome Cox brought his sisters over to hear me fiddle. I saw Mary Jane step over the ashes we'd thrown outdoors all winter long and around our wood-pile which wasn't scarcely enough to last two days and all covered with snow. We sat in the square room cluttered with cooking supplies and dishes, our meager supply of food, our clothes and beds. Mother, Father, and I all stayed in one room all winter so there was no nice place to entertain visitors. I saw the sorry paper window curtains around the smashed out window and realized it presented an unpardonable appearance without and within. Mother was fully aware that our house looked like the very Devil and hoped to have a better one soon.

But first, Father built his barn. It was to be 21 feet by 31 feet in size with a 10-foot stable added to one end, and each half of the roof square. Hiram, Old Morey, and Lute helped hew 395 feet of timber, primarily butternut. They used Mr. Hartwell's compass to set the sills just north and south, leveled them and underpinned the two high corners with stone from the wall next to the road and two of the doorstones of the old house. John D. Perkins bored 264 feet of poplar logs, and Father laid them from a spring he'd found up in the little mowing.

I helped Father considerably, building, framing, lifting, prying, and so on. All the while he called me "horrible ignorant."

"I suppose you expect me to know all about it by paternal instinct," I said

We raised the barn in August, much to the disgust of some of the neighbors because everyone was busy trying to get in their hay. We commenced at four o'clock in the afternoon. Thirteen of the neighbors came, even Owen Raymond who had one hand slung up because it was a complete sore. The Lord be praised! I hadn't flesh enough on me to be sore. We put up the east broadside whole and the rest a post at a time. Hiram lifted the west plate on his back while they entered the posts, braces, etc., getting done at dark.

In celebration, I clasped my hands over a pole above my head and raised my chin above it—a thing I never could do before.

That year, 1851, I turned 16 on December 20. Three days later, on December 24, Mother started for Christmas Eve at the Congregational Church. It stormed and she stayed all night at Jo Darling's, not being able to come home. The road was full of snow on Christmas day. I stayed home from school with a bad cold caused by the summer boots I wore and fiddled a good deal. Father did his chores, looked at the barn, worked on the stable door in the kitchen. Mother rode up with Hiram on his sled towards night. Had she not got the chance to ride, she would have stayed away all night again.

We hadn't had anything but the shivers for a week. I believed I wouldn't go to school much that winter, but when I did go, I'd study. I'd gotten as far as simple equations in algebra. I didn't believe any scholar would learn a cent's worth by the way they studied.

I helped Father work on his stable, which was not yet

half done. He was a slow team. Our jaws continued. Mother said I was so impudent that she wasn't going to live in the house with me much longer! I thought it very probable, for doubtless she would soon go to the poor-house and I to the Devil. I didn't care anything about her scolding, only it sort of provoked me to have her keep talking.

Then in April, we moved out of Mr. Hartwell's house and into the half-torn-up house by the barn, as I'd predicted.

Father and I loaded the small stove, two beds, some chairs, drawers, and a lot of trunks into the wagon. Mother tried to get the hens and cats but the hens escaped their box and couldn't be caught again and the cats scratched like the Devil and she had to let them go.

There were only two rooms that were in decent shape. Our yard was a perfect barn-yard all around.

Father said the house was good enough for him and if we didn't like it, we might leave. And if Mother hadn't spent five dollars going to singing-schools with Hartwell (almost fifteen years before), riding out with him no less, we could have the windows all full of glass.

It was the poorest inhabited house in town, but it seemed settled that it was to be our permanent home even through the winter. Oh it was abominable! I wrote in my journal, "I'm of a good mind to clear for Oregon. It will be a mean thing to live in this house next winter. It strikes me 'twas a queer way to tear a house all to pieces that he was going to live in, for the want of a few boards. There is one thing however that Mother says we shall have and that is some window-curtains, for they cost only 10 cents each."

As if the condition of the house wasn't bad enough, I was dumbstruck to learn that we owned only half the house. The Frinks owned the other half. Mrs. Frink sent a letter that read, "Pleas Mr. G.P. Cobb if your a minter sen down $12 towards my part of the house. I'll wait a spell for the rest—if not I'm going to tare down my part of the home next week Monday."

Father averted the catastrophe by giving the Frinks my watch, a box of honey, one dollar cash, and his note for $6.50, due in six months with interest. I thought Father got the best of the deal but the Frinks were so devilish poor they had to accept it.

CHAPTER 34

COMING DOWN LOW IN EVERY WAY

That winter I wrote in the common room where the fire was. It was mighty uncomfortable in the old house. The air was chilly, dusty and stinking. Impure air from below the floor came up through all the holes and mixed with the air we breathed. And to make the case worse there were always potatoes or parings, apples, pumpkins, or something of the kind swept there and rotting so as to give the air an unnecessary stench. I felt like I was breathing bad air continually and catching cold all the time.

After much jaw on the subject, Father finally got some glass to put in the windows. From his point of view, it was an extravagance, it being so much easier and cheaper to fill the windows with old clothes, and also—as he contended—so much better to keep 'em filled with old clothes than not to keep 'em filled at all. He had the day before offered Ed Woodward 75 cents for a miserable old drum and wouldn't listen to getting half that worth of glass.

That summer was a dry one and our home spring was a resort for frogs and snakes, unfit to drink in any way. I filled our pail and tea-kettle with water from a glorious spring over in Hosea's pasture, which was at least a quarter mile from the house.

Father continued to do little on his farm. One Saturday that fall, it showed rainy in the morning, and although it amounted to little or nothing, the threat induced Father to stay in the shop. Then, suddenly, he brought my writing to a pause by exclaiming, "We must get a load of wood–go to covering pump logs–dig our longjohn potatoes– secure our corn."

"Glory to the highest! We can get what little corn the mice haven't got and perhaps we should try to get half a peck of apples at the ends of some squirrel holes," I said. It's no wonder Father was always mad at me.

I was so angry with Father that I spent most of my time writing music in my Great Book, spending many whole days on it. My Great Book then contained at least 700 tunes. They were all I had in my memory and possession and so I needed to beg or borrow some new music books.

Chas Raymond paid me 50 cents for some work I did the previous fall, and Father let me have 10 more cents. I immediately went down to the Green to buy Musician's Companion No. 3. I didn't even stop at school that day, which made Mother indignant. She said it was pure folly to stay out of school, but somehow I didn't like a schoolhouse. I stayed home for another week copying music into my Great Book but had to keep mighty still or raise a jaw from Mother, who was always nearly mad even at having me 'round.

He had an axe and a large pack on his back. He was a pitiable looking object, inquiring his way to a family whom he thought lived in Barnard. Father didn't offer him anything to eat, but got him a lot of cider, of which he drank two large tumblers brim-full almost instantly and another tumbler soon after.

We were coming down low in every way. Father split up logs Lute had drawed to our door. We'd intended to sell them but our wood supply was too small to be selling. We were out of anything to eat. We couldn't even feed an old man who came along and wanted to stay the night. He had an axe and a large pack on his back. We told him we had no spare bed—we might have said and no food—and directed him to Grow's. He was a pitiable looking object, inquiring his way to a family he thought lived in Barnard. Father didn't offer him anything to eat, but got him a lot of cider, of which he drank two large tumblers brim-full almost instantly and another tumbler soon after. The man told wonderful stories about the war of 1812 in which he said he fought at Niagara, but he got so many men into his armies that he ruined the whole.

Since the commencement of my journal, I never felt so miserably situated. I broke the crystal on my Anchor Escapement watch. Everything was undone and it was wintry to the last extreme. It was so cold that our clock stopped. I moved my bed into the main room. I wore all my clothes and tried to keep warm by determining not to be cold. I besought the Lord to make me warm. I finally concluded being cold was unavoidable if not unendurable. I couldn't work with any degree of animation or even stay out of doors on account of the cold. I thought I'd rather die than do anything in such weather. It seemed if I had steady employment and a comfortable atmosphere, I could do more than two men, provided I worked for my own advantage of course, for pure selfishness would be at the bottom.

I laid abed reading and again, contemplated running away to Oregon. The broken watch wouldn't matter if I starved to death enroute.

Chapter 35

"Adversity is the First Path to the Truth"

I wrote in my Great Book but my journal hadn't stopped by a condemned sight. Late that winter the weather turned gloriously dark and cloudy with a little rain coming down. I learned that Henry got the mumps and I thought "Glory to God. I must have caught them from him." If I had the mumps for a fortnight and ink and paper and my book, along with the pleasing thought that I hadn't ought to be outdoors working, I would get out the light

I shut the paper up in my colt-skin trunk and picked up
Sardanapalus, *wondering if things could get any worse. I read:*
I know not what I could have been, but feel
I am not what I should be—let it end.

stand and read and write. I could make a devilishly interesting work of fiction, although my previous attempts were enough to sicken a skunk.

Mother sneered at me when I was writing and told me it was foolery. My conscience bore evidence to that fact so strongly that remaining entirely idle often seemed better than writing. But afterwards, when I couldn't get the time back, I was sorry I didn't write. I loved to write. I almost lived to write.

Every day I felt my neck and cheeks. But alas! No swelling.

"Adversity is the first path to truth," wrote Lord Byron in *Sardanapalus*. I'd found the book at Henry's house. His words described my state of mind.

I was almost sick from doing nothing. I wanted to write but if I was not working, then writing seemed to be a foolish expenditure of time. I knew the discomfort of writing and resting without anything to rest from. So my greatest obstacle to writing became a continual inclination to do something else.

When I was at work, it seemed as though I had a perfect right to spend a little time writing. When I had the most to do, I was the most inclined to write. If I was busy 16 hours in the day, as I wished I could be, I would write more than if I was busy only four hours.

Oh! It was too bad to think of having worked so long on my foolish journal. I'd grown round-shouldered and crooked-necked, and continual writing with my right hand had put my shoulders on different levels. That was why I was so bashful. And what would it amount to? It seemed to me I was going to be a crittur like a Hodgman I had seen hanging 'round—no home, never to work, and miserable. I knew I never could live by labor nor have a chance to educate myself. I had no mechanical ingenuity and thought I must live by my writing. As 'twas, I would do it on a miserable scale.

I took up my paper and wrote, "I must pen something or die." Even with such a strong commitment to writing, I shut the paper up in my colt-skin trunk and picked up *Sardanapalus*, wondering if things could get any worse. I read:

I am the very slave of circumstance
And impulse—borne away with every breath!
Misplaced upon the throne—misplaced in life.
I know not what I could have been, but feel
I am not what I should be—let it end.

If I'd been in Lord Byron's place, I would have done exactly what he did. I would do the same as it was, but on a miserable scale. I was cautious as the Devil. If I committed a roguery I would never be detected—never. I wrote, "but this is nonsense. I will live as long as I can, and as long as I do live I will keep something of a Journal. And if I must die or raise hell and risk being hung, I will raise hell and risk being hung. I will always give my memoranda exactly true, and never get further from the truth in speaking of things than I have here. I'd decided on that course some time ago."

*Facing page: Photo courtesy of
Woodstock History Center, Vermont*

Part Four

Chapter 36

Joining the Band

Oct. 24, 1852 ... The sun shone out clear and free, no clouds being in the way on the day my life changed.

A brass band was getting up on the Green and Chas Raymond came up and offered me a place! He said by Father's paying my share of $20, I could join. Father, if left to himself, poor as he was, said he would pay it. But Mother thought 'twould be nonsense and I thought she was probably right.

Henry told me to get me a horn immediately. But alas! "Where would we find the money? Besides," I said, "I heard only Sons of Temperance belong to it." The Sons of Temperance were respectable members of society in Woodstock.

"You've never played a horn. Who would you be among those men?" said Mother. "With that money, we could buy four barrels of flour or two heifers."

"It's not only Sons of Temperance," said Chas Raymond. "You'll see."

If I joined 'twould cost $30 that winter. And mother was right, who would I be with the others! What fun would it be for me? None. What good would it do? I shouldn't ask Father to do it for me. But hadn't I ought to let him? That was the question. If he made the decision and the Band thought it foolish—and they would—then I wouldn't have the foolery of it laid to me when I'd had no hand in it.

I put off thinking about it until the next day. I had no doubt I could learn to play as well and carry as good a part as any of 'em, but that wasn't anything compared with other qualifications, of which money was an essential one. I couldn't stop thinking about it.

The next day at noon, Mrs. Cox came over with a letter from Charles D. Anderson on the Green. He'd sent it up by

Jerome Cox, directing Mr. Chas Cobb to "come down immediately and tell Lull if you wish to join us. Lull is going to Boston after musical instruments."

But Dr. Chase had already come up to ask Father if I would join and Father said I would and gave him $8, all he had towards the $20 due. He told Chas Raymond to find out if they would admit me and to come up Sunday to tell of it. So it appeared as though, through Father's contrivances and doings, I was likely—unless I unhallowedly interfered or wasn't taken a fancy to—to become a member of the Br-a-s-s Band.

I asked Father how he intended to pay for it, and he said he was owed some money. Father approached Mr. Hartwell, who owed him $3 for labor and keeping his calf. He went to collect $1.22 from Lish Raymond for helping to load logs. He asked George Cox for $3 and also John D. Powers and others. Father succeeded in raising $9.

Then Father asked Chas to pay $5 for the grafting Father had done for him and the calf-keeping and another 46 cents to boot, plus $3 he owed me for work. I thought Chas wouldn't think much of paying Father $8.46 when Father owed him $28 for the house we had bought from Charles and were living in. But

Then he sold 256 bushels of winter apples at the Green. We had more apples than anybody else in town that year, for a fact, thanks to the grafting Father had done two years earlier, the grafting I'd criticized so.

Father said he hadn't promised to pay for the house for another three years.

Then Father took 256 bushels of winter apples down to the Green to sell. We had more apples than anybody else in town that year for a fact, thanks to the grafting Father had done two years earlier–the grafting I'd criticized so.

I chopped up the last of the woodpile and got up into the orchard and piled a bushel of cider apples. In such weather as that, my work without a frock and mittens wasn't worth a damn and I stopped at Hiram's to warm myself and stayed till nine o'clock playing checkers, coming out behindhand two games. Chas Raymond was at Hiram's and said I must go down to meet the Band the following Saturday night and get my instrument. Only two of the members knew me and I thought the rest would probably be astonished. I wrote in my journal that night, "I shall also know more of the Woodstock Brass Band, & to their sorrow they'll know more of me."

We went down to the Green with the horse and lumber wagon. It was dark and raining hard. The band met in the Windsor County Courthouse. The building's air of authority made me acutely aware of my greenness and I was struck with the absurdity of my being there. Men milled about the practice room, joking, blowing into their instruments, confident and well-dressed. Among them were merchants, a doctor, manufacturers, and a printer from the Green. They knew each other, were accustomed to each other's company. They didn't smell of the barn or wear dirt from the fields on their clothes. They were used to eating things like oysters and had lace curtains, rugs, more than one oil lamp, sheds filled with firewood, and barrels of flour in their butteries.

I saw Father in his devilish ragged old overcoat. I could see the whole length of his bare arms through the shirt-sleeves and his elbows sticking out a number of inches. He usually left it in the wagon rather than wear it into a house or store. I noticed where he'd tried to patch it because, the fact was, Mother didn't do much mending. These were all the clothes he had.

I stood apart from Father, ashamed of his clothing and more ashamed of myself for standing apart. The men of the band looked at us, some came up to greet us. Erskine Woodward was there, son of the great Solomon Woodward, who owned the woolen mill and was worth at least $30,000. He lived in a mansion on Mountain Avenue. Fred Whitney, Dr. Chase and others were there, none of whom cared a cuss about money and had joined the band for the fun of it. I could see that then. I began to doubt that we'd ever play for money.

Chas Raymond led us to a man seated with a ledger. I recognized Charles Anderson, who owned the clothing shop on the Green where Father had bought me my coat. "This here's young Cobb," said Chas.

Anderson looked me over. "The band's full. We don't need anybody else."

Father pulled $9 out of his pocket.

"I paid Dr. Chase $8 for his horn. This is the rest," said Father. "I was told I should bring it down."

Anderson didn't reach out for the money. We found out that when the band met later that evening, they would see if they would ADMIT me to membership and if they decided to do thus, I might come down and get my instrument. I thought that settled before. It seemed in going down, that we got wet for our pains and that was all.

Chas Raymond said he would come up Sunday and tell whether they took me in or not, so that day, all I did was to look for him, paring apples and listening for the steps at the door. I put up twenty strings to dry. But Chas didn't come that day.

The next day I looked out for Chas all day, but he didn't come that day either. We put seven barrels of winter apples in the cellar from a total of 370 bushels we'd harvested. I was glad to see that Father had improved the cellar by boarding it up with layers and putting dirt between them for insulation. Still, he had more to fix and wood to get to the door or we would freeze to death.

The following day the sun never came in sight. I husked some and dug potatoes, working till dark. The snow didn't hinder much and we hand-sledded the potatoes down to the house and got 14 ½ bushels into the cellar. They summed up to 54 bushels. We never did so well before. Still, Chas didn't come.

Finally, on Wednesday, Father went down to the Green. At three o'clock in the afternoon he came home carrying my E♭ alto sax horn under his arm. Glory to God! I'd been admitted to the Band!

I blew on it so much that I felt rather tremulous. I could

make quite a number of notes. Henry said I must be darned careful about blowing on it too much. "The way to get one's fingers used to the fire, isn't to stick 'em in and hold 'em there!" he said.

However, I discovered that I couldn't blow a low $E\flat$ because the horn had a bruise. It seemed that Chas Raymond swore indignantly to the fellows about tucking off an imperfect instrument onto me because they didn't think I was smart enough to notice. This raised enough of a muss that Charles Anderson and three band members came up to our house to see about the horn. They took two wrong roads but finally arrived.

They came in and stepped carefully over the holes in the floor and around the pig Father and Hiram had killed and hung in the kitchen. They looked at the basket hanging above our small stove where Mother was keeping four three-day-old chicks that our cat had got hold of. She called them Stickup, Polliwog, Bobtail and Rotten-egg.

"We had no intention of using you mean," said Anderson. "It's as much for the Band's interest as yours that you should have a good instrument."

I was grieved that they found reason to announce such a thing. I thought they probably wished they'd never taken in "the cuss."

When they left, Mother said "I'll bet those band members are having a good laugh about the looks of this house. I don't think they'll be coming again." That was rather too likely and it made Father about seven-eighths mad.

I had two objectives uppermost in my mind during those early meetings with the band. One was to play better than anyone else, and two, to avoid being made a fool of. To accomplish the first, I wrote a gamut for my horn in every key imaginable and, with diligent practice, got so that I could blow the notes of one octave and one or two above and below without any effort. Within a week I found I could blow even the troubling low $E\flat$ perfectly without any trouble. Father told Anderson the horn was all right, so as to get out of the scrape about wanting a new horn.

The second goal would be harder, maybe impossible. I wanted the band members to know me as their equal.

Chapter 37

Astonishing the Band

I was devilishly disappointed to find out what poor musicians they were. The trebles sounded like crows squawking.

The band members took it for granted that I was as poor a musician as any of them, or at least no better, judging by other things about me, I supposed. At our first meeting Chas Raymond got me to play the galop alone, and I did it well. But no one paid any attention or said anything about it, they were so busy tooting. Six seconds later, they were all still as death, listening to Dan Stearns, a merchant on the Green to whom Father owed $66, try to play the easy first part, although he couldn't come within a rod of it. Even though I could play my part right straight through, I still felt like an object of ridicule to those who couldn't play hardly at all. Henry Burns, who worked at Chapman's Drugstore and took the position of first tenor which

I'd wanted, condescendingly wanted to know how I got along, encouraged me to persevere etc. I was devilishly disappointed to find out what poor musicians they were. The trebles sounded like crows squawking.

Meanwhile I had to work to avoid appearing a fool. Erskine Woodward told me I appeared "rather consumptive." Nahum J. Haskell, a book-binder on the Green, said, "What, Cobb, you don't belong to the band, do you?" in a tone that implied that I'd gotten above myself.

They thought I wouldn't realize I was being insulted, not giving me as much credit for penetration as they ought. I wanted to say, "You could work hard for three years and still wouldn't be able to read music as well as I can today." It would have been the truth. I wrote in my journal that night, "I will ASTONISH the Woodstock Band, so help me God."

Alonzo Bond, a celebrated band leader from Boston came to teach us. He played his saxhorn like lightning. We were told to refer to him as Professor Alonzo Bond.

He left us with some music. I practiced constantly. When Bond returned in December, Haskell failed to play the air of No. Five Galop while I played it note by note. None of the trebles could touch parts two or three of the Galop. They asked me to play the treble and I played it four or five times. I thought Haskell and Anderson were amazed to see that I was inferior to no one musically.

We wouldn't let anyone but band members inside the practice room. A crowd of men and boys always stood outside the door to listen to us play, Father with them. Even though we weren't creating any decent music yet, people were thrilled by the blustery sounds compared with the plain fiddles and melodeons we were accustomed to hearing. Owen Raymond announced at the closed door one night that he was a feller that had come down four miles to hear the band play and he was coming in! All hands laughed. But they didn't let him in. The band even turned Henry away, which made him mad. Father said the boys knew my horn.

Now that I belonged to the Woodstock Band, Father had the idea that I shouldn't have to play the fiddle for disreputable local dances. "You'll spile the fiddle," he said, but I went to some anyway, even to earn as little as 25 cents for an evening's fiddling. We needed the money. Bond's lessons cost each of us $2. He said we'd get our money back when we'd completed 12 lessons and could give a concert. I thought that idea was pure nonsense, although I began to hope that I could get some decent clothes to perform in. My only stockings were all used up and my coat, which might have lasted a year longer if it had been decently mended, was worn out. And we still hadn't paid for it. Even so, Father settled for a new coat at Anderson's. It cost $4.75. He'd come down with 24 cents, so must have charged the rest.

I bought a good pair of gloves for 25 cents from Geo Grow who wanted to buy some ammunition and shot it all away, and more too, before night. Those gloves were the most comfortable article of clothing I'd ever owned.

Our first practice with Bond in December was in Stevens' dining room. We couldn't meet at the court-house as planned because an obstinate jury was arguing there and argued all night. Bond didn't have to play my part a single time. He played a good part of the time on Haskell's horn, which made Haskell so mad he had to keep wiping his eyes! Bond called No. 8, "A Serenade in Three Parts," "most beautiful," but I couldn't discover the beauty of it, for I thought we made it sound most damned miserable. The No. 7 quickstep that we played was good. It had "Nelly Bly" in it. The No. 10 had "Dearest Mae" and "Carry Me Back to Old Virginia."

After Bond gave us lesson number 12, we went out into the road and played "Home Sweet Home," "Auld Lang Syne," "God Save the Queen," and "Yankee Doodle." It was our first public performance, a tradition started by the old band when they'd taken their twelfth lesson. Mr. Foster carried us in his wagon up to the Flat and all over the Green with his four-horse team, gratis. But we soon found we couldn't do much playing while travelling, because the mouthpieces kept joggling about.

The last night of Bond's instruction, Anderson spoke to me about coming to an oyster supper. I said I didn't care anything about it and that Father was waiting. I didn't know what they thought of my going off nor did I care much, seeing that I should always do the same partly from inclination and partly from necessity. I left my horn with Bond so he could try to exchange in Boston. "I wouldn't take it as a gift," he'd said. "It isn't worth a copper." That night was cold and Anderson loaned me a buffalo coat to wear home. I tried to refuse but he made me put it on.

I also missed the Windsor Brass Band's First Annual Ball. Alonzo Bond's Quadrille Band was to supply the music and I would have liked to go but tickets were three dollars, which of course made it impossible.

Oramel Cox visited the last day of 1852 and told that he'd heard I could play the best of any member of the Band! I wrote in my journal that night, after thawing my ink over the stove, "As for me, I've joined the Woodstock Band, and that's enough. I need not do anything more."

Chapter 38

Not a Great Greeny

I began arranging tunes, first in six parts, which were too few, and then leaped to 28 parts, which was nonsense. I settled on eight. I bought small books to write the parts in, one for each member of the band. I worked steadily and then abandoned it as useless labor. I thought my tunes were dead. I didn't know enough to make an open bass, a simple rhythmic accompaniment, or the oom-pah.

By then Bond had noticed my efforts and advised me to work on good melody parts and gave me a book of arrangements to study. He also wanted me to help Dan Stearns, who couldn't get his part right.

The book fell out of my coat somewhere on my way to practice—a short-lived crisis that Father bailed me out of, just as he'd fixed so many things that had seemed hopeless before. He inquired at several houses along the Green, found the man who'd picked it up, and paid him a fourpence for its return.

Money continued to be a problem. We still owed some to the band. I began accepting pay to copy music for members of the band, whereas at first I did it to gain good will. Father collected another $1.25 from someone and mended boots for Old Maid Priscilla for 25 cents and another pair for 34 cents. He gave me a dollar to take down to the band.

The road was so thick with ice the night I went down to pay my bill that the horse couldn't stand up to go a rod, so I walked down to the Green instead. I had on my thin boots and I couldn't keep right side up. As I walked along I noticed the sound of threshing all around that came from the top of the snow freezing solid and shrinking in the cold, causing it to pull apart all over. I turned over a chunk and watched it slide down the hill at a fearful rate, shivering to pieces.

I found that my bill was $4.76 and we were to have 12 more lessons of Bond. Oh, misery! Stearns said to the band in general that if anyone was out of funds, he'd pay the bill and take his pay back from the profits of playing. This made me feel even more ashamed about my embarrassed financial condition, knowing the comment had been directed at me.

Erskine Woodward and Liberty Marble, a 34-year-old saw-miller from English Mills, who was married to Solomon Woodward's daughter, engaged Father to make boxes for their horns. This caused him to enter a horn-box mania. He worked day and night on the everlasting boxes. They were fine ones, with stuffing, lining and a lock that held the horns so securely that they might be thrown down stairs without damage. Our horns were so light, they were easily dinged with the slightest of knocks.

Our first concert was scheduled for Friday night, May 5. Father scoured the horn. I cut and oiled my hair. We got a white collar and a pair of white gloves at the Green and I borrowed a white vest. I inspected myself in a looking glass, hoping for improvement in my appearance. I looked best when viewed from the front. But when seen from one side, my forehead looked more retreating, my nose more vice-versa and my neck more crooked. As always, my shoulders were round and my back, hollow. But from a distance I guessed I looked as well as average.

We met at the courthouse, marched over into the Methodist meeting house, and instantly struck up. We were disappointed at the number in attendance. Some people listened from adjoining houses without paying. Also, we'd given editors and ministers complimentary family tickets, which let in about

30 folks gratis. Receipts for the evening were $60.15, $60 of which Bond pocketed for his lessons.

I wasn't as scared as I expected to be. I played to my satisfaction, though I didn't play my solo, "Song of Eva," very well. Bond also had me help Dan Stearns by playing his part an octave below. I'd practiced it to a great rate.

Anderson pressed me to keep the white vest in exchange for copying some music. I refused but he stuffed it into my horn box without my knowing of it, so buying all my new things only came to 30 cents.

The band offered me the position of first tenor and in order to take it, I had to buy a new horn. Belonging to the Woodstock Band had elevated my status on Rum Street so much that Henry and Alden offered to buy the horn and box. The new horn beat my other two all hollow even though it had been devilishly misused. Father had a difficult time pulling out the slides and repairing the bruises. It was smaller but heavier and far handsomer. It sounded rather mournful and I found that the high part was difficult to play.

When some of the members came with new rotary valve horns, Father said I should get one of those. He wanted me to stay at the forefront of the band's improvements.

The band even hired Henry Perkins to carry me down to a marching practice. I didn't know if it was because they wanted to help me—I had to come farther than any of them to practice—or whether they saw how much I needed it. Mr. Sweet, a shoemaker from Norwich who drilled us, said I made more music than any of the others. At the conclusion of one of our practices, we played some tunes in front of Dr. Chase's house on Mountain Avenue and he gave us ice cream, the first I'd ever had. His house looked far different from our old castle!

I marched home that day, playing my horn all along Rum Street, and when I passed Henry's house, the women who'd been quilting there all came out and marched around with me.

Austin English invited me to his house to play the horn. Anticipating Father's objections, for he didn't want me taking the horn anywhere but to band practice, I wrapped it up, taking some pains to keep it out of sight and cut through the woods towards English Mills. I waded a brook that was more of a stream than I'd anticipated, forty feet wide at least and eight

*I marched home that day, playing my horn all along Rum Street,
and when I passed Henry's house, the women who'd been quilting there
all came out and marched around with me.*

inches deep on average, and arrived there just at dark. Austin had a book of airs with complicated basses, so I tuned my horn to him, and we made music far beyond my expectations. The folks were quite pleased, and they got Mrs. English's parents, Mr. and Mrs. Cone, to come and hear it.

On my way to band practice one day, I found some boys playing ball in Aunt Prudy's mowing on the flat. Solomon Wyman made me stop and said if I played a tune, he'd carry me halfway to the green. I supposed of course that he had business there but after he had completed the journey and got turned round, I discovered that he had come so far on purpose to bring me! And before that, Crayton Ainsworth got me to go into his part of Aunt Prudy's house and play his baby a tune.

I was becoming celebrated as a musician and was arranging music so diligently, that it took most of my time. I lost all interest in fishing or anything else that took me away from my music. It got so that I dreaded seeing visitors come up Rum Street.

CHAPTER 39

PLAYING WITH THE GREATEST BUGLE PLAYER IN THE WORLD

Solomon Woodward engaged the legendary Boston musician, Ned Kendall, to play with us for a week and accompany us to Weston, Vermont, for our July 4th performance in 1853. We considered him worth the $50 we were to pay him, for Ned Kendall was the greatest bugle player in the world according to some accounts. He had been leader of the renowned Boston Brass Band and famed virtuoso player of the keyed bugle. Bond said, "I'd rather hear Kendall make one good tone than to hear any other player in the world play an entire concert."

Bond started us practicing on arrangements sent by Kendall's son-in-law, E.K. Eaton. Anderson's eyes bugged out when he saw the sheet music with tunes arranged in 18 or 19 parts. My part was the air and I played it well. But the trebles couldn't play the right notes at the right times and they couldn't keep up to tempo. Finally Bond told us to put the music away. "It's too hard and t'will hurt you to practice on it."

When I first heard Kendall play, I was disappointed. I couldn't hear anything extra about his tones, even though they were played on his silver E♭ bugle. He'd been sick, so maybe he couldn't play as well as he once could. But his reputation was widespread and people came from towns all around Woodstock to hear our outdoor concert. The village erected a platform in the middle of the park and hung lanterns all around it. Boys gathered, firing crackers and blowing quills. We played our poorest tunes during the first half of the concert and most of the decent folks left. Kendall played two airs that didn't sound great and then we played our choruses in a broken-down way.

Afterwards people came up and said we did nice—but I was poorly satisfied.

We redeemed ourselves at the Weston village July 4th concert. We rode there in Foster's four-horse omnibus, the boys in the band bawling and yelling insults to every person we passed once we left Woodstock. We rode down steep hills and footed it up the steep pitches, stopping for dinner in Ludlow and waiting for the horses to bate. We stayed in Weston for two days. I slept only about six hours and ate and drank all I wanted, paid for by the town. My entire expenses were four cents.

Mighty steady, honest people lived at Weston. I didn't see a row, fight, or quarrel, and nobody drunk. I could play in comfort too, not worried about my face being a little dirty or my collar out of shape. People didn't look me all over.

On July 4, we put on our gloves, belts, and caps at the tavern and went out to the street. We marched around the common and tents, surrounded all the time by a crowd of boys, then we marched up towards the grove a half mile south of the village. Men and girls dressed all in white filled the road on each side, standing on spruce boughs spread all around. I never saw so many good looking girls out of doors at once before. We marched into the grove, surrounded by boys.

The celebration was principally got up by folks who had gone from the town years before—lawyers and merchants from Boston, New York, and the west. These were self-sufficient men, not extremely well-educated but pretty well off, as folks who went from the country to the cities generally were. A minister from New York delivered a grand oration. Those who came from Boston brought $300 worth of fireworks.

We musicians stood on a platform of three layers of boards set on two tiers of sap-tubs. The platform stood on a slight hill, and just as an old man got up to pray, the upper layer of boards got shoved down hill so the sap-tubs tipped over. All the tubs tumbled down and rolled all about. Needless to say, some of us tumbled down with everything else, bruising the bells of our horns. That delayed the old man's prayer for a good while!

Ned Kendall was our star attraction, recognized by those from Boston as he climbed up to direct us, holding his famous silver bugle. We began with "Hail Columbia." I didn't play my parts exactly as Bond had written them but made additions of

We musicians stood on a platform of three layers of boards set on two tiers of sap-tubs. The platform stood on a slight hill, and just as an old man got up to pray, the upper layer of boards got shoved down hill so the sap-tubs tipped over. All the tubs tumbled down and rolled all about.

my own. Kendall played like the Devil, as well as any man could. He put in about 32 extra notes at the end of a strain, and they came in grand too. Our playing sounded gloriously.

We marched back to town playing all the while, and played while everyone went into the big tent. Not less than 800 ate and each paid 75 cents. They put us up on a six-foot high platform around the center pole of the tent. We'd prepared to play after 13 regular toasts, but the toasts went on much past that, so we improvised by playing 16 measures of our other arrangements each time. After our music, they fired a cannon. The big men, one after another, got up and told what they'd done and about their world travels. They advised the rising youth of the town to go and do likewise! But our music was the best part.

The folks expected a dance, but when the musicians didn't come, they asked me if I would fiddle. I did so gladly, knowing I'd be paid extra for it. We got three fiddles and a bass viol and a melodeon and Haskell whistled. We'd struck up "Money Musk" just as it started to rain. The rain kept up so hard that after 10 minutes it leaked through the tent and everything got wet, but still people danced and continued dancing for a long time, finally spending the rest of the night in the meeting house!

The next morning Kendall was too sick to accompany us to Springfield where we were to give another concert. We were greatly disappointed at losing the $100 fee. But, buoyed by our success, we gave three cheers for Weston as we drove out of town, followed by a stage full of people from Boston, who answered in high style.

That night, lying in bed, I imagined I could hear every part of Bond's Grand March all together and trace each part distinctly alone at the same time, it had been so effectually pumped into me that day. That was an exception and a wonder.

Chapter 40

Broken Up and Scattered

Tarbell informed us that a C. Dinsmore who lived out of the village was just about gone with consumption and being a musician himself, he wished us to stop and play a tune before his house. It was the last music he would hear on earth for certain.

We played often that summer of 1853. We held a concert in South Woodstock, then played at the county fair, riding down to the trotting course in Blake's meadow in a wagon, playing in a half-jolted-to-death style, followed by a procession of carriages half a mile long.

Daniel Tarbell Jr. hired us to play in South Royalton for $50. He was so rich that the South Royalton Bank issued its own paper bills with Tarbell's picture on them. One handsome incident occurred there. Tarbell informed us that a C. Dinsmore who lived out of the village was just about gone with consumption and being a musician himself, he wished us to stop and play a tune before his house. It was the last music he would hear on earth for certain. We got everyone into the wagon, including Dan Stearns (who was drunk), and we stopped outside Mr. Dinsmore's house. We played several tunes and, at last, "Auld Lang Syne." We played first rate. Even Stearns seemed to rouse up a little. I saw tears shed on the team behind us and a couple of children in the yard followed suit.

That November, Chas Raymond left the Band to work for Hezekiah Smith in Lowell, Massachusetts where Hez was making sewing machines. The Band's playing had died down, and things were continuing as shiftlessly as usual at home. I'd gotten some kind of rash and itched and scratched all over. I looked like I'd been hetcheled, being spotted and striped with a rather dirty-looking red. I wondered if it might be the measles.

As well as I could make out by two looking glasses, I was a most pitiable looking object—slim, crooked, homely, yellow, and in every way most ungainly.

The tooth that Dr. Chase had filled for me that August was in full discharge of all its duties and some more. Still, sometimes it ached cussedly, and I couldn't touch it with my fingers. But, glory to God, it didn't jump and vibrate. The main horror of the toothache was that I couldn't affect, stop, or modify it by any possible action of the mind or muscles. I divided mankind into two classes, those who had experienced the toothache and those who hadn't.

At home we were reduced to eating the same thing for every meal—potatoes, bread, and nutcakes. We were once so low on lamp oil that I had to borrow a candle of Mrs. Grow, which was pressed into use immediately. Our house hadn't been improved very much and Mother continued to complain. Finally, after a lecture from Father, Mother said she wouldn't stay and be grumbled and jawed at any longer and walked out of the house and down the road to the Green where she stayed four days binding shoes for Eaton. She swapped the binding for cloth for a new gown. While she was gone, Father set up our big stove, and we added boiled beans and hulled corn to our meals. He also got glass for the windows and even bought a new overcoat.

Others in the neighborhood were also going to wreck and ruin. Sarah's new baby girl died of the croup, her fourth child to die. Henry and Father continued to talk about going to California. The Jim Cox family sold all their stuff at auction. Their premises looked sadly decayed. Jim Cox had a family of about a dozen boys around the same time that Father and my uncles were growing up on our side of the hill. Both families, ours and Cox's had suffered similar fates, both broken up and scattered. None of the boys in either family, by then men, were worth more than a third or half as much as their fathers had been.

That December, I received a letter from Chas Raymond, asking me to work for him in Lowell. I decided to go. I wrote a letter telling him so and sent it down to be mailed with Hiram but forgot to give him nine cents so it didn't go post-paid as was becoming the custom. Postage was three cents in advance and five cents not in advance.

Upon hearing of it, I suddenly became indispensable to the Band. Anderson said that without Bond and me, they couldn't give a concert. He offered to give me any place in the Band that I chose and to find me employment. He also offered to play my arrangement of Reiff's Quickstep, a gamble because his part was too low and Henry Marsh said I should have retained the air which was beautiful. The drummers also grumbled. I knew I'd improved on it but didn't say so. When they struck into it and played a piece, they found to their astonishment that it chorded! I was as much astonished at my powers of composition as were the rest of 'em. They played it many times afterwards–as often as any tune they'd got.

Suddenly it seemed that I was living easy and contentedly at home, but it had gotten to be an old story. I needed a change. I thought I'd try it on and would be satisfied as long as I was taken for a person born in Christendom. But if I was supposed to be a heathen, then I would go home in disgust.

Chapter 41

Tempests of Sweet and Magnificent Sounds

I saw the flamboyant Jullien's Band that "charmed all ears with tempests of sweet and magnificent sounds," according to The New York Times *although I didn't agree.*

On January 30, 1854, I bid farewell to my schoolmistress, attended a farewell dinner at Anderson's and left the band and Woodstock feeling victorious, bound for Lowell, Massachusetts. I had just turned 18 years old.

Chas and I worked for C.A. Durgin, making sewing machines. I arrived, only to find that Chas didn't have any particular thing that he wanted me to do. He meant to have me putter around, clean the shop and learn, go to school perhaps. The work was drudgery and erratic, and I had little interest in it. I learned nothing worth telling and had soon worn out my clothes. After four months, Chas returned to Woodstock, leaving me alone.

When I left Woodstock, I had $21.13 in my pocket. I bought a rotary valve tenor horn which soon had one valve spring and a tip broken, leaving me with little money and a poor instrument. I joined the Lowell Brass Band, having heard how they earned $4,000 playing in the streets alone, but that was a few years earlier when David Hall was its leader. We earned very little.

Nevertheless, Boston was the epicenter of brass bands, and I played with some of the best musicians in the country including two days in the prestigious Boston Brass Band uniform. I saw a whale, tasted salty ocean water, played at a muster, and heard sedate classic works by German composers and Italian operas played by the renowned Germania Band. I saw the flamboyant Jullien's Band that "charmed all ears with tempests of sweet and magnificent sounds," according to *The New York Times* although I didn't agree. I thought Julien's red upholstered podium and gilded chair too showy, the music hall too grand, and his renditions too flamboyant. None of this entranced or even half satisfied me.

And then by the Gods, Father wrote that he'd sold his farm on Rum Street. There were no apples in the orchard, only four hives of bees had wintered, and his crops had been devastated by grasshoppers. He was going to work for Whitney in the machine shop at a dollar a day. The sale was effected about April 28, 1854. God! What a decline! And yet I hoped it would prove an advance.

Jackson Street where I lived was like a tunnel between tall dark buildings. At shift changes, the streets teemed with strangers who hurried to their jobs with little notice of those around them. When "Angel Gabriel" Orr came 'round causing excitement against the Irish, the ignorant devils I worked and boarded with, sided with Orr. Their talk was violent and unreasonable. They hooted at the press when it maligned Orr's actions and got indignant at me. Knowing what was what about it, I opposed Orr's and everyone else's anti-Catholic sentiment, being naturally obstinate and disposed to help the weak side, especially if it was the right one, as always. I concluded the people in Lowell were less intelligent on average than those I saw at home.

My prospects at work and playing music continued to be unpromising as the summer advanced. Unless I resorted to desperate means, I knew I would live a mean, inferior life. I began to long for the stumbling recitations and off-key fiddle solos at the North Bridgewater schoolhouse, for bouncing along in the back of a wagon trying to keep my horn to my lips, for the cheers of small boys and the satisfaction of out-thundering the Windsor Cornet Band.

And to my surprise I realized how much I wished to be hunting gudgeons with Geo Grow! I thought of the old folks at home and the good old times forever gone. It almost filled my eyes to think of that happy period of my life.

I told Smith I wanted to leave and he urged me to stay, talking of fiddling and bookkeeping lessons and of keeping accounts and selling breeches. But I had little confidence in any of his promises.

When I got an invitation from Anderson offering me employment in Woodstock, I decided to go. Father sent me five dollars and I left Lowell. I knew I would never again be a boy — never.

I learned I was down to 144 pounds after dinner when I weighed myself at the machine shop. I was almost six feet tall and my coat set on me like a shirt on a crooked beanpole. I had misgivings as to my shoulders and when I looked in the glass, I was astonished at my miserable appearance—white in the face, snotty-nosed, and hair uncombed. But I had 32 teeth in my head yet.

I got a job in the machine shop. There I was, solitary and absent-minded, but, God help me, honest, inoffensive and thoughtful. I gained 12 pounds and soon I could hold a common chair at arm's length back-handed. No one in the shop could do it but one other, and he was a giant. If I'd been good-looking and easy-minded, I should have been happier and weighed more, but I feared that case was past cure.

Work was not unpleasant and I learned much about making tin machines and was offered more jobs on them. My career as a musician flourished. I was treasurer of the Woodstock Brass Band and played with their Serenade Band. We traveled throughout central New England. That winter my playing brought in $227.65.

All my uncles had sold their farms on Rum Street and moved to the Flat. I was satisfied that they'd improved their affairs.

CHAPTER 42

RAKING DOWN THE CROWD

I'd gained in music sufficiently to form my own band, Cobb's Quadrille Band. There were five of us, all young and tough. The other four players were handsome and well-built. I didn't include myself in that group.

By the winter of 1855, I'd gained in music sufficiently to form my own band, Cobb's Quadrille Band. There were five of us, all young and tough. The other four players were handsome and well-built. I didn't include myself in that group. The girls particularly admired our caller, whose hair fell to his shoulders and who called out the prompts in a way that got almost everyone up dancing

We made a sensation. I played my old thunderstruck fiddle, as it was meant to be played, like thunder, while the horns added trills and crescendos. We played quadrilles, waltzes, contra dances, and polkas, traveling all around central Vermont. So much did the village of Norwich, Vermont, like us that, although for a dozen years scarce four dances had taken place, all hands old and young, orthodox and universalist, danced 10 times that winter. We made a sensation everywhere we went.

The *Spirit of the Age* called me a "young musician of great promise." After one dance, it said, "the Cotillions which were mostly arranged by Mr. Cobb, were in excellent taste and

THUNDERSTRUCK FIDDLE

every part was executed with a skill and ease that would have indicated old and experienced occupants of the Orchestra." That was extravagant praise.

I remember one particular dance, in English Mills, where we raked down the crowd. It had snowed heavily. The horse barn was so filled with sleighs Father took our team over to Mr. Pilcher's barn. I wasn't sure they'd let us leave it there. Mr. Pilcher agreed but Mrs. Pilcher told us "Dancing is an evil to health, character, and happiness because it leads to temptation. You should be at home engaging in singing, reading, and discussion, especially about mathematics and sentence construction." I wanted to tell her that we'd played at the ladies' tea party at the town hall and even they ended with a dance in spite of hell and religion–but I didn't out of respect.

Our music was loud enough to be heard half a mile away. It was a glorious night. Between my fiddle and the horns, the caller's prompts could barely be heard. We played old tunes – "Chorus Jig," "Captain Jenks," "Caledonia," "Money Musk," "Hull's Victory," "Virginia Reel." Someone opened the windows and the breeze made the oil lamps flicker against the walls. Mrs. Pilcher complained the next day to the selectmen but nobody paid her any attention.

I knew nearly everyone. It was an important night for me. That night they saw that I wasn't a greeny from the hills anymore.

At three o'clock in the morning I took up my cornet and a player from the Reading Band got up and played "Fisher's Hornpipe" on his clarionet with me. He was a great player, no doubt about it. We never stopped from the first note of the figure to the last, and seldom played a part alike twice. I'd never played the horn more catawampussingly.

Some of the boys in the band set aside their instruments to dance. I was no dancer–never considered myself graceful enough. And I thought I was too homely. Then a girl bowed to me, a good-looking girl I'd not seen before. I returned the bow and joined the dance–the first time for either. We played until dawn.

I played with Cobb's Quadrille Band for many winters. Some of the original players left, accusing me of being fidgety and fault-finding. I wasn't always easy to get along with. Even so, the *Spirit of the Age* called me one of the best musicians in the country and a "band in himself."

My reputation continued to spread, and by the age of 22, I was skilled enough to be hired to teach the Tweed River Brass Band in Pittsfield and the Rochester Brass Band, as Alonzo Bond had taught the Woodstock Cornet Band only six years before.

Charles Cobb's relationship with other musicians was often rocky, given as he admitted, to being fidgety and fault-finding. Cobb's Quadrille Band and Hough's Quadrille Band competed for engagements in central Vermont and New Hampshire in the late 1850s. Although often at odds, each recognized the musical expertise of the other and sometimes played together such as they are here. This is a remarkable undated photo, probably from the 1860s, of some of the best musicians of the time playing together in Hough's Quadrille Band. Charles Cobb is in the upper left and Hough, of Lebanon, New Hampshire, in the center front. Woodstock's Owen T. Marsh, plays the bass in the upper right. The other players are Owen Densmore of Chelsea, Vermont, and W.H. Straw of Claremont, New Hampshire.
Photo courtesy of Woodstock History Center

Chapter 43

Teaching the Tweed River Brass Band

I was to be paid the impressive sum of $50 to provide three days of instruction to the Tweed River Brass Band in Pittsfield, Vermont. It hadn't been so long before that I'd been paid 75 cents for a full day of hoeing and considered that a good wage. It had surprised me when L. Beard arranged for me to teach, for Beard's uncle was a Reverend, and the Pittsfield old folks were very strict about music and dancing.

Ransom Durkee, the band's leader, appeared startled when I walked in the door the first evening, for I was a mere boy and so slim I looked like I'd wear myself out after an hour. But my appearance was deceptive. For I was a worker.

Two solemn boys met us at the door with their hair slicked back and faces scrubbed clean. I could see the signs of a mother who wasn't obliged to work constantly without an hour's intermission for weeks together, a mother who wasn't worn down by poverty and labor and could tend to her children properly.

At 22, I stood taller than most men, but weighed only 147 ½ pounds regardless of the fact that I ate more dinner than any other two people. Even with my shoulder braces, which I wore so as not to appear so stooped, I looked homely and poor as a scarecrow. Back home in Woodstock, Vermont, a worker at the machine shop put his hand on my chest when I was lying on the woodbox and swore I was deformed. "No naturally formed chest sticks out forward so," he'd said. Another old man there said I had an excellent chest and that I "would outlive the lot."

The Tweed River Band consisted of 19 men, shopkeepers and farmers prosperous enough to pay for instruction and an instrument. Musical ability wasn't necessary. The older members talked pretty insulting to each other, though in joking style. The younger ones stood self-consciously apart, looking poor, sober and green just as I had the first time I met with the Woodstock Cornet Band.

They were an unpresuming lot, less showy than the Green Mountain Brass Band at Rochester, Vermont, who I'd instructed the week before. The Green Mountain folks had treated me well. One of the more forthright members said I was not near so good a teacher as someone they'd had earlier, but he acknowledged that I was a far better player. I admitted I was no teacher at all, but I got that band along faster than they ever got along before. It was by persevering effort and determined labor though, not the musical talents of the band members.

The members of the Tweed River Brass Band found their seats and began tooting. I listened, noticing those who could express themselves plainly, who was tooting ad libitum. The second E♭ cornet wore stupendous pantaloons and looked pretty tough but blew half-heartedly. He'd been displaced from the position of first E♭ cornet by a saucy little cuss who imitated his way of speaking—"I du jest's I'm mind tu," glancing around to see who'd found him amusing.

After rousing a couple of the members who'd arrived drunk, I directed the band to play a polka quadrille they knew. Predictably, it sounded like 19 cats squalling as though they'd gotten their tails pinched. The treble went squizzlety squitt, squizzlety sh__. Every player had his own idea of notes and timing. Even when the first E♭ horn played the air correctly, it sounded wrong.

It took me back six years, when Alonzo Bond must have heard the same sounds from our Woodstock Cornet Band. I had my first horn then, a $20 E♭ alto sax that was worthless according to Bond. It had one open sound that was imperfect and completely spoiled the instrument, but I learned to play on it, and I thought my music sounded impressive, although I probably squawked as badly as some of the Pittsfield musicians in front of me.

"It's not blowing that produces sound. It's the vibrations of the lips," I said, directing my advice to a player who blew with all his might and main. "Never use the tongue to end off the notes suddenly. Let 'em ring." Then finally, "Noise is not music! You don't want to drive your audience away." This, I confess, may have been spoken more heatedly than necessary.

Toward the end of our session, I demonstrated how to play a scale on my $76.37 E♭ German Silver Horn. Its valves were quick and smooth and I played like lightning.

That night I went home with Durkee. He lived in a good farmhouse with straight fences and glass in every window. Two solemn boys met us at the door with their hair slicked back and faces scrubbed clean. I could see the signs of a mother who wasn't obliged to work constantly without an hour's intermission for weeks together, a mother who wasn't worn down by poverty and labor and could tend to her children properly.

Mrs. Durkee looked disappointed when she saw me. As I said, I was thin and my forehead slanted back most devilishly so that my head was nearly all behind and my nose stuck out awfully. I'd always been self-conscious about my appearance, so much so that when I was younger, I lacked the courage to look a man in the eye or answer a question that was asked of me. I often aroused excitement or nostalgia with my music but it wasn't the same as appearing substantial from the beginning. I'd once written in my journal, "It is well that folks can't swap bodies, for if they could, I should soon cheat someone I fancy."

We sat in the square room. The boys looked longingly at my horn, gleaming in the light from the oil lamps. Young Frank stretched out his hand to touch it and Mrs. Durkee looked at him warningly. After a moment Durkee asked me to play something. I'd been expecting it. I was often asked to entertain when visiting someone, even to entertain babies in their cradles. I pointed the bell away from my audience and played the "Cracovienne Quickstep." Feet tapped around the room. I played "My Lodging Is On The Cold Ground" and I saw Mrs. Durkee wipe her eyes. I finished with increasingly complex variations of "Yankee Doodle" and the boys cheered.

"That's how we'll play one day," said Durkee, smiling

broadly. Mrs. Durkee looked at me with admiration. I was accustomed to people's surprise. Young Frank Durkee asked me if it could be true that I'd played with the Boston Brass Band.

"Yes," I answered. He looked awestruck.

"He knows David and Rhodolph Hall and Ned Kendall too. He's played with all the greatest musicians," said Durkee. "

"And at such a young age," said Mrs. Durkee. "How did you learn to play so well?"

I didn't know how to answer. My self-confidence drained away. I felt like I did as a boy, unable to answer a question for fear I would stammer incoherently. I wished I could write an answer down and hand her the paper. I could always write better than I spoke. "I sang at singing schools with my mother," I said. "Took lessons in fiddling of Leverett Lull in Woodstock. Studied with Pushee in Lebanon. Then Alonzo Bond came from Boston to teach our band in Woodstock." That was my musical life condensed into 34 words. But back home, I had a trunk filled with journal pages that told how I'd arrived at that day. The Durkees didn't have time to hear how my orthodox Christian neighbors reviled my fiddle playing, my shame when I played at drunken dances for a dollar, going without flour to pay for lessons, always trying to rise above the label "great greeny," shouted by boys on the Green who knew a poor hill farm boy when they saw one.

After my third day instructing the Tweed River Band, I returned briefly to Rochester, then headed home, walking four miles to Tuppers where I was to catch the stage to Woodstock. I'd earned $50 for just three days of work, 100 days of work for a farmer.

CHAPTER 44

THE LIFE OF A MUSICIAN

But unfortunately, my success was derailed. I had started taking a drink of whiskey the first thing on arriving at a dance. I'd also begun to look over the female property and Boston wasn't a slow place to find any such thing.

At the end of every winter, when the dancing season came to a close, I was offered positions in various bands. Although I hated leaving Vermont again, in 1858, I accepted an offer from David and Rhodolph Hall with the Boston Brass Band. I started the season playing first tenor horn, which would have been an easy summer of playing. But when the second E♭ horn player left, Hall asked me to take his place. I had to devote all my attention to supporting that part which was full enough for me to do. It ruined the fun and the summer's playing was, contrary to my anticipation, hard work.

One of our most glorious performances was in the July 4th celebration on the Boston Common. The particulars were written about in the newspapers. Four brass bands with 72 musicians, played magnificently together. Light Artillery accompanied "Hail Columbia," and the six cannon came in just right. The fireworks representing the burning of Charleston, were never so good.

I had reached the pinnacle of band playing in the country, playing in the best position in one of the best bands anywhere. David and Rhodolph Hall commanded high salaries for all of us. We played at Cleveland, Portland, Island Pond, Montreal, Kingston, Toronto, Hamilton, Buffalo, Dunkirk, and Fredonia and at some places twice, on our way out and back.

But unfortunately, my success was derailed. I had started taking a drink of whiskey the first thing on arriving at a dance. I'd also begun to look over the female property and Boston wasn't a slow place to find any such thing. When I got a dose of the clap at 21 Endicott Street, my band business took a decided turn for the worse. I was hard up, apprehensive, and low spirited. Very few in my situation would have played every job that fall, but I did.

I hadn't realized the value of my health until it was lost. I swore by the living God I would stick to a different text from then on. I was conscious of my disastrous condition, fully, and too much so. I could not bear to return home looking and feeling as I did, hard up and very thin, so swore off all indulgences and stayed away until I'd gained to 145 pounds.

I was thankful for one thing during that time. I had never abused myself when I was small. To that I owed my general firm health and unsurpassed wind. I knew nothing in the world was so injurious and nothing seemed so weak and shiftless as to fool away a particle of health. But even so, as I grew older, I began to give way about every two weeks and always under self-protest, although probably not enough to make any difference. I marked such failings with a star in my journals. Every time, it spoiled my peace of mind for a day or two and I vowed to stop it, although I knew it really was of little consequence. But enough of that, although it was more important than 99/100ths of my memoirs.

When I finally returned home, I played continually, traveling from one party, dance, levee, ball, singing school, or tea, to another, always in demand. The Woodstock Cornet Band knocked the other bands stiff at Bradford Muster. My old tuba raked down all the bass.

I never played so well as I did at a ball in Newport, New Hampshire, January 5, 1860. Lip first rate, nice company and our caller, Colby, did good service in calling a polka quadrille. But later that night the hotel took fire in the garret and burned to ashes. I lost my cap but nothing more. Colby helped me get my team out of the barn.

Another devastating fire occurred in Woodstock a month later, destroying nearly all of the shops in Edson's Row. It was the day of the Woodstock Light Infantry's annual military ball at Gilman Henry's Hotel. The day had been cold and very windy. A fire started in a garret of one of the stores and burned $30,000 worth of property opposite the tavern.

The ball was held anyway although only 30 couples attended. Hiram appeared there with Cynthia. I was surprised to see them, considering Cynthia's reputation. Sarah Cobb had died four years earlier of "ulcified" teeth according to Granny Morey. She was only 33 and reduced nearly to a skeleton. She should not have been seen. I never knew any woman to bear what she had. After her death, Hiram gave their daughter, 15-year-old Caroline, to George Raymond's family.

One week in January I fiddled six nights in a row and worked in the machine shop four days. One bitterly cold night I walked home from Barnard 11 miles over the hills, breaking through 10 inches of snow half the time. I got home at noon and worked that afternoon in the shop. When Aaron Whitney saw me he said "It's the sure and inevitable ruin of a man, morally and physically, to become a musician."

I said, "It's unhealthy but as for my morals, pshaw!"

One night a Captain Brown gave me a ride home from Barnard when the thermometer was at minus 45 to 50 degrees, as cold as was ever known. I froze one ear severely. He told me about the China experience in Boston, where he said that girls could be bought for from $50 to $100. He'd gone down there once and come back married. I wished I was in Boston with him. The boys in Vermont had an idea that no womankind would draw me a rod, but they didn't know me.

The next summer, the Boston Brass Band invited me to play the tuba on their European tour. I turned down the invitation as well as those from the bands in Lowell and Springfield, Massachusetts, and with the New Orleans Burlesque Troupe because my old symptoms had returned. Also, Anderson offered me a bass-horn worth $70 and the ladies got up a levee with a promenade concert and raised a large amount–$143.50. Woodstock was increasingly showing their support for the cornet band.

I was at work clapboarding Father's house when Isaac A. Priest drove up and wanted me to ride to the Green with him to help a circus band play the menagerie into town. I knew everyone in that band and they persuaded me to travel with them for the season for a dollar a day. I went because I wanted to see the country. I played with circus bands often in the following years, always returning to Woodstock for one day to play for muster. I meant not to fail of that on any account.

By the end of the summer season, I had enough money to discharge my debts and $408 to buy the house next to ours for Mother's sister who intended to move to the Flat. Hiram had married Cynthia, much to my amazement, and I let him live in the house until spring when Aunt Polly would arrive to help Mother. Mother was so blind she could hardly read, although she was only 51.

The threat of war eclipsed dancing in 1861 and I played half as much as the previous winter. But my troubles were thrown into the shade in August when I learned a draft of 300,000 men to go to war for nine months was pending. A three-year company had been recruited from Woodstock the previous year, but nearly all were from out of town. Geo Grow had enlisted, but he was so miserable and mean that they discharged him. C.J. Winslow came home boxed up. Seth Winslow went out to get him home and found him dying with consumption. He weighed only 70 pounds.

Hiram enlisted, also Rufous Holmes, Ed Woodward and others, some of them to avoid the draft and also to get the $50 the town had offered for volunteers and $25 from the government. But money would never make me go to war. I studied my options and finally became satisfied that, if drafted, $50 would clear me by state law. It was hard to find this out as lawyers kept so still.

I refused Silloway's offer to play with the circus that summer because their tour would take me through Canada. I didn't want people to think I'd skedaddled. A good many men had run away to Canada, especially from back towns.

Chapter 45

Finding a Wife

I wished I could court someone. I ached all the time to talk to a girl. I saw Seth Winslow and A. Whitney walking out with girls on Sundays but I dared not.

Another reason for staying home was to get acquainted with the girls. I wanted an opportunity to squeeze 'round one of them. I thought I could do it in pretty decent style although I'd been away so much that I hardly knew the girls at home and they still thought me of slight account. But fellows were mighty scarce and small potatoes at that. None of them had done any better than I had.

    I had hardly spoken to a girl in Woodstock until one day, Elizabeth Cobb, Norman's girl, came into the machine shop. She was then 17 and a credit to the Cobb family. We weighed ourselves. I went 148 ½, she, 149 pounds. When she left, I was spoiled for the day.

    I wished I could court someone. I ached all the time to

talk to a girl. I saw Seth Winslow and A. Whitney walking out with girls on Sundays but I dared not. I wondered what the devil was the reason. I was as smart in every way as either of them. I could buy Winslow out clean in half a day. Physically I was entirely ahead of him. I had more stamina than both of them four times over.

    Nevertheless, I did not feel as much of a man at home in Woodstock as when I was off playing. And slights still cut me. I was up to Montpelier to play with Fale's band for a couple of balls and was walking out on the street alone, thinking of my affairs, when I met two strangers. They both laughed involuntarily. What in hell they saw I couldn't tell. Once again, I wished for independence of spirit, satisfaction in behaving right up to the handle, and not caring for slights. But I had not that faculty. I could only swear to myself that I would make them even in time.

    I had one last bust at 21 Endicott Street in Boston where I paid five dollars for capotes and a chance to try one. After that I vowed to discipline myself, restrain my passions, keep as cheerful as possible, and never go back one step. I didn't suppose I'd get another chance to use them anyway as there didn't seem to be hardly any girls at home and what there were, kept entirely out of sight.

    I knew I must have a mate or I would fail to behave myself so got Charles Hutchinson, who then had a photograph car at the Bethel House, to take 12 small pictures of me, with some idea of giving them to girls. They looked better than I thought they would.

    I made a list of girls. I thought I might send one of the pictures to Ellen Francis Knight, an old schoolmate who used to like me but who'd moved away. Another was Sarah L. George of Barnard, age 19 or 20. I took her to the Thanksgiving Ball at the Bethel Depot House where I played and afterwards wrote her a letter and included one of my pictures. She answered it and I wrote again and so on. She said more than I dared to. She wasn't very handsome, nor very smart, nor worth anything but it was a great satisfaction to believe that if I wanted her I could have her. I certainly felt better than I did when I had no reason to suppose that any woman in the world ever would want me to look at her. But I wanted a girl of spotless integrity and of that, Sarah could not boast.

I went over to Brewsters one night and fiddled some. My old thunderstruck fiddle still served me well and I hoped to impress Mary and Abby Brewster. Even though it didn't amount to anything, I would have given 25 cents for some excuse to go again.

I thought of such things more than going off to fiddle. By then, it was no novelty to play for a dance—not even a big one, although I liked the pay as well as ever.

Sunday evening, November 9, 1862–I wrote at my desk to make myself understand myself. The danger was in forgetting what I was after and I did forget for days together. Journalizing kind of cleared my brain and raised the fog. I could see better how I stood when I stated the case in black and white, than I could by merely considering my position.

It was a stormy miserable day and the first snow was on the ground. I felt my time to be worthless, so I could write without feeling foolish and shiftless. My things laid around in confusion which showed that I was lazy. Still I couldn't sit down to read a piece an inch long without my conscience starting me up to do something—although there was nothing I was willing to do.

As I wrote, I realized that time was indeed revenging me. I worked in the shop and behaved myself. I put up my tools and kept my work in good order. My position as a musician was secure. I was offered enough music jobs—once even a European tour with the Halls (although it never came off) that I had no fear of failing. I was no heavier than a year ago, a trifle over 150 pounds in coat but I was quite healthy and certainly gaining in looks.

Father and Mother no longer needed to worry. I had paid off Father's mortgage. I had paid E.A. Wood for finishing the clapboard work on Father's shed and for painting the house and fence. When the shingling was complete, Father's house looked good. I bought $22 worth of blinds and got trusted for a new carpet for the parlor, the first and only one we ever had. I had got a new stove. Father had needed $10 to go to Boston with a load of hay and I gave it to him easily. I'd hired a barn—21 by 31 feet in size, built behind our house. The carpenters left it without doors or floors and Father was to finish it. But he was still a slow team and it was a long time before it was done although I no longer cared so much.

Father had given $400 for his house and I thought it

worth $1,000 after improvements. The value of land seemed to be increasing rapidly. I thought folks on the Flat were becoming aristocratic. Hiram had deeded his share of 31 acres on Chubback Hill to me. We'd bought it together for $1,075. I gave him a note of $161.36 and assumed his promise to support Grandfather's wife, Hannah Richmond, as long as she lived.

I would be 27 years old in little more than a month. I had taken a walk up Rum Street that afternoon, noticing the light snow on the hills, the buildings abandoned or gone altogether, only cellar holes marking where they'd been.

My goals had come down since I'd walked along that same road singing, so many years ago. Then I'd been optimistic about becoming president. By the year 1862, I felt that nothing would satisfy me as much as an untarnished reputation and capital enough to live on.

I stopped writing in my journal after that night. It was time to devote myself to my final goal–that of finding a wife to help take care of me. And I did. Within two years I was married. I have a daughter, Ada, and son, Charles, and now, as I'm approaching old age, a granddaughter, Winifred Cobb. My cousin, Henry Cobb, who'd nearly died of canker rash, had married Ada. I live in the house I was born in and will probably die here. I still have the thunderstruck fiddle and a little hair trunk which I open occasionally. It smells like my old bedroom on Rum Street, of lamp oil, wood and smoke. I check to make sure my journals are still whole, noticing the dirty threads that bind the pages into books. Sometimes I open one and look at the small hand-writing that fills every page.

I remember how valuable I'd considered my writings to be. I wanted to know that 50 years in the future I could open them and know they told the truth, the whole truth and nothing but the truth about that which could no longer be seen. Those years have passed and knowing that I kept that promise, my journals are indeed, as valuable as I'd hoped they would be.

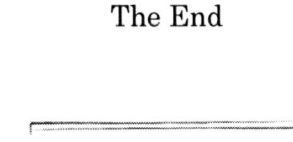

The End

Epilogue

The Years After 1863 – A Band in Himself

Last known photograph of Charles Morris Cobb (lower left). Don E. Thomas is the only other person whose identity is known (lower right).

From Charles Cobb's final transcribed diary, written in 1862, we learn that he was 27 years old, owned an estate worth $1112.37, including two pieces of land and a new barn, and was ready to find a wife.

Two years later a 24-year-old woman named Lucy Jane Shaw, known as Jane, left Northfield, Vermont, to work in a sewing shop in Woodstock. She sewed during the day and went out during her free time, sometimes with Caroline Cobb, Charles' cousin. She kept a diary, so we know she went to a Mendelsohn concert, to meeting, a husking, picking butternuts and for rides.

She lived in a boarding house with other young women and her diary contained the names of young men who called on her. There were many. Wales Johnson went home with her often. Willie Vaughan called on her, John Cone and then Fred Parkhurst. "We gals all had calls," she wrote on the first day of Fred's visit. "Every room was occupied." Wales Johnson eventually married Caroline Cobb. Fred Parkhurst moved away and he and Jane exchanged letters for a while.

On December 6, 1865, she stayed home for the afternoon getting ready to go to a ball at Bridgewater. Everyone from the sewing shop went. They had a gay time. It's quite likely Charles Cobb was one of the musicians. We don't know what happened in the intervening years, but he and Jane married in 1867.

Together the couple raised two children, Ada and Charles. Jane died in 1876, and in 1877, Charles married Mrs. Eunice Thomas, a widow.

Charles' writings after 1862 are ledgers containing records of money earned and spent, records of debts, lists of performances and songs played. They include an interesting account entitled "unnecessary expenses and losses," all evidence of his life-long concern about money. These account books are stored at the Woodstock History Center.

Charles was a solid citizen. His obituary describes him as having "a very active temperament." His name is mentioned often in local newspapers in connection with various musical events. The *Spirit of the Age* called him "a band in himself".

Charles and his father increased their land holdings in the years following 1861 when Charles bought his first piece of land on the Flat for $100. Land records show at least 10 purchases in the hills around Woodstock, including on Rum Street. Before Gaius died in 1891, he gave Charles the old Grow place on Rum Street and another 10 acres consisting of a meadow with an old house and barn and an orchard enclosed by a stone wall. He also gave Charles the bee house land where Charles had spent so many warm, sunny hours playing his thunderstruck fiddle and watching for bees to swarm.

Charles died in the same house he was born in, in West Woodstock on March 7, 1903, of pernicious anemia, a condition that wasn't recognized medically until 1849, and for which there was no cure. Upon his death, Charles had 400 acres and had spent at least $8,800 on property.

He continued to write in his Universal Musician or Great Book of Music for his entire life and he also wrote a book of poems.

Charles Cobb (far left middle row or fourth from the left in the photo) continued playing with the Woodstock Cornet Band for many years. This photo was taken some time after 1884 when the Norman Williams Library was built. Photo courtesy Woodstock History Center.

Charles Cobb's obituary in *The Vermont Standard,* March 19, 1903, recounts his later career: "Having inherited an unusual musical talent from his mother, he at an early age began his musical career, for at the age of seven he was copying music and when only nineteen was teacher of a brass band. Soon after this he went to Boston and played in Hall's brass band. On his return to Woodstock he learned the machinists' trade and was employed in A.W. Whitney's machine shop until 1869, with the exception of one year's travel with Wambold and Whitby's circus. His evenings during the time he worked in the shop were given to his music, writing, playing and teaching it. In 1869 he went to Smithville, New Jersey, and after remaining there a year he returned to Woodstock. In the summer of 1872 we find him at the Crawford House, White Mountains; in '76 and '77 he traveled with Beedle's Bell Ringers; in '79 he was employed in the Estey Organ Shop at Brattleboro, where he organized a band. Since the year 1883 he has been in Woodstock the greater part of the time.

"Mr. Cobb had traveled nearly all over this country and Canada with different musical organizations, playing various instruments including cornet, violin, tuba and clarionet, with great skill. He composed songs and wrote a number of poems. In 1865 he became a Mason, remaining a member through life.

"Mr. Cobb was a good neighbor, and in his dealings was always strictly honest and square. He will be greatly missed among his musical friends, and in our community."

Today Charles' Rum Street is accessible primarily to mountain bikes, snowmobilers and hikers. It is now called Von-

Today, Rum Street is known as Vondell Road and is closed to vehicles much of the year.

Cellar holes are all that remain of a struggling community of poor hill farmers who tried, and finally failed at farming on Rum Street, outside Woodstock, Vermont in the 1850s. This is probably the cellar of the home of Elijah (Old Grow) and Ruth Grow and their son George.

dell Road and meanders up through Vondell valley, ending at the Vondell Reservoir built in the 1960s. A new road skirts the edge of the reservoir, branching northeast toward Prosper, becoming Cobb Road and further on, Grassy Lane. The more north-easterly branch climbs the steep hill to the site of the old Cobb family homestead and Charles Cobb's last home on Rum Street.

Trees have grown up, filling in the old pastures and hayfields. The buildings are gone, but stone-lined cellar holes remain, along with old maples bordering the road. Stone walls that wind through the woods mark property lines of long ago. The road up over the hill and down to the Cox District School remains, and the fields have been kept clear and the stone walls maintained. It's private land but signs welcome hikers and skiers. The area around what was Charles' sugarbush still provides a magnificent view towards the west. A beautiful old stone arch stands where Charles may have once boiled maple sap.

Cellar holes are all that remain of the houses lived in by the Cobbs and their neighbors, the Raymonds, Moreys, Clapps, Shaws, and Grows. Near the cellar hole that was beneath Charles' last home on Rum Street, is a well or privy pit, partly filled with woody debris. Some of the cellar holes are stacked stone walls of foundations and others are shallow pits, the stone walls barely discernible. They would be easily missed were it not for maps.

The evidence of Cobb's musical life has fared better. In 1930 Helen Hartness Flanders had the job of recovering old songs in Vermont, passed on from one singer or fiddler to the next through the generations. She wrote, "Tragedy and comedy, gleams of old incidents seen through the veil of years, sounds of vanished laughter and the silences of old sorrows, vision and faith, too—all these and more are hidden in the old ballads."

Flanders recounts a meeting she had with Mrs. Hawkins of Reading, Vermont, during her years of searching out old music. "[Mrs. Hawkins] left the room murmuring something about a book. She returned with a most amazing compilation. It was a heavy, calf-bound book, entitled *Universal Musician* by C.M. Cobb. She had saved it from a bonfire of his papers in the yard after his death 'because he had put so much work into it.'"

"Work, indeed!" continues Flanders. "Six hundred pages of closely penned stanzas and music notation could have involved a lifetime. Every inch is used by this eccentric musician to set down words and airs, fiddle tunes, and calls for dances."

"In black ink Mr. Cobb transcribed all he knew of a ballad. A tune was written where a margin gave space. Another song comes to mind. This he sets down in red ink between the lines in black ink. Another group of stanzas is crowded into another small section of a page, every word readable though in miniature letters. Words are packed 'every which ways.'"

Flanders persuaded the Vermont Historical Society of its importance as a treasure of Vermont folk music and persuaded them to buy it for $25. It's in their collection today. At some point it was rebound, but all its contents are original.

Charles called this *Universal Musician*, his "Great Book." He wrote somewhat dismissively of it in his journals: "This volume which appears so like a great bible is only a

Charles' cousin, Henry Cobb, narrowly survived the canker rash outbreak on Rum Street and later, married Ada, Charles' daughter.

Music Book." To which Flanders replies, "But what do we find? A great spread of what was currently sung a hundred years ago. This book has genuine personality. Had this book gone up in flames, so would have passed the heart and soul of an itinerant musician and ballad-monger."

Ada L. Cobb

Ada Cobb and her daughter, Winifred Cobb, at their home in Woodstock in the early 20th century. Photo courtesy of John Beauvais and the Cobb descendants.

*Rum Street resident Lucius Raymond with Ed Shattuck
wearing a straw hat, working near the Green.
Photo courtesy Woodstock History Center.*

People in Charles Cobb's Journals

Charles mentions more than 200 people in his journals. These are a few of them.

Anderson, Charles B. - Woodstock Cornet Band secretary for many years, recognized Charles' talent early on although Charles often railed at what he considered Anderson's mismanagement. Owned a clothing shop on the Green where Charles bought his coats, usually on credit.

Bond, Alonzo - band leader from Boston who taught many small-town brass bands in the mid-19th century. Taught the Woodstock Cornet Band when Charles first joined in 1853.

Chase, Dr. Henry - the dentist who filled Charles' tooth so it was "now in full discharge of all its duties and some more." He lived on Mountain Avenue in Woodstock in a grand house that looked "far different from our old castle." An active and influential participant in the Woodstock Cornet Band, he helped Charles join the band and supported his participation.

Churchill, Laura - born in about 1820, the daughter of Joseph Churchill, a house painter, and his wife, Clara Eddy. Laura was either idiotic (according to the census) or "high-minded" (according to Charles), or "weak-minded or odd" (again according to Charles). Everyone seemed to agree that she was unconventional, wearing fewer clothes than other women and going about bare-headed even in the rain. She often visited Rum Street, particularly Henry and Laura Cobb, sometimes staying for lengthy periods of time. She was a friend of noted author Mary Gibson (Winnie Woodfern), who'd lived with the Churchill family as a child upon the death of both of her parents. In her later years Laura and Mary Gibson (Mary Francis in the 1880 census) lived together in English Mills. She died October 27, 1885.

Churchill, Nathan T. - Charles described him as a "Farmer 1 ½ miles from the Green at the junction of our road with the river road. Much better looking person than men will average. Worth [$]3,000 at least. Married but has no children. Something of a farmer politician tho' he is no lawyer. Makes no speeches &c and does his business for the people & no party but yet he has always been elected to office by the Whigs & no one else." 1860 census listed him as a farmer with about $2,800 worth of real estate and $4,000 in personal property. Married to Elizabeth. President of the Ottauquechee Savings Bank, starting his term in 1858. Contributed $500 to replace the wood rail fence around the village green with an iron rail fence in 1878.

Churchill, Oramel - born about 1810, lived on the Flat with his sister Priscilla. Needed his "boots mended" more often than anyone, until Charles realized it was a euphemism for going upstairs to his father's shop for cider. Great friend of Gaius Cobb, teller of gossipy stories, and farm-hand whenever help was needed. "The most entire and professional drunkard that I have ever clapped eyes on" wrote Charles.

Cobb, Ada - the daughter of Charles Cobb and Lucy Jane Shaw, born January 18, 1868 and died May 4, 1921. Lived with and cared for her grandfather, Gaius P. Cobb, during his declining years. Married Henry Eugene Cobb in 1896, when she was 28. Had a daughter, Winifred S. Cobb, in about 1898.

Cobb, Benney - Charles' great-grandfather, born in 1764 and died June 28, 1817, in Woodstock. Benney moved from Middleborough, Massachusetts, to Woodstock in about 1790 with his wife, Azubah Shaw, and sons Elias, Isaac, and Gaius. In 1798, the Direct Tax census noted that the family had improved 20 of their 75 acres and built a 20 by 30-foot barn and 34 by 16-foot house. The land was valued at $488 and taxed $1.39. The house wasn't taxed, indicating that it probably didn't have much value.

Cobb, Betsey - Charles' aunt, whose "appetite mastered her" with symptoms similar to bulimia that included eating, vomiting and eating again. Her father tried to remedy his daughter's condition by locking her in her room. According to Charles, she escaped by climbing out the window and never again returned to the family home. "Result, a constitution wrecked, a life thrown away and made a burden to the community. Admitted to the "insane asylum" at Brattleboro but treatment failed and she was supported by the town. Verily all intemperance comes not of rum alone," wrote Charles. Lived with various families on the Flat. Gaius Cobb and his brothers paid the town for her board, a financial burden that contributed to the loss of their farms.

Cobb, Betsey Palmer - Charles' paternal grandmother, born in 1785. Married Gaius Cobb at the age of 20 and moved into the family homestead at the top of Rum Street hill. From Calais, Vermont, where she appeared to have been an active member of a church. Left a collection of letters which Charles acquired, including those from an admirer, Mr. Kingsley, who wrestled with the Lord's displeasure over his feelings for Betsey. Her sister, Mary Palmer, pressed her to "pray for me that I may live more to the glory of God than I have done in time past." Raised five sons and two daughters to adulthood.

Cobb, Eddie (Norman Edwin) - born about 1835, the son of Norman Cobb and Mary Elizabeth Cobb. Went to Cox District School with Charles until, at the age of eight, when his father married Emeline Morey, was sent away to live with the Aldrich family in Nashua, New Hampshire. In 1851, was learning the blacksmith trade in Amherst, New Hampshire. In 1860, lived in Milford, New York, and was worth $100. Married to Harriet A. from Massachusetts, and had two children, George and Mary.

Cobb, Elizabeth - was two years old when her mother died. Sent to be cared for by Emeline Morey and when her father married Emeline, was sent to live with Aaron W. Whitney's family on the Flat. She was three years old at the time. Grew up to be an attractive and hard-working girl. "Elizabeth is always busy at work I see, about something," and "Elizabeth Cobb do credit to the Cobb family," wrote Charles. Later, worked at Solomon Woodward's woolen mill in Woodstock.

Cobb, Emeline (Morey) - arrived on Rum Street when her second husband "ran away," leaving her with two children. Married Norman Cobb, Charles' uncle, and immediately sent Norman's own three children away to live with other families, an act that Charles never forgave, at least during his journal-writing years. Prone to telling tall tales, many of them very funny. Charles wrote "It is impossible for Emeline to live in a neighborhood long with any one, and much more in a house, without lying about them." Born May 13, 1815 and died February 20, 1901.

Cobb, Elias - moved to Woodstock from Middleborough, Massachusetts, with his father, Benney Cobb, thus Charles' great-uncle. Built the house Charles' family rented from Mr. Hartwell. A deacon in the Baptist Church, then elder in the Christian Church, ordained in 1808.

Cobb, Frederick – the eldest son of Hiram and Sarah Cobb, Charles' beloved cousin whose fiddling, at less than five years of age, started Charles on his musical career. Born in 1844 and died at the age of seven during an outbreak of canker rash.

Cobb, Gaius Palmer - father of Charles Morris Cobb who appeared to prefer shoe-making and carpentry to farming, except for beekeeping, at which he excelled. Won top prizes at the local county fair for his honey. The eldest of his siblings and therefore sometimes assumed fatherly responsibility for the care of his brother's families, after the elder Gaius Cobb's death. Relationships with his judgmental teen-age son, Charles, and wife, Lucia, were often frought with difficulties. The Woodstock History Center has a fiddle that he made. Lived on the Flat most of his life after losing his farm on Rum Street. In the summer of 2010 an instrument dealer in Boston bought a fiddle inscribed with G.P. Cobb, Woodstock, Vermont, 1893. It was made two years before Gaius' death. Born in 1807 and died in 1895.

Cobb, Gaius C. - Charles' paternal grandfather. Moved to Woodstock from Middleborough, Massachusetts, with his father as a young man and helped build the original family home "in a back place, and on very high ground, overlooking everything and North and West of it are three high hills, which keep the wind off grand." A big man, over six feet tall and more than 200 pounds. Described by Charles Dana in his *History of Woodstock*, as a "man of much native shrewdness of mind, quick-witted, always ready with an answer." Married Betsey Palmer on February 7, 1805, and moved into the family home with his parents, raising eight children to adulthood and taking in neighborhood boys as well. "According to Hiram's tell the lot used to have good times," wrote Charles. Many years later, his granddaughter, Caroline Cobb, wrote in a letter to her niece, Winifred Cobb, "My Grandfather was industrious and a successful farmer. He used to go to Boston by team with farm products." Gaius C. Cobb attained success as a farmer, largely through the sale of merino wool. After the death of his wife, he married Hannah Richmond. Gaius' death in 1846 left his sons with the financial burden of her care which was a part of the reason Charles' father lost his farm.

Cobb, Henry Eugene - son of Hiram and Sarah Cobb, born 1848 and died 1932. Married Ada L. Cobb, daughter of Charles, in 1896. Had a daughter, Winifred S. Cobb. A gentle man, he left papers in which he wrote "free this country from the scourge of slavery" and "read, be wise and live." According to an old news clipping reprinted in a local newspaper in 1960 (name of newspaper lost), "Henry E. Cobb of here [West Woodstock] lost a cow last Saturday. She got into a lot of apples and ate herself full, becoming so drunk that she never came to. Even with her three stomachs she couldn't arrange the matter." (From John Beauvais, Henry's great-grandson)

Henry Eugene Cobb in his later years. Photo courtesy of John Beauvais and the Cobb descendants.

Cobb, Henry Mower - born October 22, 1808 and died August 8, 1892. Charles' uncle and influential in young Charles' life. Lived in the family homestead with his wife, Laura Smith Cobb. Their only child died as an infant. The most financially successful of the brothers, innovative and sensible. Loved to argue and stayed out all night discussing philosophy and mechanics. The 1850 census listed his real estate as having a value of $1,200, the 1860 census as $2,000, and the 1870 census as $3,400 in real estate and $1,500 personal property. Played the snare drums or bass drum for the Woodstock Artillery. "I worked for Henry and like a good fellow too, as he used to tell me stories and converse with me. I learned from him, more than I ever did at school," wrote Charles. His drum is in the Woodstock History Center's collection.

Cobb, Hiram Orlando - Charles' uncle, strong and rather larger than his brothers, weighing 170 pounds or more and 5 feet 11 inches tall. Farmed on Rum Street. First wife was Sarah Morey Cobb, with whom he had seven children. Two survived to adulthood. Lost his farm and moved onto the Flat where he worked as a machinist and carpenter. Enlisted with the Woodstock Light Infantry Company B, 12th Regiment on August 19, 1862, and mustered as a private October 4, 1862. Served for nine months. Married Cynthia and had a son who died young. His obituary described him as "A man of quiet life, minded his own affairs." Born February 22, 1819, and died May 22, 1890.

Cobb, Hiram and Sarah's children - **John Andrew Cobb**, born 1846; **William Orlando Cobb**, born 1849; and **Frederick Carlton Cobb**, born 1844, all died of canker rash in 1851. Caught the disease, now commonly called scarlet fever, in Bridgewater, where it was about. People were so afraid of it that they stayed away from the children's funerals. Small gravestones mark their burials in the southeastern corner of the Shaw Cemetery on the hill above the Flat (now West Woodstock). Sarah Cobb's grave is nearby. She lived only a few years after the terrible loss of her children. A quiet cemetery on a dirt road, surrounded by a moss-covered stone wall.

Cobb, Hosea Orlando - born in 1819, the smallest of Charles' uncles. Never married and although he visited Rum Street often, didn't play a significant part in Charles' life. Died in 1873 in Smithville, New Jersey, where he lived in the home of Hezekiah Smith, Laura Cobb's brother, and famous inventor of woodworking machines. After the death of three of Hiram's children, Charles wrote, "I never knew how inferior Hosea's character is to Hiram's. (I don't mean as regards knowledge, honesty, or anything of the kind, but independently of all these, some folk's characters are great, and other's small). I don't think Hosea considers he [Hiram after the deaths of his children] lost anything, only the funeral expenses."

Cobb, James Alphonso (Jim) - was seven when he was sent away to live with Gustavus Marsh upon the marriage of his father, Norman Cobb, to Emeline Morey. Lived with various families in Woodstock and maintained contact with Charles.

Cobb, Laura (Smith) - a spiritual seeker and keeper of the Smith family Bible. Sensible and kind, she took a serious interest in Charles, offering him advice and sugaring down his sap. Helped her husband, Henry Cobb, with his farming, an unusual practice for most of the wives on Rum Street. First to wear bloomers on Rum Street. Her only child died as an infant. Sister of Hezekiah Smith, a famous inventor. Born August 21, 1810 and died September 15, 1892.

Cobb, Lucia Emeline (Cobb) - mother of Charles and wife of Gaius Cobb, was born a Cobb in 1810, probably in Chateaugay, New York, and died 1885. Shared a common ancestor with Gaius seven generations earlier, Henry Cobb, who'd came to the new world from Reculver, Kent, England, and married Patience Hurst from Amsterdam, in Scituate, Massachusetts, in 1631. Among their children were John, Lucia's ancestor, and James, Gaius' ancestor. Both their ancestors eventually lived in Middleborough, Massachusetts. Lucia's grandfather, James Cobb, moved to Woodstock in about 1777, and Gaius' grandfather, a few years later. Her father, also James Cobb, was brought up on a farm near Pogue Hole on Mount Tom. She had two sisters, Susan Isman (wife of Aaron Isman) and Polly Woodruff (wife of Sam) and a brother named Charles Morris Cobb who moved to Sheridan, Michigan. Charles and Polly were born in Woodstock before their father left for Chateaugay, New York. James died while fairly young, after which, her mother, Joanna, married Daniel Chase. They had a son who, in 1851, lived in New Hampshire.

Cobb, Lucy Jane (Shaw) - born November 1, 1838, and died September 18, 1876. From Northfield, Vermont, she moved to Woodstock and worked in a sewing shop. First wife of Charles Cobb. Parents were Asa Alonzo Shaw and Abigail Tinkham. Mother of two children, Ada Cobb and Charles Cobb.

Cobb, Lyman - the Lyman Cobb branch of the family were descendants of Benney Cobb's son, Binney Cobb. Binney settled in English Mills and had a son named Lyman, who also had a son named Lyman who was born in 1820. According to family stories, he made $3,000 in the California gold rush (almost $80,000 in 2015), and bought his own farm in English Mills. Married Mary Graves of English Mills. Died young and Mary carried on the farm. Her daughter, Ida Nannie, married Milo Lewis. They had a son named Rupert Milo Lewis who kept the farm until the 1960s when he sold it. He had two daughters, one of whom was Marion Ruth Lewis, mother of the author of this book. English Mills is now Prosper.

Cobb, Norman Meacham - Charles' uncle, born July 4, 1811, and died June 24, 1887. Norman's first wife, Mary, died October 6, 1842, at the age of 29. Remarried Emeline Morey who brought her two children to the household while sending Norman's children away to live with other families. Did not prosper on Rum Street so moved to Illinois, then returned to the Flat where he worked at the machine shop.

Cobb, Sarah (Morey) - Hiram Cobb's first wife, daughter of Lydia and Andrew (Granny and Granther) Morey. Had six children with Hiram, four of whom died while young, three of them in the canker rash outbreak of 1851. She died November 8, 1856, at the age of 33.

Cynthia - a girl Charles' age on the Flat who was widely believed to be "public," and thus, the subject of much rumor and speculation. "CYNTHIA'S character is so ESTABLISHED that it is beyond all comment or Question," wrote Charles.

Spent a lot of time on Rum Street, often helping the Old Maids, who she was related to. Cynthia was the second wife of Hiram Cobb.

Daniels, Reuben - acquired part of Bennett's Mills on the Flat in 1831. The business became known as the "machine shop" under the firm name R. Daniels & Co. and was a primary employer for men on the Flat, including Charles Cobb and his father and uncles. They manufactured "carding-machines, spinners, shearing-machines, pickers, and other articles of the same character." (Henry Swan Dana, *History of Woodstock, Vermont*) One of the first trustees of the Ottauquechee Savings Bank in 1847. In the 1850 census his real estate was listed as being worth $5,500. Charles wrote "Reuben Daniels lives in a very fine large house." His son was John Daniels who went to school with Charles.

Dodge, Jo - lived in half of Hiram Cobb's house and lost two of his three children during the canker rash outbreak. Mrs. Hannah Dodge was a Morey, Sarah Cobb's sister.

English, William Austin - Charles' friend who lived in English Mills with his father, William S. English, a rake-maker with an estate worth $1,000 in 1850. By 1860, his real estate was listed as worth $4,500 and personal property, $4,000, by the United States census. His rakes were widely known. He made from 300 to 800 dozen a year, continuing until 1884. His home and factory was in English Mills. Austin became a physician, practicing in Hartford, Connecticut.

Frinks - a "devilish poor" couple who owned half the house that Charles moved into with his parents in 1852. Threatened to tear their part down that winter unless Gaius Cobb could pay them $12. He paid with apples, a watch, a box of honey, one dollar in cash and his note for $6.50 due in six months with interest.

Furber, Dr. Zopher Willard - born in Dublin, New Hampshire in 1806 and graduated from Castleton Medical College in 1829. Known to doctor the poor and occasionally called upon by residents of Rum Street.

Gibson, Mary - was born in 1835, orphaned as a toddler, and raised by Joseph Churchill, a Woodstock house painter. Joseph's daughter, Laura Churchill, was a great friend of Mary's throughout their lives. Charles often met her when she was visiting his aunt Laura Cobb. Mary Gibson used the writing aliases, Winnie Woodfern and later Mary O. Francis and Margaret Blount. Daniel Cohen studied and wrote about her importance as an early writer of stories in which girls were independent adventurous heroes. Much of what we know about her comes from his study, *Making Hero Strong Teenage Ambition, Story-Paper Fiction, and the Generational Recasting of American Women's Authorship* (Journal of the Early Republic, Volume 30, Number 1, Spring 2010, 85-136). Mary described herself as a "romp" (tomboy) and briefly attended Thetford Academy in about 1850 or 1851 and by 1852 had moved to Boston, "where she began writing for literary newspapers, mainly under the pen name, Winnie Woodfern. She published poetry, prose, sketches and stories in weeklies and *Waverley Magazine*." Her career as a writer continued on to New York City and Great Britain. Later in life she moved back to English Mills where she lived with Laura Churchill in what has been speculated to have been a "Boston marriage." She continued writing stories under the pen name Margaret Blount into the early 1900s.

Graves, Mary - Charles thought she was the best-looking woman in Woodstock. Married Lyman Cobb, Charles' first cousin, raised eight children and ran her farm capably as a widow for many years after her husband's death, sometimes acting as a fence viewer to decide property disputes. She was the author's great-great-grandmother.

Graves, Emma - Mary Graves' sister who lived near her in English Mills. A schoolmarm in local schools, never married and died in her 30s. Kept memoranda in the 1860s and 1870s with brief intriguing entries, some of which are included in this book.

Grow, Geo - three years older than Charles, lived on Rum Street with his parents Old Grow (Elijah) and Ruth Grow. Known on Rum Street for his hunting, he was also known to be rather lazy. Frequent visitor at Charles' home and participant in many of Charles' adventures. Born in approximately 1832, he married and in 1860 had two daughters, Elizabeth, born approximately 1858, and Ella, born in 1860. In 1860 he was listed in the census as being a farmer worth $100. A soldier in the Civil War during which his wife kept Hosea Cobb's house. Enjoyed a brief period of local fame for acting as a spiritual medium during the rapping craze of 1852. His parents believed the rappings to be the work of the devil.

Hartwell, Isaac - a very good singer and taught singing schools. Encouraged Charles' interest in music. Also performed official duties such as writing deeds, negotiating disputes, and administering wills. Sarah Hartwell, his wife, lived at the Vermont Asylum for the Insane in Brattleboro, dying there at age 41 on May 16, 1852. Buried in the old section of the Prospect Hill Cemetery in Brattleboro, known as the poor section and containing many people who died at the asylum. Her grave is one of the few marked by a stone. Charles' family lived in Hartwell's house on Rum Street and Lucia Cobb did his housekeeping. Mr. Hartwell later married Sally C. Cox. His son, Isaac N. Hartwell, died in 1854. "It is an additional misfortune to him I suppose and a heavy one. Isaac N. hadn't sufficient regard for himself to live - his mind was the ailing part," wrote Charles.

Haskell, Nahum - a book binder and book seller on the Green. He belonged to the Woodstock Cornet Band. Made the book Charles wrote about music in and called his *Great Book of Music*. This book is now at the Vermont Historical Society and is called *Universal Musician*.

Hazen, Dr. Edwin - son of Elder Jasper Hazen, among the first medical students of Dr. Benjamin Palmer in 1840 in Woodstock, high priest of the Ottauquechee Chapter of the Masons. Cared for Hiram and Sarah's children during the canker rash outbreak. Lost at least one daughter of his own, possibly two, during the outbreak.

Holmes, George Byron - born in approximately 1827. Had "fits" that were blamed on his over-eating. His mother sent him to the Brattleboro Asylum for the Insane where they "made out to diet and reduce him down so as to break the fits." He was brought home where his fits and overeating returned. "John Raymond took him to Boston to consult with a celebrated Doctor and received information that he must be fed lightly and regularly and nothing more nor less," wrote Charles. Listed in 1859 census as being worth $1,000. He died in 1860 at 32 years of age.

Holmes, Elvira - well-to-do widow and staunch orthodox Christian on the Flat. Highly critical of Charles' fiddling as well as dancing, card-playing, gambling, and alcohol. Born in approximately 1803 in Massachusetts. Her real estate in the 1850 census was worth $2,000. She had two sons, George Byron and Rufous Addison, who was Charles' friend. "She is a good woman but has made her children snappish, foolish, ignorant & foppish and to pay for all this perhaps a little superstitious, and very green. I don't like that sort of religious education. One ought to be learned common sense, reason, reading &c so as not to be quarrelsome & foolish," wrote Charles.

Holmes, Rufous Addison - born approximately 1836, lived on the Flat with his brother, Byron, and mother, Elvira Holmes. Friend of Charles. In the 1860 census he was a harness maker, worth about $1,700 and married to Lucy E. from New York and living with his mother and brother.

Caroline Cilinda (Cobb) Johnson - born April 6, 1845, and died in 1936, the daughter of Hiram and Sarah Morey Cobb. Narrowly survived the canker rash (scarlet fever) outbreak of 1851. After the death of her mother in 1856, Caroline lived as a servant in the home of George and Mary Raymond on the Flat. Hiram lived nearby. Married Wales N. Johnson and in 1874 had a daughter who died the following year and a son, Hiram, who was born about 1882.

Johnson, Wales - Friend of Charles on the Flat. Became foreman at Daniel's machine shop in West Woodstock in 1876 when Reuben Daniels died. Bought the shop in about 1879. He and his wife, Caroline Cobb, built a stately home on the Flat, now the Jackson House Inn.

Kendall, Edward (Ned) - a mid-19th century music celebrity for his skill on the keyed bugle and leadership of the famous Boston Brass Band. Considered to be the greatest bugle player in the world. Caused a sensation when he played with the Woodstock Cornet Band at the July 4th celebration in Weston, Vermont, in 1854, which was Charles' first brush with the exhilaration of playing to a wildly enthusiastic audience.

Kidder, Moses - pastor for The Christian Church, a beloved man in Woodstock, gentle, wise and kind, who, in his lifetime gave 2,458 funeral sermons during the years he was minister of the church, 1847 - 1890. It was Moses Kidder who, in 1854 at the American Christian Convention in Cincinnati, Ohio, as chairman of a committee to determine what the Church's beliefs were, laid the Bible on the altar and announced that the Bible was the committee's report. "We believe the Bible," he said (J. F. Burnett, *The Origin and Principles of the Christians*, 1921). Officiated at many Cobb burials.

Leach, Marcus and Susan - both born in about 1810 and lived in the next house south of Charles Cobb in the Cox District. Susan and Lucia often visited each other. Marcus was a farmer and Susan Leach made and sold soap (appropriate to her name).

Lull, Leverett - Woodstock music teacher who wrote songs and dedicated them to people in town. "The Child At the Grave" to Mrs. Laura B. Simmons, "The Farmer Sat In His Easy Chair" to Mrs. Norman Williams, and "Green Mountain March" to Frederick Billings. Charles' first fiddle instructor.

Morey, Andrew and Lydia (Granther and Granny) - born in about 1785 and moved onto Rum Street in the 1840s. Often lived with their daughters' families, Emeline Cobb and Sarah Cobb. Granny Morey's colorful personality, outspoken views and outlandish behavior caused no end of trouble on Rum Street. They were exceptionally poor. She once vowed revenge on Lucia Cobb because "a worm if trod on would turn." One day Charles wrote, "Granny Morey is down here this morning with terrible news that Old Morey is drunk, and carryin on most orful &c &c --and she wants him tooked care of." Granther Morey had left 9 or 13 or 15 children, 58 or 76 grandchildren and 7 great-grandchildren - and had been "knocked 'round enough to kill 10 men. ... It can't be wondered at that he's been a drunkard most of his days," wrote Charles.

Pilcher, Mrs. - a fictitious character brought to the story to represent the common wisdom about maintaining a happy home at the time. Her views came directly from the book, *Woman in Her Various Relations,* published in 1851.

Powers, Dr. Tom - born in 1808, son of Dr. John D. Powers, was a physician worth $4,000 in real estate and $2,000 in personal property in 1860. Elected state representative to Montpelier in 1850, serving three terms and as speaker of the house. Involved in temperance and editor of the *Vermont Temperance Herald* and then the *Vermont Temperance Standard* until 1854. Appointed government assessor for the second district of Vermont and performed this duty for nine years.

Pushee, Abram - well-known band leader and teacher of fiddling and dancing in Lebanon, New Hampshire. Born in approximately 1791. In 1860, listed in the census as a musician with $3,500 in real estate and $2,000 in personal property. Charles traveled to Lebanon to study the violin with Pushee, his first contact with the larger world of musicians. "Pushee is an infidel, but that don't make me think any less of him, only that all 'great men' i.e., smart cusses, pretend to be very religious. Also he swears considerable," he wrote.

Raymond, Almira Augusta (Cobb) - Charles' aunt, born January 29, 1825. Married Chas Raymond and had two children, Mary and Henry. "Almira's boy (3 y. old) is the noisiest devil I ever saw," wrote Charles. Lived on the Green and visited her brothers on Rum Street often and participated in the life of the community. Inherited land and a house from her father which was managed by her husband. Died on December 31, 1883.

Raymond, Chas - born November 18, 1820 and died January 10, 1902, he married Almira A. Cobb, Charles' aunt, in 1844. Industrious and respectable, he lived on the Green and farmed the Rum Street land Almira inherited. He took an interest in Charles and was instrumental in providing many of Charles'

Lute Raymond operated a mill on Rum Street. This photo, taken in the later years of his life is courtesy Woodstock History Center.

opportunities as he grew up, including working in Lowell, Massachusetts, and joining the Woodstock Cornet band.

Raymond, Lucius (Lute or Luke) - born about 1824, ran a saw mill on Rum Street with his father Elisha (Lish) Raymond. His farm abutted that of his grandmother, Priscilla Raymond, and his aunts, collectively called the Old Maids, with whom he was often in "mortal strife." In 1850 Charles wrote, "Lute is 25 years old and almost a giant. If he had been like Ed Woodward he would have been a smasher but he is a first rate fellow."

Raymonds, the Old Maids – a family of sisters, (Susan, Sylvia, Sarah who was labeled "idiotic" in the 1850 census, and Elvira) and their mother and grandmother who carried on their own farm on Rum Street. The grandmother, Priscilla Raymond, was born in 1766 and married John Raymond, known as Fiddler John. They left Middleborough along with others who settled in Woodstock. John Raymond died in 1804, leaving his wife and a large family including Priscilla, Chester, and Elisha. They were very poor, with land worth $300 in 1850. Old Priscilla Raymond died at 91 in July of 1857. They owned horses, raised sheep, harvested hay, drew wood with their oxen, made maple sugar and grew potatoes and corn.

Scales, George - born in approximately 1828, worked as a peddler and lived on the Flat in 1850. George wanted to make his living as a fiddler, tried to form a partnership with Charles in the fiddling business, failed at that, and left Woodstock, gathering a reputation that spread back to Rum Street (being tarred and feathered for being where he oughtn't, losing his clothes and ending up in Four Mile Grove, Illinois, with two women, one dressed as a man and the other who'd left her husband).

Shaw, Benoni - became friends with Charles when they were spelling competitors and continued through their shared interest in music. "Mr. & Mrs. Shaw are not handsome but they are good folks and their way of living contrasts very strikingly with ours. They have everything right - live in a good house - and thrive." They were overcome with emotion once when Charles fiddled some old tunes while visiting Benoni.

Simmons, Austin - school teacher, district clerk and medium during the rapping craze of the 1850s. Controversial figure with followers who attended meetings to watch him lecture while under the influence of controlling spirits and opponents who tried to prevent such meetings. Was (at least) once pelted with eggs by a group of boys.

Smith, Hezekiah Bradley - brother of Laura Cobb and instrumental in Charles' life by offering him his first job away from Woodstock at his manufacturing business in Lowell, Massachusetts. His spectacular life continues to provide fodder for articles. It seems most likely that he had an eighth grade education, was a fiddler and had a cabinet shop in a former tannery building on his father's farm on the Flat. He married Eveline Verona English and had five children. He was an inventor and manufacturer of sewing machines and his own inventions - a mortising machine used in the manufacturing of blinds and woodworking machinery in Lowell, Massachusetts and Lebanon, New Hampshire. In Lowell, he met a mill girl, Agnes Gilkerson, and moved with her to Shreveville, New Jersey, a town he'd acquired after a major fire, and renamed Smithville. Apparently, his life there was scandal-ridden, and marred by troubles with his children and his political career (he represented New Jersey as a Democrat in the House of Representatives from 1879-1881) because he married Gilkerson without a legal divorce from his wife. Nevertheless, he continued to manufacture wood-working machinery, advancing the practice of woodworking from hand-made to machine-made. Born July 24, 1816, in Bridgewater, Vermont, and died November 3, 1887, in Smithville, New Jersey.

Thomas, Alden - born in approximately 1825 and lived on the Flat, often working as a hand on Rum Street, although not known as a steady worker. In Charles' opinion, Alden was a "spendthrift, a sabbath breaker and a profane swearer. He is rather mean but is the best informed of the three." "The three" referred to the Thomas cousins on the Flat–Milton, Alden and Mosely. In 1860, he was working as a farm laborer with $200 worth of property.

Thomas, Bezer - farmed on Rum Street before Charles began writing his journals. Bezer was the victim of many of Charles' and his friends' Slab City Lyceum stories. Charles wrote he was pious, Godly and staid like old church-going men and women.

Thomas, Milton - son of Prudence and Andrew, a machinist in 1850, brought up in the nurture and admonition of the lord according to Charles. "Milton ... is more foppish, or in other words, he can sing, &c and is more suited to the company of girls than Alden. ... Milton not having ever been allowed to look (out) of a Meeting house on Sunday &c now lazes round playing cards, gambling, dancing &c spending his wages and more too: But he is honest, and generous some yet he will cheat a little."

Thomas, Mosely - son of Prudence Thomas, "brought up so green and tight that he never enters company. ... About being economical, I notice that he has got the double chin in some degree." Often worked as a hand for Charles' uncles and father on Rum Street, as long as he was sure of being paid.

Thomas, Mrs. Prudence Cox - born in approximately 1792 in Massachusetts and widowed in 1850. She lived on the Flat and was well-off, with real estate valued at $2,600 in 1850. She and her husband, Andrew, were "devout members of the orthodox church." Mother of Milton, Louisa and Mary Thomas. In 1849 Charles wrote, "She is called prudence, and that name is exactly right."

Thompson, Zadock - from Bridgewater, Vermont. He was an Episcopalian priest, prolific writer, historian, educator and especially, naturalist, who was perhaps the first to write and speak seriously about man's destruction of the environment. He wrote many articles and books. A "preeminent nineteenth century student of Vermont" (*Zadock Thompson and the Story of Vermont*, J. Kevin Graffagnino).

Whitney, Ed - was born about 1817. His escapades as a "horse jockey" and reformed alcoholic figured prominently in the life on Rum Street. Known for his skill in swapping.

Whitney, Aaron - foreman of the machine shop on the Flat for many years and as such, was recognized as a leading authority on and advocate of temperance and voting Republican. Raised Norman Cobb's daughter, Mary Elizabeth, after her mother died.

Willis, Mrs. Jim (Nancy Morey) - one of the Morey sisters who sometimes lived on Rum Street with one of her sisters, Emeline or Sarah. She had several children. Her son Warren Willis went to the gold diggings in California sending home alternating news of riches and hard times.

Wood, Sam - Overseer of the Poor in Woodstock who was responsible for the care of indigent residents by sending them to the poorhouse or finding families who would care for them. Was sometimes called upon to help the people of Rum Street.

Wyman, Ashley - born in about 1802, was a successful farmer on the Flat, father of Solomon Wyman and several girls, Clara, Susan, Julia, and Mary Ann. His farm was valued at $2,500 in the 1850 census.

Wyman, Solomon - Charles' friend who lived on the Flat and frequently visited on Rum Street. Charles wrote, "He flatters himself that he is superior to me – he knows he is – and maybe he is – I shan't pretend to say he ain't but yet it seems to me that he will wake up sometime and find himself rather weakly."

Chapter Notes

1 NOTHING BUT THE TRUTH

- Charles Cobb's journals are at the Leahy Library of the Vermont Historical Society in Barre, Vermont. They were transcribed by Michael McKernan in 1988 as part of a Cate Fellowship research grant from the Vermont Historical Society and are available on CDs. His untranscribed memoranda and later journals of expenses and income are at the Woodstock History Center.

2 A SMALL BOY ON THE FLAT

- The river that flows through the Flat, now known as West Woodstock, was called the Quechee. In 1908 it was named the Ottauquechee and remains so today. It has also been labeled the Watrock Quitchey, Wasserqueeche, Waterqueeche, Water Quechee, Waterqueechy and Ottâ Quechee.

- Gaius Cobb, Charles' father, invested in the Vermont Beehive patented in 1841 by John Weeks of Salisbury, Vermont. As Mr. Weeks explained in his promotional material, it was "the first improvement by which honey could be gotten without destroying the bees." For this invention, Weeks received a silver medal from the American Institute of New York. Weeks also wrote a manual of beekeeping which sold more than 20,000 copies. (Vermont Beekeepers Association, vermontbeekeepers.org.)

- The Stage Road, now Route 4, was improved between

1829 and 1835 when it became a turnpike connecting Woodstock with Sherburne (now Killington), Mendon and Rutland beyond. A toll gate to pay for road upkeep was to be established in Sherburne Hollow.

3 THE MOVE TO RUM STREET

- The value of Benney Cobb's estate in 1817 was $1,297.89, comparable to approximately $19,751 in 2015.

- The Cobb Heritage

Charles Cobb's ancestral roots were in Kent, England, where his ancestor Henry Cobb, a single 33-year-old man, came to America. He landed in Plymouth in 1633 and joined the Pilgrim's church. He helped build the town of Scituate, Massachusetts. He later moved to Mattakeese, now Barnstable, in the Colony of New Plymouth. His home was similar to others in the community, a stone lower level for fortification against attack and wood second story. It was built on a lot of seven acres. He planted crops on the common land and grazed cattle on his 75-acre great lot. Henry Cobb took part in governance of the new town, serving as a town officer, a member of important civil and military town committees, as a representative to the colony court and in the office of senior deacon. He was later ordained Ruling Elder in the Barnstable Church. He was a "useful and valuable man" (Massachusetts Historical Collections, Second series, Vol. IV, 247).

At the age of about 43 he married Patience Hurst, daughter of a deacon and tanner, and sired seven offspring including John and James, Charles Cobb's ancestors on his father's and mother's sides respectively. They had large families and so did their offspring, creating a web of Cobb families who spread throughout America, families that today fill thick books with complicated lines of descent.

John Cobb's offspring remained in Barnstable working

as bricklayers and masons for five generations. From there, they moved to Middleborough, Massachusetts and then to the hills north of the Flat in Woodstock, Vermont.

James Cobb's descendants stayed in Barnstable for several generations as well, then moved briefly to Middleborough, Massachusetts and then to Woodstock in 1777. He and his wife, Sarah Simmons, built their house of logs near Pogue Hole on Mt. Tom. When Moses Sampson was shot in June of 1781, he was taken to James' farm. The frame dwelling, put up in 1793, was placed a little below the log hut and remained there until 1886 when it was removed by Payson A. Pierce. "After Deacon James Cobb left the farm it was owned and occupied by Eliphalet Thomas, who stripped the place of much of its valuable timber. Afterwards it fell into the possession of O.P. Chandler, Esq., who conveyed to Hugh P. Howe, Mr. Howe to Edward Dana, in the fall of 1863. The farm was carried on, after that date, by Charles Dana, till the summer of 1884 and in the fall of that year it became a part of the magnificent domain of Frederick Billings, Esq." (*History of Woodstock Vermont*, Henry Swan Dana, 188).

James Cobb occupied this farm until 1810. His son, also named James Cobb (born February 20, 1781) married Joanna Raymond (born July 5, 1782), daughter of Sylvanus Raymond. Sylvanus served as a drummer in Captain Nathaniel Wood's Company, Colonel Simeon Cary's Regiment, at Roxbury, Massachusetts, on April 1, 1776, when he was 19. He moved to Woodstock in 1780. James and Joanna Raymond were Lucia Cobb's parents.

Lucia had two sisters, Susan Isman (wife of Aaron Isman) and Polly Woodruff (wife of Sam) and a brother named Charles Morris Cobb who lived in Sheridan, Michigan, in 1850. Charles and Polly were born in Woodstock before their father left for Chateaugay, New York, where he bought some property and cleared it of trees. He died there when he was fairly young and her mother remarried and moved to New Hampshire.

- Benney Cobb was the first of Charles Cobb's ancestors on his father's side in Woodstock. From the list of things in Benney's estate upon his death in 1817, it is possible to recreate a picture of the family's home. The women sewed fulled cloth into long dresses and bonnets. Benney Cobb wore stockings, a linen shirt, and trousers secured at the knees with buckles. Wooden barrels, bags of corn, and tubs filled with meal and maple sugar, stood in the kitchen. Wool skeins spun by the women from the family sheep hung from the rafters. A brass kettle and three-legged cast iron spider were set on coals in the big open fireplace where water was heated and food seasoned with pepper from the pepper pot and salt from the salt cellar. Food was set out on pewter plates and eaten with spoons and forks. The table was pine and covered with a plain table cloth and circled by four wooden chairs. Azubah and Betsey Cobb strained bits of debris from the bucket of milk from their black and light red-colored cows, then scooped the top layer of cream into tin or earthen milk pans for churning in the butter barrel. Old Benney wore spectacles to read the Great Bible, family Psalm books or from an old sermon. A plug of tobacco was packed into a corner of his mouth. The family slept on feather mattresses laid on a weave of cords and covered with sheets, flannel blankets, and a quilt, their heads on feather pillows.

4 CHRISTIAN TO THE VERY UTTERMOST

- The *Christian Messenger* was a publication of the Christian Church and read by many of the Cobbs on Rum Street. It encouraged the free exchange of ideas and individual interpretation of the Bible as well as abolition of slavery.

- William Miller, a preacher and farmer from Poultney, Vermont, predicted that Christ would arrive in a great cataclysmic event and the world would end in

1843. It was a widespread movement with a large Vermont following. He based it on his studies of Biblical prophecies, particularly Daniel 8:14. The movement was known as Millerism.

5 WAXING INTO A GREAT GAWKEY

- Whipping was an allowed method of discipline but the practice was beginning to be questioned and even forbidden at some schools.

- In the 1850s, about 12 small district schools were scattered throughout Woodstock, ranging in size from schools such as that on the Flat with more than 40 students and the Cox District School with 12 students in 1852. (Map of Windsor County, Vermont, 1856.)

- Schools were supported by taxes paid by families who could afford to send their children to school, a system that probably restricted attendance of poor students. Attending school was not compulsory and although parents were encouraged to insist that their children attend school regularly and to be on time, most of the large boys, including Charles, attended only the winter term.

- The first Superintendent of Common Schools in Vermont, Horace Eaton, who was from Barnard, only a few miles north of Woodstock, would have probably agreed with Charles Cobb's assessment that the Cox District School was a "mighty inferior affair." In an 1846 report, Eaton described small scattered rural schools as a "paradise of ignorant teachers." Teacher salaries were negotiated and were often higher for better attended and more desirable village schools than poorly attended rural schools. In the 1850s male teachers were paid about $12 a month, about the same as a farmer would expect to earn, and women were paid less than half that. At about that time, Horace Mann's theories of education reform began to take hold in Vermont and were supported by Eaton. These included equal educational opportunities for all children through tax-supported schools and high-quality teachers through higher pay and training in normal schools. ("A Brief History of Public School Organization in Vermont," David Cyprian, 2012.)

- In 1867 school attendance became compulsory for all children between 8 and 14 years of age. It wasn't until 1864 that the Vermont legislature mandated that common schools not charge pupils and be supported by taxes.

7 THE WAYS OF THE MAMMOTH MAN

- Lyceums were popular during Charles' time. They were groups formed to educate adults through lectures, entertainment, performances, debates, and writing.
- The cemetery in the Flat–now, West Woodstock–that Charles played in, is now known as the Hendee Cemetery.

8 THE WOODSTOCK-SHADIGEE TOUCH-HOLE OLD-IRON COMPANY

- Charles' reference to firing the anvil referred to the old practice of setting one anvil on top of another that had been placed upside down so gunpowder could be poured into the hole at the bottom. The gunpowder was lit and the upper anvil launched into the air and crashed back down onto the lower anvil, creating a loud bang, appropriate to July 4th celebrations.

9 MAKING THE CIDER RUN

- Blue-y or blue, was used by Charles to infer excessive swearing.

- Phthisic, as Charles used it, was a term for asthma.

- The Cobbs made a small amount of water cider by pouring water over the pomace left after the apples were pressed for whole cider. In 1851, Hiram, Gaius, and Charles Cobb made 5 barrels of whole and 1 ½ barrels of water cider.

- Liquor laws

    In 1844, liquor vendors needed to be licensed. People who were drunk could be arrested and jugged.

    In 1847 Windsor County, Vermont, passed Act 24 granting judges the "power to grant licenses only for medicinal, chemical or mechanical purpose." Small beer and cider were exempt. The law wasn't stringently enforced and was often evaded. The exception on medical use was handy for that.

    In 1848, the previous year's vote was narrowly reversed. In 1849, the referendum was again reversed and prohibition returned, though, as before, cider was exempted. In 1850 a permanent ban on licensing alcohol for beverage purposes was passed through Act 30.

    In 1852 Vermont passed "An Act Preventing Traffic in Intoxicating Liquors for the Purpose of Drinking." The law prohibited the sale of cider to habitual drunkards or in "places of public resort." Otherwise, cider could still be sold, manufactured, or used. Woodstock joined other large towns in Vermont by voting in favor of the law (348 yes to 277 no), while most small towns went against it.

    In 1853, Vermont became a dry state when voters ratified the Vermont Prohibition on the Sale of Intoxicating Liquor Act. Still, alcohol could be served in homes as long as it didn't lead to drunkenness.

10 WASTING WISDOM

- Groups such as the Christian Church appeared during and after the second Great Awakening. The Christian Church strongly emphasized personal experience and conviction based on individual understanding of the Bible instead of more traditional denominations that focused on inherited beliefs expressed in creeds and preserved through ecclesiastical authority. Nancy Pearcey wrote in her book, *Total Truth*, that these groups were unduly influenced by the American passion for individual freedom and defiantly abandoned some of the safeguards of more collective and time-proven structures. This was in contrast to the older Congregational Churches that broke with the Church of England and emphasized local autonomy but were still much more respectful of traditional creeds and other elements of church history. (Ed Wheeler, pastor of Valley Bible Church, Middlebury, Vermont.)

- A report on the well-attended Christian Church baptism in 1808, is in the publication, *Herald of Gospel Liberty*, "Extract of a Letter from a Brother in Woodstock (Vt.)". Portsmouth, New Hampshire. Vol. 1, Issue 1, Page 3,4. August 5, 1808.

- Religion was often argued and highly valued but its formal practices were casually observed by the Cobbs. Norman, Hosea, and Laura were members of the Christian Church under the ministry of Elder Jasper Hazen followed by Reverend Moses Kidder. Lucia Cobb was a member of the Congregational Church. If a religious service was needed in the Cobb family, Reverend Kidder was most often called upon.

  For an excellent discussion of the Christian Church in New England, read James Gardner's "The Christians of New England." He wrote that when Vermont was formed, it had a reputation of offering "liberty, democracy and hope" for the poor or a "dangerous place of free thinkers and irreligious barbarians," depending on one's point of view.

The Cobbs fell into the first class. Charles followed in the footsteps of his aunts, uncles, and grandparents, discussing religious and philosophical subjects while working and visiting. He read their copies of the *Christian Messenger*, Barton Stone's publication that supported study and rational thought, to support his arguments. Sometimes, his opinions led to conflicts with the Orthodox Christians in his community.

By the time Charles was born, the Christian Church was well established in Woodstock. In the early part of the century, Abner Jones whose family had settled in Bridgewater (he later taught school in Woodstock), and Elias Smith who also lived in Woodstock for some time, had separately rebelled against dogmatic teachings from the pulpit. The two men worked separately and together to establish and extend the reach of the new Christian Church.

Elias Cobb became an elder in the Christian congregation that started in English Mills in 1806, an early, if not the first, Christian Church congregation in Vermont to remain active for more than a short time. He was joined by Binney, Azubah, and Betsy Cobb. Charles wrote many of his journals while living in the house Elder Elias Cobb built.

The Christian Church's liberal democratic leanings suited the Cobbs. The church allowed ordination of women, opposed slavery and departed from the simplicity of a cappela singing by introducing instrumental music, all controversial at the time. The church's leanings were so democratic that Jasper Hazen refused to use the self-important title "Reverend" before his name. By the mid-19th century, the Christian Church had moved to a meeting house on Pleasant Street in Woodstock. In 1843 it was one of the largest of its kind in Vermont. Elder Jasper Hazen baptized people in an outdoor baptistery in the back yard of his house on Elm Street. His son-in-law, Moses Kidder, succeeded him and served as pastor for many years. He was well respected and known to be kind and thoughtful.

11 MICE WERE THICKER THAN PUDDING

- Charles mentions four people who had typhoid fever or typhus during the years he was writing his journals, one of whom died. The two illnesses are entirely different and it isn't known whether Charles used the correct word for the illness experienced by Laura Cobb and others. Both would have been greatly feared. Typhoid fever is caused by a bacteria that's spread by contaminated food and water and contact with an infected person although the Cobbs didn't know that at the time. Charles said his Aunt Laura got the typhoid fever as a result of having the mumps. Considering that the Cobbs used water from easily contaminated streams, springs and shallow open pit wells, its occurrence is not surprising. Typhus fever is also a bacteria, but spread by lice, chiggers or fleas in crowded conditions. It occurred in America but wasn't as common as typhoid. It seems unlikely that Laura had typhus fever.

- Zadock Thompson could have had Rum Street on his mind when he wrote about his observations about man's effect on nature in 1842 in *History of Vermont, Natural, Civil and Statistical*. He most certainly could have been referring to Geo Grow when he wrote, "We are of the opinion that all birds, without a single exception, are to be regarded as friends to the farmer and gardener, kindly provided by Providence to prevent the undue multiplication of noxious insects, and we cannot too severely reprobate the barbarous practice in which boys are permitted to indulge, of shooting birds for amusement. It is a practice which should be discountenanced by every friend of his country – by every friend of humanity." Thompson was a poor farm boy, born in 1796 and raised in Bridgewater, just a short distance over the hills from Rum Street.

His early awareness of man's effect on nature wasn't widely appreciated and stacks of his *History of Vermont* remained unsold. It wasn't until George Perkins Marsh of Woodstock published *Man and Nature* in 1864 that the destruction people were wreaking on the environment became widely noticed.

- Thompson also wrote a Vermont *Gazetteer* in 1824. The Cobbs owned a copy that Charles used to follow the action along the Connecticut River and through the Green Mountains as he read *The Rangers, or the Tory's Daughter, A Tale Illustrative of the Revolutionary History of Vermont and the Northern Campaign of 1777* by Daniel P. Thompson.

- Zadock Thompson was a lecturer at the University of Vermont and appointed Vermont State Naturalist in 1853. His death in 1856 brought tributes from within and outside of Vermont. His papers and collections of natural history specimens were donated to the University of Vermont. Refer to Kevin Graffagnino's, "Zadock Thompson and the Story of Vermont" for an excellent history of this remarkable but largely unknown man.

12 THE ESSENTIAL SKILL OF SWAPPING

- Charles was a meticulous keeper of lists of expenses and income throughout his life. He listed these family assets in 1849 when he was 13 years old.

    ~ Livestock and feed consisted of a horse ($80), dun cow ($15), a black cow that was a "little sick" ($10), two calves ($6), 17 roosters and 5 hens ($2) and a pig weighing about 35 pounds ($5). "The value of the cattle was their worth in October. We don't call the cattle what they will be worth in the spring, because of the value of the hay they'd consumed over the winter."

    ~ 5 tons more hay than was needed for the winter so valued at $25. Charles also listed 10 bushels of corn worth $5 and 10 cords of wood on the road to the green worth $10.

~ 15 swarms of bees ($75) in a bee house ($30). The bee house land was worth $2.

~ Other

Wagon-House	30
Wagon	60
Wheels	16
Rake	8
Sleigh	22
Two Ploughs 6 Chains 3	9
Shovels Axes Hoes	5
Sap Tubs 6 Measures 1	7
Harness	22
Saddle	5
Cart, Old Wagon &c	15
Boards & lumber	6
Barrel, tubs	12
Father's Tools	32
Old Thunderstruck fiddle	18
Red Fiddle	6
Boxes 5 & Bows	5
Melodeon & Music (Book $5)	28
1 stove	10
1 stove	3 1/2
1 stove	2 1/2 (gave 15)
High Draws	5 (gave 8)
5 chests	5
2 tables, chairs 5 (or $12)	10
Bedsteads & bedding	28
(Rather little) Pencils	12
Dishes	5
Pots & Kettles (cost 25)	6
Storage boxes &c	6
Clock (cost 20 or 25)	5
Silver spoons, Gold Beads	
500,000 articles, not in this list, worth 10c apiece	

Combined with the value of our small personal

possessions and excluding the value of our land, I figured we were worth $600 (about $17,250 in 2015).

14 POLITICAL DISQUIETUDE

- The Whigs preceded the Republican Party, largely disappearing by the election of 1856, when the two major parties became the Republicans and Democrats.

- The Locofocos were a political group that split from the Democratic Party in the 1830s. By 1852 they were again part of the Democratic Party but a distinct vocal faction.

- Charles' predictions for the election of 1852 were correct with the exception of Mississippi.

- Austin English criticized Pierce for fainting at the Battle of Contreras in Mexico when his leg was crushed after being thrown from his horse.

15 FIDDLING AND MY GREAT BOOK OF MUSIC

- Charles' *Great Book of Music*, as he referred to it in his journals, is now called *Universal Musician*, and is at the Vermont Historical Society. The contents of this book are available to the public on microfilm through inter-library loan. Refer to Helen Hartness Flander's articles, "Songs Alive" and "The Cobb Manuscript of Reading, Vermont" available in the Middlebury College Library Special Collections for more information about Charles Cobb's place in the musical history of Vermont in the second half of the 19th century.

- *The Musician's Companion* by Elias Howe, was an affordable set of music books containing cotillions, marches, quick-steps, hornpipes, contra dances and songs for all instruments as well as descriptions of dance steps.

16 HILL FARMERS

- $2,000 is approximately $57,500 in 2015 dollars.

- The Cobbs promised to pay their father's widow, Hannah Richmond, $60 dollars a year which is approximately $1,700 in 2015.

17 THE ABODE OF SATAN'S POVERTY STICKENS

- Charles knew a remarkable number of people who spent some time at the Brattleboro Retreat, called the Vermont Asylum for the Insane or, more casually, the Brattleboro lunatic asylum. Two went for eating disorders and at least one for a nervous breakdown. The grounds were beautiful and large, opening in 1834, with 49 acres of meadows, gardens, dairy farm, and river-front and expanded in size over the following years. The hospital emphasized good nutrition, employment, recreation, and culture in a family setting. Patients had private rooms and use of a bowling alley, chapel, gymnasium, and many other forms of entertainment. It was among the first psychiatric hospitals to treat mental illness humanely and healthfully, considering it a medical condition rather than the result of sin or immorality. (Wikipedia and Stephen Sanders, Historic Preservation Consultant, http://www.crjc.org/heritage/V02-34.htm)

- The mid-19th century was a time of transition from cooking over a fire in a fireplace to cooking on a wood-burning stove. Lucia used both, sometimes the fireplace in the kitchen or a big stove set in front of it, and sometimes the smaller wood-burning stove in the square room.

- The Cobbs took their melodeon, a small reed organ held in the lap with buttons to press rather than keys, and fiddles with them to neighborhood sings and other get-togethers where music was often performed and sung. Charles also often played both the melodeon and fiddle for visitors at his home.

- The buttery was a small room, typically used to prepare and store food, bathe, and wash clothes in cold weather but the Cobbs used theirs for storage.

- My grandparents, who were Woodstock, Vermont, farmers, referred to the unheated upstairs room of their farmhouse as the chamber and the unheated downstairs room off the kitchen as the woodshed chamber. The woodshed chamber held firewood. The upstairs chamber was used as an extra storage room for odds and ends of un-used household items.

18 THE FARM YEAR

- Maple sugar was priced at about 7.2 cents per pound in 1850, equivalent to about $2.01 in 2015. (*Trends in the American Economy in the Nineteenth Century,* National Bureau of Economic Research, 1960 and The Federal Reserve Bank of Minneapolis Consumer Price Index 1800-2008)

- Charles' spiles, made of branches with soft centers such as sumac, and wooden buckets would be replaced within the next few years by metal implements. His evaporating kettle was soon replaced by evaporating pans. An early patent for a metal evaporating pan was issued in 1858 and in 1859 the first patent for metal sap spouts was granted. Metal sap buckets were introduced in 1875.

- Charles Cobb's first arch seemed to have been a limb supported by poles or trees, from which his boiling kettle would have hung. His improved arch may have been similar to the stone arches with three closed sides and an open side for inserting firewood, that can still be found in the hills around Woodstock. One still existed in 2016 very near Charles' boiling place.

- In 1850, Charles made about $8 worth of sugar which would have been about the same as the cost of a good overcoat, a ton of hay, a rifle, a spy-glass, or a trombone. It paid for Leverett Lull's $5 worth of fiddle lessons with some left over.

- Wire fencing wasn't available until the late 19th century.

- Eva Crane described a Vermont beehouse. "Every one so far as I remember had a bee-house – an open shed 12 or 15 feet long by 4 or 5 feet wide, open on the south side and boarded up on the north side and also the ends ... there were two shelves, one near the ground and the other about 3 feet above on which the hives were set. Sometimes, setting up at one end of the house, there was the section of the trunk of a tree 6 or 8 feet long that had been brought in from the woods with a runaway swarm in. ... Hives for the most part were made of boards of uneven widths, or straw ... The size or capacity of these hives varied from a half bushel to two bushels or more ..." (*The World History of Beekeeping and Honey Hunting*, Eva Crane, 1999)

- Charles compared the worst of anything to Tophet, an Old Testament Biblical reference to the valley of Hinnom, near Jerusalem, where children were offered as sacrifices. The word was analogous to "hell."

- The drink that made Charles sick was a version of switchell or hay-maker's punch.

- Laura was the only woman mentioned in Charles' journals as having worn breeches. Wearing pants were unusual but not unheard of among women of the time.

19 NORMAN COBB LEAVES WOODSTOCK

- Norman Cobb referred to public land given to the Illinois Central Railroad in 1851. The railroad sold the land to encourage farmers to ship products on the railroad. The railroad was 25 miles south of Norman's location in Four Mile Grove.

21 MOTHER'S SICKNESS

- *The Practical Cook Book* by Mrs. H.M. Robinson published in 1864, has a recipe that was probably similar to the method used by Lucia Cobb for her milk-emptyings bread.

"Take a pint of new sweet milk, add to it boiling water, until it is as warm as the finger can be borne in it, a tea-spoonful of salt, and flour to form a batter a little thicker than for griddle-cakes. Mix in a pitcher or small tin pail, place it in a kettle of warm water, and keep it at as nearly the same temperature as possible. If it becomes thin and looks watery, stir in a little more flour. When risen, which will be in about five hours, take a pint of warm milk, and the same of warm water, or all water if preferred, and stir a stiff sponge; when cool, add the emptyings, and a small tea-spoonful of saleratus if you chose, and place it where it will keep warm. When light, mould it as soft as possible into loaves, taking care that it does not become cold during the process; let the loaves rise and bake."

Milk emptying bread was described as having a "sourish taste" in a story called "Tom Wilson's Emigration", in *The Literary Garland, and British North American Magazine* from Toronto, Canada, published in 1847.

Fourteen Weeks in Chemistry by J. Dorman Steele, published in 1872, said milk emptyings develop yeast if kept at 90 degrees. A recipe from *The Complete Bread, Cake, and Cracker Baker* published in 1881 attributes the rise of milk emptying bread to spontaneous fermentation.

This spontaneous fermentation was a result of the multiplication of wild yeasts in the air and in flour, which wasn't known about at the time. It's quite likely that milk-emptyings bread was similar to modern sourdough bread.

- Sick headaches would be called migraine headaches today.

25 TREMENDOUS BAD TIMES

- Canker rash was a dreaded childhood disease. In Benjamin Colby's *A Guide To Health* written in 1846, he could have been describing Hiram's family when he said of canker rash (a form of scarlet fever, also called putrid sore throat), "These forms of disease combined, have prevailed to an alarming extent in different sections of New England, consigning to the tomb the fond hopes of many a devoted parent."

  Doctors claimed the disease wasn't catching, but people certainly suspected otherwise, even though they didn't understand how it was spread. They didn't know about germs, invisible streptococcal bacteria that clung to hands, bedding, and utensils and could be picked up and carried to others. They attributed contagion in a vague way to "noxious air" and "filth."

  The people of Rum Street carried water from a dug well, spring, or brook or melted snow for all their household needs. Water was precious and used sparingly, so thorough cleaning of people, hands, tables, utensils, bedding, and everything else was difficult.

  Although researchers were inching toward an understanding of the germ theory, it wasn't until 50 years later that a 1900 document issued by the Michigan State Board of Health advised isolating those with canker rash symptoms and avoiding contact with "infected clothing, rags, hair or paper or by any of the discharges from the body of a person afflicted with the disease", and further advised hand-washing and sanitizing eating utensils and clothing and bedding with zinc-solution and hot water and other methods of good hygiene." Germs were still not understood.

  Today scarlet fever is easily treated with antibiotics.

- Some of the residents of Rum Street are buried in the Shaw Cemetery in West Woodstock. It's located on a small hill along Wyman Lane, a dirt road parallel to Route 4, and is surrounded by a mossy stone wall. Gaius and Betsey Cobb are buried there along with Henry Cobb and Laura Cobb and some of her family.

  Three small tombstones can be seen in the southeastern corner of the Shaw Cemetery, marking the graves of W. Orlando Cobb, AE 17 months; J. Andrew Cobb, AE 5 years; Fred C. Cobb, AE 7 years. The taller stone of their mother Sarah Morey Cobb, stands in front of the graves of her children.

29 THE RISE AND FALL OF SPIRITUALIZM ON RUM STREET

- *Spiritual Philosopher, The Spiritual Telegraph,* and *The Celestial Telegraph: Secrets of the Life to Come,* were periodicals devoted to the study of the spirit world beyond the grave. Rappings and knockings were popular among some Woodstock residents but largely denied, ignored, or dismissed by many, judging by lack of reference to the spiritual circles in local newspapers of the time.

30 FROM THE WOMEN'S PERSPECTIVE, HELL RIGHT HERE ON AIRTH

- Married women could not vote or own property during the time Charles was writing his journals. Single women could own property.

- Girls under 18 and boys under 21 could be indentured to a master for food and clothing in exchange for labor and service. This was the situation Norman Cobb's children found themselves in and also, later, Hiram Cobb's daughter, Caroline Cobb. Charles said Hiram "sold" his children. Caroline was officially indentured to a Raymond family in Woodstock. In later years she referred to them as her aunt and uncle, suggesting a close familial relationship.

- Divorce was legal, although there was a social stigma

attached. Women often simply left their husbands. Married women had some control over inherited real estate after 1847 but could not control personal property, even their own clothes and household goods, and could not control their own earnings.

- Daniel A. Cohen studied Mary Gibson's long career as a female story writer and published his findings in "Making Hero Strong; Teenage Ambition, Story-Paper Fiction, and the Generational Recasting of American Women" in the *Journal of the Early Republic*, Volume 30, Number 1, Spring 2010, pp. 85-136, University of Pennsylvania Press, DOI: 10.1353/jer.0.0136. He also edited a book of Mary Gibson's stories called *Hero Strong and other Stories*, University of Tennessee Press, Knoxville, 2014.

Mary was born in 1835, orphaned as a toddler and raised by Joseph Churchill, a Woodstock house painter. Joseph's daughter, Laura Churchill, was a great friend of Mary's throughout their lives. "Mary described herself as a "romp" (tomboy), briefly attended Thetford Academy, and moved to Boston where she wrote for literary newspapers under the name, Winnie Woodfern and others, including Mary O. Francis and Margaret Blount. She wrote for *True Flag*, the *New York Ledger* and *Reynolds's Miscellany* in England. Her life was an early example of girls who rebelled against the rigid mores of society. In the Federal Census of 1880, Mary Gibson was listed as Mary O. Francis, a story writer, living in English Mills with Laura Churchill, next door to Sylvia Raymond, one of the "Old Maids" from Rum Street and two doors down from Mary Cobb, Lyman Cobb's widow.

31 GOLD

- Matthew Kennedy's ore was found in what became known as the Taggart vein about five miles west of Rum Street in Dailey Hollow. While some rich pockets were found, the gold was unevenly distributed.

39 PLAYING WITH THE GREATEST BUGLE PLAYER IN THE WORLD

- In the 1850s, Ned Kendall was considered one of the greatest bugle players in the world. Among brass musicians, he was a superstar, famed player of the keyed bugle, the horn that was being replaced by valved horns in brass bands by 1853. Kendall had been the leader of the renowned Boston Brass Band, and was, in 1853, leader of the iconic Boston Brigade Band. His name is still spoken with reverence among enthusiasts of old time brass band music and stories told about his life are now folklore. Once he posed as an unassuming stranger and tricked a horn player into a competition where he played so magnificently, that his opponent claimed only the "devil or Ned Kendall" could have played as he did. A famous keyed bugle–coronet musical duel with Patrick Gilmore, celebrated band-leader in 1856, has become legendary.

The beginning of the brass band movement paralleled the development of the keyed bugle in the early 1800s, the instrument Ned Kendall played so brilliantly. Early brass bands using the keyed bugle and its lower-voiced counterpart, the ophicleide, and by the 1830s, were supplanting woodwind bands at popular events. Brass bands, easily heard outdoors, naturally achieved great popularity in the days before there was electrical amplification of music. In the 1840s, more melodic and technically facile valved instruments were being developed and introduced to brass bands. The first of these were coiled instruments, called cornets, followed by saxhorns, a larger general category of valved bugles that produced tones in all voice ranges, from soprano to bass, all with similar qualities of sound. They were also fairly easy to play. As cornets and saxhorns became more readily available in the second half of the 1840s, small amateur brass bands began to be formed in small towns throughout New England. By the 1850s, it was a significant popular movement. There were many bands like the Woodstock Cornet Band, many of them taught by Alonzo Bond, and competition for music jobs was increasing. Brass bands, with their rousing showy performances of light classical music, quadrilles, quicksteps, gallops, polkas, mazurkas, schottisches and waltzes, along with patriotic songs and marches, became popular musical attractions, especially at outdoor celebrations–picnics, bandstand concerts, fairs, circuses, firemen and fraternal events, and musters. The musicians were generally merchants, tradesmen, and working class folks such as Charles, people who could afford to buy an instrument and learn to play it relatively easily. It was a social movement that brought music to all people.

41 TEMPESTS OF SWEET AND MAGNIFICENT SOUNDS

- John Sullivan Dwight, a famous music journalist in Boston in the 1850s, decried the rise of blustering brass bands that had cast aside the mellowing influences of woodwinds, but he agreed that the music was glorious; "The experiment (of blustering brass bands rather than the more mellow woodwinds) succeeds beyond doubt or cavil ... the music might be better, with larger and more especial organization, but under the circumstances it has been very good, and has been drunk in with every sign of attention and delight by a continually increasing crowd of listeners. There could not have been fewer than ten thousand persons, of all ages and classes, on the common the two last times."(*Dwight's Journal of Music,* 1853)

44 THE LIFE OF A MUSICIAN

- A good night's pay for playing music in 1858 was five or six dollars which would be about $138 to $166 in 2015.
- Charles' description of getting venereal disease was oblique but revealing. It had apparently happened at

a brothel at 21 Endicott Street in Boston, a location that is now a park. A recent study of artifacts found in a privy at a brothel that existed at 27 and 29 Endicott St. in Boston between about 1852 and 1883 reveals that a Dr. Padelford, a homeopathic doctor "considered to be crackpotty at the time," and married to a Mrs. Lake who listed her profession as prostitution, prescribed copaiba oil and silver nitrate as treatments for venereal diseases. (http://www.bu.edu/bostonia/web/brothel/)

- Charles calculated his Father's house on the Flat to be worth $1,000 in 1861 which would be about $26,600 in 2015.

- The (David and Rhodolph) Hall Family Papers in the collections of Henry Ford Museum and Greenfield Village were edited by Robert E. Eliason and can be read online at the Yankee Brass Band website. The concert Charles described is also described in the "Hall Letters of July 28, 1858 from Rhodolph in Boston to Lucy in New Haven." He wrote,"We had a glorious 5th in celebration the finest I ever saw in Boston or elsewhere. The Monster Concert on the Common in the morning was all could be expected the particulars you have read no doubt. The 4 Bands ie. 72 musicians (all brass) played well. Hail Columbia with Lt. Artillery accompanyment. The 6 canon came in just right. The Fire works were never so good, representing the burning of Charleston &c."

45 FINDING A WIFE

- Charles Cobb's descendants donated Lucy Jane Shaw's diary and other Cobb family memorabilia to the Woodstock History Center.

CPSIA information can be obtained
at www.ICGtesting.com
Printed in the USA
FFOW03n1329151117
43538103-42283FF